AF706884

AUTONOMOUS VEHICLES

Self-Driving Cars and the Law of Canada

AUTONOMOUS VEHICLES

Self-Driving Cars and the Law of Canada

NATHAN BAKER

with contributions from Jaye Hooper

IRWIN LAW

Autonomous Vehicles: Self-Driving Cars and the Law of Canada
© Nathan Baker, 2021

All rights reserved. No part of this publication may be reproduced, stored in a retrieval system, or transmitted, in any form or by any means, without the prior written permission of the publisher or, in the case of photocopying or other reprographic copying, a licence from Access Copyright (Canadian Copyright Licensing Agency), 56 Wellesley Street West, Suite 320, Toronto, Ontario, M5S 2S3.

Published in 2021 by

Irwin Law Inc
Suite 206, 14 Duncan Street
Toronto, Ontario M5H 3G8
www.irwinlaw.com

ISBN: 978-1-55221-580-7 | e-book ISBN: 978-1-55221-581-4

Cover image: Adobe Stock

Library and Archives Canada Cataloguing in Publication

Title: Autonomous vehicles: self-driving cars and the law of Canada / Nathan Baker with contributions from Jaye Hooper.
Names: Baker, Nathan, 1982– author. | Hooper, Jaye (Jaye Elizabeth), author.
Description: Includes bibliographical references and index.
Identifiers: Canadiana (print) 2021032855X | Canadiana (ebook) 20210328568 | ISBN 9781552215807 (softcover) | ISBN 9781552215814 (PDF)
Subjects: LCSH: Automated vehicles—Law and legislation—Canada.
Classification: LCC KE2095 .B35 2021 | LCC KF2209 .B35 2021 kfmod | DDC 343.7109/46—dc23

Printed and bound by CPI Group (UK) Ltd, Croydon, CR0 4YY

1 2 3 4 5 25 24 23 22 21

SUMMARY TABLE OF CONTENTS

DETAILED TABLE OF CONTENTS

ACKNOWLEDGEMENTS

The onset of the COVID-19 pandemic and the immediate closing of in-person court appearances left me with less work in the traditional sense, but also left me with a wife working on the frontlines in healthcare and two young boys learning from home. I started the book because I wanted a distraction during the hard times. The encouragement from my wife, Amy, and understanding from my two boys, Josh and Oli, gave me the fortitude to accomplish something extra during the lockdowns and helped me keep my sanity. I want to thank Jaye Hooper for her amazing contributions, especially her chapter on civil liability issues. Jaye's contributions were invaluable in keeping me thinking past my comfort zone of criminal law. I want to thank all my editors, especially my mother Connie and the various proofreaders at Irwin Law who had to go through things so often. I am a terrible editor, and your hard work is especially important at bringing my thoughts together in a cogent form. The technology involved in autonomous vehicles is still developing and the law will develop with it. The joy of the common-law is its ability to evolve with the changing times. Autonomous vehicles will be a real test as they continue to progress.

Nathan Baker
August 2021

It is tough to admit, but as I stayed home with my family in the weeks after the onset of the pandemic, relatively safe and secure compared to most, I did not handle the shutdown well. A busy, productive professional with two over-scheduled kids still at home, I suddenly found I had nothing to do. Nathan Baker, a terrific friend and valued colleague, threw me a lifeline: could I contribute to a legal text on civil liability issues for autonomous vehicles? This allowed me to focus on something other than work being at a standstill. I will always be grateful to him for this opportunity and his extraordinary patience.

I could not have undertaken this project without the support of my husband, Paul, who continues to have my back whenever I try something new. My kids, always a source of inspiration, continually push me to step outside of my comfort zone. They are the reason I get up every morning, and I would not have finished this without them.

Jaye Hooper
August 2021

INTRODUCTION

The automobile has been arguably the most impactful achievement of the twentieth century. It has allowed freedom of movement for people and goods, generated urban development, and created industries. Canada, with a small population spread over a huge geography, is highly dependent on the automobile. Consequently, technology has a profound impact on the use of automobiles across the country. Drivers in Canada may encounter dangerous winter weather, long stretches of flat prairie, and twisted mountain roads. Driving in Canada, or anywhere, is "an inherently dangerous activity, but one that is of both legal and . . . social value."[1]

The vast majority of Canadians live in urban areas; nonetheless, to allow an automated vehicle to function well, a staggering number of kilometres of road would need mapping. This would be a difficult and expensive process. Converting non-autonomous vehicles into automated vehicles over time and the public appetite for the technology will influence their impact. Some of the benefits of automated vehicles become exponentially greater at higher levels of automation and with higher rates of acceptance by drivers—overall safety is more enhanced when highly automated vehicles are used by greater numbers of people. It may be that

1 *R v Roy*, 2012 SCC 26 at para 34, referencing *R v Beatty*, 2008 SCC 5 at paras 31 and 34.

until automation reaches a critical mass, its widespread adoption will fail. Yet, whatever the degree of acceptance, the law will have to be able to deal with not just the commonplace but also the rare and unique. Were the usual operation of a motor vehicle to lead to the frequent need for court intervention, driving would cease. A balance of regulation and freedom has allowed the Canadian driving experience to emerge.

Autonomous vehicles, or self-driving cars, are becoming more commonplace. The idea seems futuristic and far-fetched, but every day we come closer to realizing such technology in everyday life. Many aspects already exist and are integrated into existing conveyances, in the air, on the ground, and on the water, to varying degrees. There is a joke that new passenger airplanes are staffed by a pilot and a dog. The pilot is there to feed the dog, and the dog is there to bite the pilot if he tries to touch the controls. Will law be the biting dog?

In flying, shipping, and rail travel, automation has been adopted much more aggressively than in the automotive industry. The degrees of automation and their adoption have been much slower in motor vehicles, largely due to the high number of vehicles that would be affected and the cost involved. But automation has been creeping into driving since the advent of the automobile. Cruise control was pioneered in Wilson-Pilcher vehicles in the 1900s through use of a governor (a governor is a widely used device in automobiles that "governs" the amount of fuel being used and so acts as a cruise control). Anti-lock brakes appeared in the 1920s, seeing widespread adoption beginning in the 1970s. Even the intermittent windshield wiper, patented in 1964, is a form of automation that takes control from drivers, allowing them to focus on more imminent issues while moving. Society loves automation, and it loves new gadgets in vehicles. Although a level of control is being surrendered, when done properly automation can increase the safety, comfort, and enjoyment of the driving experience.

It is expected that drivers will take certain steps to ensure the safety of others. For example, drivers must signal lane changes and turns. Brake lights are required. Communication between drivers is a legal requirement. As every driver knows, however, this relies on other drivers as much as on themselves and is affected by the lowest common denominator. The worst drivers, whether careless or inexperienced, can affect the best ones, and a lack of communication has caused many accidents. Automating communication between vehicles is an obvious next step.

People worry about losing control but rarely consider how other drivers' unsafe or erratic actions may affect them. In the United States, the National Highway Traffic Safety Administration and the National Transportation Safety Board are calling for devices to be installed in vehicles so that they communicate their locations automatically in order to prevent collisions. There will be issues surrounding privacy, safety due to hacking, and reliability, which are discussed in different parts of this book.

Further automation is where driving is headed. While vehicles move at increasingly higher speeds and people are preferring to spend time connected to their phones to communicate and to entertain, steps will be required to ensure that drivers pay an appropriate level of attention. But, in the longer term, automation will be needed to accommodate safety and comfort. Proper automation will allow vehicles to move more quickly and safely by removing the risk of human error, and the law will need to adapt to deal with this. Civil liability may shift from drivers to manufacturers. Criminal acts will be changed by a "new normal" surrounding criminal intent. How would all of this be affected, for example, by a person's decision to take control of the vehicle rather than rely on automation? What if the person relies only on automation? Both are potentially risky. A new area of law will be needed and with it a new assessment of how current law can be adapted to that end. The authors hope that this book will be a ready resource as courts and litigants begin the journey down this new road.

It is important to recognize that one of the greatest strengths of common law is its ability to grow with and adapt to the changing circumstances of society. Common law can look to existing rationales to justify decisions regarding novel and dynamic situations. Concepts such as third-party liability in both criminal and civil matters already exist. The application of these principles to new technologies will be the question that this work seeks to address. What an autonomous vehicle is, how the level of automation affects legal outcomes, and what legislative gaps exist are also addressed.

Understanding automation is key. As already stated, *automation* does not necessarily equate with *autonomy*. Driver input will be required for some time. Technology is evolving, and over time it will continue to take over more parts of driving. To naysayers who believe that further automation is not likely, it can be pointed out that the desire for safety has always generated technological advances. It was unthinkable to drivers in the 1960s that a seatbelt would be a required safety device; airbags were a premium feature in the 1990s, and are now standard; backup cameras were considered high-end technology in the early 2000s, but they are now required safety equipment on every new vehicle in North America.

Over the coming decades, the law surrounding motor vehicles is going to go through profound changes as autonomous vehicles become common. Issues of law deriving from advances in technology will arise. The definition of *autonomy* will arise as we move to find new solutions to age-old problems, which range from gridlock to human error. With the transition to, and ongoing evolution of, autonomous vehicles, the law will have to adapt accordingly.

Autonomy can promote safety. It maintains a degree of predictability that human decision making often lacks. Speeds on highways may go up, but with autonomous vehicles human perception and reaction are taken out of the equation. In situations that might otherwise stop human drivers from driving safely, such as bad weather, vehicles will use sensor suites to communicate with each other and maintain safe distances, replacing the driver's need to make a decision. Accidents caused by fatigue will no longer be an issue. Much of the carelessness or poor reactions of drivers will become irrelevant. But this is a huge undertaking that will require widespread adoption of autonomous vehicles before the greatest benefits are realized. It cannot be a piecemeal process but rather a ground shift that revolutionizes the driving industry. The benefits are obvious. Imagine a world with no traffic jams, no motor vehicle accidents, and people travelling more quickly and safely than ever before.

Issues of legislation unique to Canada will arise as autonomous vehicles become more commonplace. The overlapping of federal and provincial heads of power will need to be considered. Although civil rules and regulatory offences involving vehicles are a provincial responsibility, changes to criminal law and transport safety law will be required at the federal level. Vehicles will need to meet federal safety standards, whereas drivers and perhaps the self-driving programs themselves will need to be vetted to provincially acceptable standards. Just as drivers require a licence from the province in which they reside, the self-driving car may need to meet certain criteria based on its level of automation, its intended use, and a host of other criteria. The development and implementation of automated technology to remove human drivers will require a national strategy that preserves the constitutional division of powers for regulation.

Some provinces are taking steps to prepare for this overlap of jurisdictional issues, hoping to gain from their openness to such vehicles as early adoption and the willingness to be used as a testing ground may lead tech companies to set up shop in some of these regions first. The equipment required in a vehicle is typically dealt with by Transport Canada, but much of the enforcement falls to provincial and local authorities.

The relationships we have with cars and traffic are as varied as the places where we drive. Automobiles, trucks, and buses and other forms of public transportation, allow a freedom of movement that was previously lacking. They affect real estate values. In Canada, the delivery of goods is largely dependent on the trucking industry. But what would that industry look like without drivers? Can goods be delivered faster and cheaper? How, and against whom, will liability be assessed? Human control over transportation may continue to exist to some degree, but the operator may cease to be present in the vehicle.

Because Canada is largely affected by its geography, anything that makes that geography more accessible, such as cars and other transportation systems, will have an impact on the country and likely require legal intervention at some point. The unique land that is Canada will also necessitate developing a system that can handle wide ranges of temperature and driving conditions that can arise in even a single day. Automated vehicles will need to deal with the realities of the Canadian environment.

The environmental impact of autonomous vehicles on efficient travel, such as a reduction in vehicles sitting in traffic, will be tremendous. The possibility of shared ownership of vehicles, the freedom of individuals to better schedule use of a motor vehicle, and the ability of the vehicle to drive itself to its next use will have an effect on the cost of motor vehicle access across income levels and lifestyles. Consider a ride-sharing app with a subscription service that allows individuals to request a pickup and ride without the need to have a driver. Consider that same app with vehicles that can go dormant when not needed rather than having taxi, Uber, or Lyft drivers waiting on their next call.

Much of North American society has been built around automobiles. Our cities are designed around them. Our economy is propelled by them. The impact and benefit of autonomous vehicles to people, to the environment, and to society as a whole will be profound. Although some of these advantages may be decades away, others may be pushed forward more quickly. Leaps in technology often occur around other societal problems. The issue of the environment or even an unforeseen event (for example, COVID-19) may fast-track the development of these technologies. Consequently, the laws surrounding them will adapt more quickly than we may expect.

The laws of autonomous vehicles have not yet been written, but their foundation is there. We just need to see it.

chapter 1

DEFINING AUTONOMOUS VEHICLES

A. WHAT IS AN AUTONOMOUS VEHICLE?

In simple terms, automation is the elimination of human labour, to varying degrees, in a given task or process. Although many aspects of vehicle operation have been automated over time, both criminal law and civil law continue to hold the driver ultimately responsible for the operation of the vehicle. As manufacturers of autonomous vehicles continue to increase the degree of decision making of artificial intelligence in order to reduce human error, the law will have to determine whether it will allow the human occupant to escape liability for any particular act, omission, or failure to act. Depending on the nature of the system implemented in a particular vehicle, different levels of care may be applied as against the driver.

Year after year, new technology has incrementally affected the focus of drivers. Early cars were controlled very simply. A steering wheel and a throttle control lever provided the minimal level of control in some of these vehicles. Developments in technology brought more complicated controls; gearboxes, clutches, windshield wipers, lights, and the like followed each other in rapid succession and offered varying levels of autonomy. Today, some vehicles automatically turn on lights or signals, whereas others operate windshield wipers. The automatic transmission is a form of automation that has shifted decision making from the driver to the vehicle. With each advance, some members of society have been reluctant to adopt them, worrying that the driver is no longer in control. Over time, however, each feature's safety and efficacy have improved, and adoption of the technology has become more widespread.

Today, an increasing number of vehicles sport features such as adaptive cruise control, lane-departure controls, and fully automated parallel parking. These technologies are generally things that the driver can turn on or off. The ability to opt in or out of the use of the automation technology gives the driver a greater feeling of control. At some point, however, the safety benefits that autonomous vehicles offer may trump a perceived comfort that some people gain from having direct control of the vehicle, and these technologies may become mandatory.

The Society of Automotive Engineers International (SAE) is the US-based organization that works on standardization in automotive construction and is referenced by governments throughout the world. SAE has been a key stakeholder in the definition of levels of automation in vehicles. Its standards and definitions have been adopted by governments in the ongoing classification of autonomous vehicles within legislation. Although SAE technical standards do not, in and of themselves, carry the force of law, the fact that many governments adopt SAE definitions as the standard to measure things against means that SAE's decisions have a significant impact.

The guiding document for automated driving is SAE's *Taxonomy and Definitions for Terms Related to Driving Automation Systems for On-Road Motor Vehicles.*[1] It recognizes the limitations of current automated driving systems (ADSs) and assigns levels of automation (see Table 1.1). At Levels 1 and 2, the ADS supports but does not replace the driver. At all times, the driver is responsible for operating and controlling the vehicle Controlling the operation of a vehicle is defined as dynamic driving tasks (DDTs). These tasks include monitoring the lateral motion (steering), the longitudinal motion (speed), and the environment; planning and responding;

---

1 SAE International, On-Road Automated Driving (ORAD) Committee, "Taxonomy and Definitions for Terms Related to Driving Automation Systems for On-Road Motor Vehicles," J3016_202104 (30 April 2021), online: www.sae.org/standards/content/j3016_202104.

and ensuring signalling. With higher levels of automation, the ADS has certain levels of fallback should the DDT be too unpredictable for the system. For example, a vehicle at a higher level of automation may still be presented with a situation that it cannot easily interpret, such as approaching an accident scene. The system then relies on the DDT fallback. At lower levels of automation, this means the human driver taking over; at higher levels, the system may be able to craft its own response, such as pulling over, activating hazard lights, and calling for emergency help.

In the following chapters, as we discuss the issues that may arise through further automation of vehicles, it is important to consider whether human behaviour may pose the ultimate obstacle to these initiatives. Most drivers like to drive. Most people like to be in control. Those who don't like to drive may choose public transportation. Although drivers have ultimately accepted existing automated functions regulating comfort within their vehicles, it is unknown whether they will want to relinquish decision making to their vehicle's artificial intelligence.

Drivers who do embrace a vehicle taking over control may not be so willing to embrace the fact that they still need to pay full attention to the road. In the United States, the National Transportation Safety Board (NTSB) has already recognized the fact that ADSs can be abused by an overreliance due to complacency.[2]

Automated vehicles provide opportunity and risk. A system is only as good as its design. The limitations on imagination at the design stage can have issues when a system fails to respond to an unimagined situation. Driver understanding of the functions and limitations of the technology they wield is integral to safety. For example, automated vehicles are being developed with complex sensing technology, but that technology may be affected by adverse weather, such as heavy rain or a snowstorm. Contrast that with a system that goes beyond the human experience and allows a vehicle to observe into the infrared and ultraviolet wavelengths of light, which may allow vehicles to see in the dark, look around corners, or detect

---

2 "Collision Between Car Operating with Partial Driving Automation and Truck-Tractor Semitrailer, Delray Beach, Florida, March 1, 2019," NTSB/HAB-20/01 (22 January 2020), online (pdf) at 11: *National Transportation Safety Board* www.ntsb.gov/investigations/AccidentReports/Reports/HAB2001.pdf.

subtle changes to road surfaces, such as icing, to determine a course of action safer than that which a human driver might choose. Only by understanding the breadth of the system can the driver put its functions to the safest use. Since a system, especially in the early days of automated systems, may not be able to react to every situation, the human driver may have to maintain an ability to operate the vehicle absent the automated systems.

No manufacturer will want to design a vehicle that becomes known for a particular fault. Consider the aircraft industry and the ongoing issues with the Boeing 737 MAX and the possibility that the plane's automated systems caused two fatal crashes, killing nearly 350 people. An automated vehicle that cannot operate safely will be quickly affected by market forces, if not regulatory reaction. Parameters important to operation will include the ability of ADSs at higher automation levels to accurately sense and respond to the wide variety of situations driving presents. Sensing technology, which at this time can be affected by impactful weather, may take greater time to develop. An automated vehicle whose sensors cannot differentiate between falling snow and a physical impediment that needs to be avoided will not succeed in Canada. To succeed in its purpose, sensing technologies will need to be able to observe and detect in multiple ways to safely provide checks and balances.

Increased road safety from autonomous vehicles cannot truly be realized until they become the dominant mode of transportation. Only then can tools such as vehicle-to-vehicle sensing technology become more widespread. This technology acts like the transponder system in aircraft. The internal processing of an ADS would allow the vehicle to note the location of other vehicles and plan around them without needing to detect them in other ways. One vehicle could tell another its location, speed, and direction. The two vehicles could then determine the most effective course of action to ensure the safety and speed of both vehicles. The widespread adoption of smartphones over the past two decades means that data is already being collected on a large scale. Pull out a smartphone and open a map. The live traffic situation being reflected comes from data pulled from millions of phones, all communicating through a central processing location to regularly update the speed and location of traffic snarls. Installing such technology in motor vehicles is not a far stretch. Combining this with the data already being mined from individuals' phones may create an even broader level of protection extending to pedestrians as well. It will not be a replacement for other sensing technology, but it may be a useful companion. Privacy concerns will exist, and the data being transmitted will need to be limited and protected in some way, perhaps through anonymization. But the fact that such technology already exists and is in widespread use by the general populace suggests that these privacy concerns can be addressed.

1) SAE Levels of Automation

TABLE 1.1 SAE LEVELS OF VEHICLE AUTOMATION[3]

Level	Name	Definition
0	No automation	All actions are controlled by the driver.
1	Driver assistance	Lateral or longitudinal vehicle motion may be controlled for sustained periods in specific circumstances. The driver is responsible for all other tasks.
2	Partial automation	Lateral and longitudinal vehicle motion may be controlled for sustained periods in specific circumstances. The driver must actively supervise the driving automation system.
3	Conditional automation	Automated control of all driving tasks with the requirement that the driver is available should unexpected issues arise.
4	High automation	Automated control of all driving tasks without the expectation that the driver will intervene, disengaging only to fail-safe.
5	Full automation	Fully automated control without any requirement for intervention or attention from the driver.

a) Level 0: No Automation

This is the most common level of automation in vehicles currently on the roadway. The driver has complete control and responsibility for all driving actions. The vehicle has no control over its actions. The driver must

3 "The 6 Levels of Vehicle Autonomy Explained," online: *Synopsys* www.synopsys.com/automotive/autonomous-driving-levels.html.

make all decisions regarding the operation of the vehicle. As the driver is responsible for all actions of movement by the vehicle, the responsibility for any and all movements is easily understood as belonging to the driver. The driver must perform all aspects of DDTs, including controlling speed, steering, monitoring the environment, planning, responding, and ensuring that proper signals are used.

b) Level 1: Driver Assistance

Level 1 automation is full control by the human driver—*hands on, eyes on*—but it allows the driver to set a particular single parameter. The most common example of this is cruise control. It is the lowest level of automation and is understood by most drivers on the roadway. Although control of a particular task is turned over to the automation, the driver is required to monitor it at all times. This level of automation also applies to adaptive cruise control because, as with regular cruise control, the driver remains responsible for all other aspects of driving, including steering and braking. The driver remains completely "in the loop" and relies on automation to perform only a single, limited task under the direct and continuous supervision of the driver. The vehicle supports the driver but does not supplant them in any way. The driver is responsible for observing and reacting to the changing driving environment and is the final arbiter of how the vehicle will be controlled. An important feature of Level 1 automation is that the system controls disengage immediately upon the request of the driver. Consider the effect of tapping your brakes while cruise control is engaged. The cruise control turns off, and full control over speed is immediately returned to the driver, without any further reasoning by the system. The system accepts the driver's override.

c) Level 2: Partial Automation

Advanced driver-assist systems fit this definition. This level is still *hands on, eyes on*, despite some automated features. Examples are Tesla's Autopilot and Cadillac's Super Cruise functions, which control both speed and steering. Partial automation may include systems that combine adaptive cruise control and lane-keeping technologies. The vehicle can maintain course and speed, adapt to make turns, avoid other vehicles, and generally drive itself in limited circumstances. The driver is nonetheless required to monitor the operation at all times, and the system may require the driver to take over in an instant. This sort of system generally requires some form of interaction by the driver to ensure continued interaction between the driver and the vehicle. Tesla achieves this by requiring the driver to interact with the steering wheel, whereas Cadillac has a system that detects gaze and assesses the amount of time a driver is focused on the road. This is the current level of technology that many people see as a form of self-driving vehicle. This characterization is not correct, however, and it reveals a poor understanding of the technology. As a result, unfortunate and dangerous issues can arise (see the NTSB report from Florida).[4]

At Level 2, the vehicle is responsible for control over the vehicle, but the human driver remains responsible for observing and reacting to the driving environment. Should the system have any concern, the driver is required to take back control in an instant. The driver's attention cannot be turned away from the driving task because the system's supports are not sufficient to allow the driver to be disengaged, or "out of the loop." Similar to Level 1, the ADS must disengage immediately upon the driver's request. The driver should feel supported by the automated technology but not confident enough to shift their attention from the task. At this level, many issues arise due to a misunderstanding of the limitations of Level 2 automation.

d) Level 3: Conditional Automation

At this level of automation, significant changes occur. As Level 3 automation is developed, it will have the greatest impact on the legal sphere and will require a rethinking of certain established areas of law. This is the first level where the automated system monitors the driving environment and the driver is expected to be allowed to turn their attention away from the task of driving. Although Level 2 automation is substantial, the driver is still expected to remain engaged at all times. Level 2 allows for hands off but eyes on. In contrast, Level 3 contemplates *both hands off and eyes off*. Level 3 has sensing capabilities that allow the vehicle to detect changes in

4 Above note 2.

the outside environment and make decisions for itself. This may include making the decision to pass another vehicle that is moving slower than the system wishes to travel. The driver must still remain available to take control should the system deem an event too dynamic to control, but the automation is of a sufficient degree to allow a person whose attention may be elsewhere to shift their attention back to the task of controlling the vehicle. At this level of automation, decisions may be made without the occupant's consideration or intervention. As a result, at this level of automation, responsibility for the actions taken may shift from the driver/occupant to someone else, such as a programmer or designer.

Audi has announced that, beginning with model year 2019, its A8 L would be the world's first Level 3 production vehicle. The regulatory process in most jurisdictions, including across Canada, is adapting and processing this development. To allow it to operate as a Level 3 vehicle, key hardware and software are being left out in North American markets until the regulatory smoke clears. However, the German model features what Audi calls Traffic Jam Pilot, which combines a variety of sensors, including light detection and ranging (LiDAR), and enhanced processing power to allow the vehicle to navigate through traffic without interaction with the driver.

When Level 3 automation is met, the vehicle takes over the observation and reaction functions from the driver along with the control of the vehicle. The human driver remains as a fallback should a significant dynamic situation require it, but, generally speaking, the human driver is not involved. At this level, the human driver cannot completely ignore the task of driving by, for example, sleeping but may be able to divert attention momentarily away from the function of driving—for example, to answer a text. The design and expectations of each vehicle will determine the legal standard to which a driver will be held. Momentary and perhaps even longer periods of inattention are likely to be tolerated, but some level of attentiveness and responsiveness will nonetheless be required.

Level 3 automation systems may still have some limitations, such as knowledge of a limited geography, operating only under a particular speed, or otherwise being unable to cope with certain evolving situations. If the driving conditions exceed the design of the system, the driver is expected to take over. The system is designed to appreciate when such a limit is imminent and require the driver to take control. If such an event occurs, the system will cede authority to the human driver within an appropriate amount of time after a request by the system for human intervention. At this level, the system is designed to disengage immediately upon the request of the driver.

e) Level 4: High Automation

At Level 4, although human interaction with the vehicle is possible, the vehicle does not require any interaction in the vast majority of situations. The vehicles are so automated that if there is a system failure or a dynamic situation, the vehicle can make a decision to fail-safe—that is, pull over and stop or consider other alternatives. The human occupant has the option to override the automated system but should not be required to do so. Level 4 technology is being developed but is not installed in any production model currently available. Legislative adaptation and infrastructure will be needed to allow these vehicles to operate in the wider world. Currently, such technology tends to be limited to very specific geography where testing is under way. This allows the vehicles to operate in well-known areas, typically at limited speeds and where other issues, such as pedestrian control, can be in place to ensure safety during development. Examples of this technology include the following:

- NAVYA, a French company, is already building and selling Level 4 shuttles and cabs in the United States that run fully on electric power and can reach a top speed of 55 mph.
- Alphabet's Waymo recently unveiled a Level 4 self-driving taxi service in Arizona, where they had been testing driverless cars—without a safety driver in the seat—for more than a year and more than 10 million miles.
- Canadian automotive supplier Magna has developed technology (MAX4) to enable Level 4 capabilities in both urban and highway environments. They are working with Lyft to supply high-tech kits that turn vehicles into self-driving cars.[5]

---

5 Above note 3.

This sort of technology presupposes that the driver is secondary to the automated system. Although human interaction could play a role in any incident that arises, generally speaking, the actions of the vehicle will be those of the automated system and not the vehicle. Assessing which mode the vehicle was operating in during any incident under legal review will shift the onus from occupant to manufacturer. As well, as this level of automation becomes more common and trust in such systems builds, judges and juries may begin to take a dimmer view of individuals who are in manual control of their vehicles during accidents, especially if a prosecutor or plaintiff can show that the automated systems could have prevented the accident. The standard of care, both criminally and civilly, is likely to shift as these systems become more accepted.

The shift in the orientation from human driver to machine driver can be further shown when considering an event where the human driver wishes to take over control of the vehicle. In some Level 4 settings, the machine may decide that it is unsafe to immediately relinquish control back to the human driver. Consider an example where the automated system was able to follow another vehicle closely due to its interaction or communication with that vehicle. The automated system may decide that the driver is not yet engaged sufficiently or that the situation is one where the human driver can no longer operate the vehicle safely. In these cases, the automated system may react in some way, such as distancing itself from the vehicle it was following, before letting the human driver take back control.

At Level 4, the human driver is almost completely removed from the equation. The vehicle systems control movement, observation, and reaction and have the ability to react to dynamic situations. The vehicle may not be able to deal with every situation in a way that continues driving, but it can react safely in any situation, though it may mean the vehicle has to stop until the dynamic situation it cannot process is resolved. At Level 4, a vehicle faced with an accident in front of it may slow down or pull over and notify emergency services as a response, whereas a human driver may navigate around the accident. The automated vehicle recognizes the dynamic situation and responds appropriately and in the safest manner. Occupants of a motor vehicle operating under the control of the ADS at Level 4 or 5 are considered passengers by SAE rather than drivers. Although the occupant could theoretically take control in a Level 4–equipped vehicle while the system is engaged, they have no input or control in normal circumstances.

Similar to Level 3, Level 4 automation may encounter a situation it cannot handle, and the system can request human intervention. If the intervention is not forthcoming, then the system is expected to fail-safe in some manner, such as slowing, activating hazard lights, and pulling over until the situation can be remedied. But if the human occupant requests to take control, the system may determine whether that is appropriate and take steps to ensure that the driver can safely do so. Only after achieving a safe condition will it then abdicate and allow the human driver to take back control.

f) Level 5: Full Automation

At this level, the occupant of the vehicle is fully a spectator. The expectation is that vehicles with this level of automation will not allow the occupant to take control. They will be able to go anywhere and do anything that a human driver could, perhaps even better than a human could. At this level of automation, the human element has been completely removed. The effect that this will have on all aspects of law will be significant. Although such vehicles could greatly enhance safety, when incidents do arise, assigning fault and responsibility will require different examinations than those that currently exist. The occupant of the vehicle would have no control over the actions of the vehicle. How, then, could the occupant be responsible for the actions of the vehicle? From a civil standpoint, any liability may be shifted to the designer or manufacturer.

Insurance concerns would change dramatically as the background or abilities of the occupant would no longer be relevant in determining risk. Instead, insurance may have to be shifted to the manufacturer. Owners would still be liable to some risk surrounding maintenance of the vehicle. They would have to ensure, and be able to prove, that they have not tampered with or altered the vehicle in a way that might create a danger. We can imagine a self-driving car that allowed the owner to control whether it could exceed the speed limit in certain circumstances. If a person allowed this, then some liability could still ensue, but it would be greatly controlled. Manufacturers may require limiters, for example. As more vehicles become more highly automated, speed limits might be modified to reflect the ability of the vehicles to react to dynamic situations faster than a human could. Separate speed limits for human drivers and automated drivers could be the natural evolution in this direction.

This level of automation is the inverse of Level 0. The driver cannot intervene in the operation of the vehicle. The human occupant could still have some input into the strategic use of the vehicle. For example, the occupant will still control where the vehicle is taking them (the destination), but the vehicle will determine how to get there (the route), and the speed, while maintaining observation, reaction, and control of the vehicle at all points. The vehicle system decides when to put the vehicle into motion and how. The occupant may have an emergency stop option, but the system will still maintain how that stop is to be initiated to prevent any danger, such as performing an emergency stop in heavy traffic at high speeds. At Level 5, the operational design domain is said to be unlimited, meaning that the vehicle system can make all of the decisions that would be made by the human driver in a Level 0 vehicle. Just as Level 0 has no system that aids the driver in the control of the vehicle, a Level 5 vehicle will have no human supporting the ADS.

B. CONCERNS ABOUT SETTING LEVELS

SAE recognizes concerns that many of the terms used in relation to automation are "functionally imprecise"[6] and therefore misleading. As a result, they are frequently misused or misapplied. These terms include *autonomous*, *driverless*, *driving modes*, *self-driving*, *unmanned*, and *robotic*. The public misunderstanding of such terms, and their misuse in marketing, has already caused harm in both the perception and use of automated systems and will likely continue to do so. In law, evidence is often elicited

---

6 Above note 1 at 34.

from people with a less than precise understanding of the subject matter. A court will likely have to consider the subjective understanding of the party or accused when considering standard of care or culpability.

1) Who Is the Driver?

The question of who is the driver is key when determining and apportioning liability, both criminally and civilly. Our current understanding of the law easily recognizes and deals with vehicles at Levels 0, 1, and 2. Levels 3 and 4 will be more problematic and will require a greater degree of scrutiny to discern whether decisions were made by the driver, the system, or some combination of the two. Whether the driver should have taken control will be a key consideration when assessing blame. There will be instances where the driver should have taken control from the system, but there will also be situations where the driver taking control may be the more negligent action. At Levels 3 and 4, the answer to the question "Who is the driver?" is not neither the driver nor the system but rather both. It will take time and real-world experience to provide a definitive answer to this question. At Level 5 automation, the driver is the system. There are already plans for Level 4 and 5 vehicles to be able to loiter without an occupant in them. In these situations, the human is no longer in control; the system is. With loiter capability, some people will not park their car but instead will allow it to roam until it is needed or find a parking spot on its own. In these situations, the vehicle is no longer under the direct care or control of the owner.

A secondary issue when considering whether the occupant or the car's system was in control at a particular point in time is the potential liability of the vehicle's owner. Although an owner is responsible for entrusting the vehicle to a competent driver and must properly maintain the vehicle, once fully automated vehicles are operational, can an unlicensed person or an impaired individual be alone during its operation? Could an owner be held responsible for not downloading software updates within a reasonable time? Certainly, the insurance industry will need to consider this interesting area of law and determine new actuarial tables to help in assessing risk.

2) Taxonomy Versus Regulation

SAE makes certain observations in its setting of levels. It notes that its actions to classify different levels are not to provide specifications or impose requirements but instead are intended to provide a common taxonomy to allow discussion and design of automated vehicles. The intent is to create a common language and standardization to allow for further development. The different levels are to meet design intention rather than to measure a particular system and assign it a level. Failing to meet any particular level does not connote a lack of safety or non-compliance but rather would just lead to a different classification of the system in question. Levels are assigned, not measured.

Some technologies automate certain tasks for the driver but are not recognized in the same way. For example, lane-drift or blind-spot warning systems do not operate on a sustained timeline. They operate in the moment to prevent a particular action, such as changing lanes when another vehicle is in the driver's blind spot. Since these systems do not control the speed or steering of the vehicle over time but instead only in the immediate event, they are not classified by SAE as automation. The difference in the legal or commonplace understanding of automation and the engineering definition is important to note. Understanding this difference may be important in characterizing a system, the decisions and actions of a driver, and the ultimate result that occurred to a trier of fact. A lane-departure system may not have allowed the driver to take a certain action that led to a different sort of an accident than otherwise might have occurred regardless of whether the system was acting over a sustained period of time. Anything that takes control of the vehicle out of the hands of the human driver may have an impact in legal proceedings.

SAE recognizes concerns regarding certain "deprecated terms." SAE has determined that these terms are "functionally imprecise (and therefore misleading)" and that "they are frequently misused by application to lower levels of driving automation (i.e., levels 1 and 2) in which the driver automation system does not perform the entire DDT."[7] These terms

7 SAE, *Taxonomy*, above note 1 at 28.

include *autonomous*, *driving modes*, *self-driving*, *unmanned*, and *robotic*. SAE states its concerns with the misunderstanding of such imprecise terms. Of course, such terms are regularly used by the public and by those marketing such vehicles. The public misunderstanding of such terms has already caused harm in the use of automated systems and will likely continue to do so. In law, where precision is often important, evidence is often elicited from people with a less than precise understanding of the subject matter. Looking to the subjective understanding of the person before the court will require resorting to these terms and attempting to relate the subjective understanding of an individual to the more objective taxonomy that SAE has set out.

chapter 2

EXAMPLES OF AUTONOMOUS OR SEMI-AUTONOMOUS VEHICLES CURRENTLY IN PRODUCTION

FIGURE 2.1 EXAMPLES OF EXISTING AUTOMATED SENSING SYSTEMS[1]

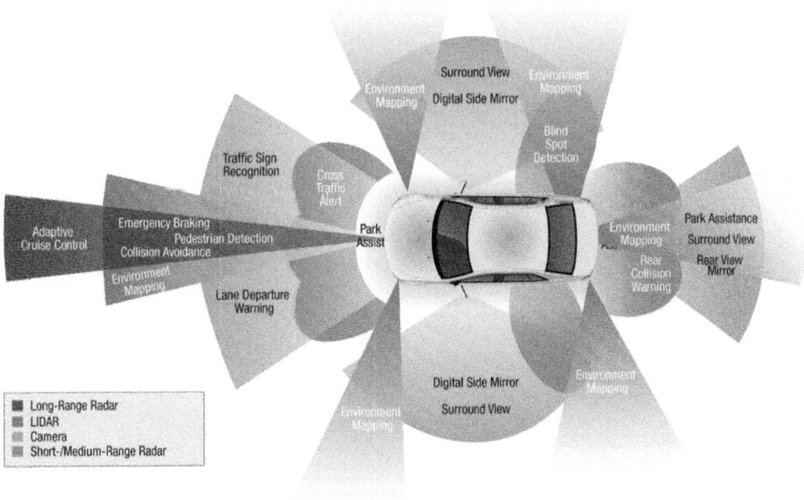

IMAGE COURTESY OF TEXAS INSTRUMENTS INC.

1 Steven Ashley, "Centimeter-Accurate GPS for Self-Driving Vehicles" (2 November 2016), online: *SAE International* www.sae.org/news/2016/10/centimeter-accurate-gps-for-self-driving-vehicles.

A. TESLA AUTOPILOT

Tesla has integrated the hardware necessary for its Autopilot feature into all of its models.[2] It notes that ongoing software updates are important to continually improving functionality over time. The Autopilot system involves the use of eight cameras that provide 360 degrees of visibility around the car to a distance of 250 metres. Furthermore, twelve ultrasonic sensors and forward-looking radar are used. Tesla states that the system "is able to see through heavy rain, fog, dust, or even the car ahead."[3]

Sensors are noted in the owner's manual to Tesla's Model S vehicle as follows:

1. A camera is mounted above the rear license plate.
2. Ultrasonic sensors are located in the front and rear bumpers.
3. A camera is mounted in each door pillar.
4. Three cameras are mounted to the windshield above the rear view mirror.
5. A camera is mounted to each front fender.
6. Radar is mounted behind the front bumper.[4]

Tesla stresses the importance of the computing power on board its vehicles. It notes that "current Autopilot features require active driver supervision and do not make the vehicle autonomous," although this is not noted as prominently as it is by other manufacturers. In the Model S owner's manual, Tesla warns of the following limitations:

- Poor visibility (due to heavy rain, snow, fog, etc.).
- Bright light (due to oncoming headlights, direct sunlight, etc.).
- Damage or obstructions caused by mud, ice, snow, etc.
- Interference or obstruction by object(s) mounted onto the vehicle (such as a bike rack).

---

2 "Future of Driving," online: *Tesla* www.tesla.com/en_CA/autopilot.

3 *Ibid.*

4 "Model S Owner's Manual: Software Version 2020.20, North America" (2020) at 79, online (pdf): *Tesla* www.tesla.com/sites/default/files/model_s_owners_manual_north_america_en_us.pdf.

- Obstruction caused by applying excessive paint or adhesive products (such as wraps, stickers, rubber coating, etc.) onto the vehicle.
- Narrow or winding roads.
- A damaged or misaligned bumper.
- Interference from other equipment that generates ultrasonic waves.
- Extremely hot or cold temperatures.[5]

A further iteration of Autopilot is the "Navigate on Autopilot" function, which suggests lane changes and other tips to try to provide a faster travelling time. This function can also steer the vehicle toward highway interchanges or exits based on user-programmed destinations.

Tesla does not restrict the use of its automated systems to any particular roadway, although it does recommend against their use in dynamic situations. Its "Smart Summon" function allows drivers to command the vehicle to come to them. Tesla states that the vehicle can navigate the complex environment of a parking lot with this function.

According to Tesla, its vehicles are already equipped with the necessary hardware to allow for full self-driving capability, and this is the company's goal. Tesla indicates that it is merely a matter of achieving the software capabilities to allow for this. It suggests that such upgrades will be made possible through automatic updates downloaded by the vehicle.

Tesla refers to programming that will allow drivers to summon their vehicle when leaving their house and then, having arrived at a destination, send the vehicle to find a parking spot on its own. These functions are not yet available but are in development.

The system in a Tesla relies on autonomous emergency braking (AEB), forward collision warning (FCW), side collision warning, lane assist, traffic light and stop sign control, and automatic high beams as its current automated systems. (The availability of some functions varies depending on the region in which the vehicle is operated.) The Model S owner's manual devotes forty-five pages to the functioning of these systems, and an informed driver would be well advised to review them.

---

5 *Ibid* at 80.

B. CADILLAC SUPER CRUISE

Cadillac refers to its Super Cruise system as "the first true hands-free driving-assistance feature for compatible roads."[6] It notes that the company has achieved more than 8 million kilometres of hands-free driving. The system is currently available on the 2018, 2019, and 2020 model years for Cadillac's CT6.

The Super Cruise system requires drivers to still remain involved in the system. It requires an active OnStar plan, active Wi-Fi hot spot enabled, a working electrical system, cellphone reception, and a Global Positioning System (GPS) signal. Cadillac's website indicates that the Super Cruise system works by using multiple systems, including its own OnStar system, light detection and ranging (LiDAR) mapping, in-vehicle cameras, radar sensors, and GPS as sensing technology for the vehicle to read the road.

The company's website also states multiple times that "paying sufficient attention" is important for the driver at all times, including monitoring whether lane markings are visible, GPS is available, and there are no system faults. Lane-marking concerns include markings being obscured by glare or poor weather conditions. Camera and radar sensors must not be covered or obstructed.

The system works through a combination of adaptive cruise control (ACC) and the forward collision system, the latter being a combination of FCW and AEB. Cadillac also has a "Teen Driver" function that must be deactivated. The system relies on a "Driver Attention Camera," which detects whether the driver is remaining attentive to the task of driving by assessing the focus of the driver's eyes. If the system determines that a driver has turned their gaze from the roadway long enough, then the system will disable itself. It provides warnings both visually, through green and then red lights, as well as audible alarms, including a voice prompt. A driver can push a button to find out the reason for the system disengagement so that appropriate action can be taken.

---

6 "Innovating the Future of Driving. Again.," online: *Cadillac* www.cadillac.com/world-of-cadillac/innovation/super-cruise.

The system is programmed to function only on "compatible highways." For example, Highway 401 from Windsor to Montreal is the most compatible but has notable gaps, including through Cambridge; from Guelph to Milton; numerous short gaps across Toronto, including from Dufferin Street to the Don Valley Parkway; and gaps in Durham and near Cobourg. Cadillac recognizes these gaps and states that it is working to fill them. Software updates are required in order to access newly mapped areas. Mapped areas in Canada remain largely restricted to limited-access highways.

The discussion of Super Cruise takes up thirty-eight pages in the manual. Of interest is that the manual provides instructions for how to delete data that the system may generate if a person so wishes. As with other vehicles, understanding the limitations of the system is key to safe use.

C. BMW PERSONAL COPILOT

BMW does not currently advertise its systems as automated but recognizes that they have reached SAE's Level 2. Automated functions include Parking Assistant, where the vehicle can park itself when a space is identified by the driver; Active Lane Keeping and Traffic Jam Assistant, which detect optimal lane changes to maximize speed; and cruise control.

The company notes that its ACC and lane-assist technology includes "support in narrow places [, which] is also available up to 210 km/h."[7] The systems provide computed solutions to allow for lane changing or suggestions regarding evasive manoeuvres in the case of obstacles detected, but the driver, not the system, is expected to undertake those manoeuvres. The exception to this is the Emergency Stop Assistant, which will take control of the vehicle to drive it safely to the side of the road if the system determines that the driver is experiencing a medical emergency.

Sensing equipment on the vehicles includes top view, panoramic view, and remote three-dimensional (3D) view. The Reversing Assistant stores data regarding the last 50 metres travelled to allow for a reconstruction of that distance to aid the driver in parking or to allow the vehicle to park

---

7 "BMW Personal Copilot: Autonomous Driving," online: *BMW* www.bmw.com.mt/en/topics/fascination-bmw/bmw-autonomous-driving.html.

itself. BMW has partnered with some parking facilities to allow the vehicle to self-park there, including on multiple floors, through highly controlled and detailed mapping of the facilities.

The system is referenced as "driver assistance functions" and relies on radar and camera sensors, like most other manufacturers' automated systems. BMW has stated that its next generation of systems will be able to detect speed limit signs and interpret traffic lights to allow speed to be regulated in an easier and more convenient manner.

D. AUDI

Audi has released the A8, the first production vehicle to have been developed for conditional autonomous driving at SAE Level 3. This functionality has been disabled in North American markets at the present time and is awaiting regulatory approval. All produced vehicles are equipped with the necessary hardware for this capability, but the software to allow use of the functionality is disabled.

Their Traffic Jam Pilot function can take over all driving tasks in slow-moving traffic up to 60 km/h on multi-lane roads with physical separation of traffic—that is, highways. This includes control over starting, stopping acceleration, steering, and braking. When the operational parameters are met, drivers are able to shift their focus away from the driving task. If the system reaches a limit beyond its operational design domain (ODD), then the driver will be required to take over.

Sensing equipment includes radar sensors, cameras behind the windshield, peripheral cameras on each mirror, a rearview camera, both peripheral and night-vision cameras mounted in the grille, and ultrasonic sensors. Of interest is that certain functions, including parking, can be remotely accessed with sensor data, including 360-degree camera functionality being provided to the mobile device of the driver.

Audi uses a laser scanner in its collection of sensing equipment. The scanner works in conjunction with other sensors. It operates to cover a field approximately 80 metres long, covering 145 degrees of view. This sensor is conceptually similar to any LiDAR system.

The A8 owner's manual has the following warnings and tips:

- The use of an assist system cannot overcome the natural laws of physics. A collision cannot be prevented in certain circumstances. . . .
- The systems may not function as expected in unusual driving situations, such as driving offroad, on unpaved roads, on loose gravel, on inclines, or on grooves in the road.
- The systems may not function correctly in unclear traffic situations, such as turning lanes, exit ramps, construction zones, rises or dips that obstruct visibility, intersections, toll stations, or city traffic.[8]

Current functionality in North America includes ACC, FCW, AEB, integrated night vision, speed limit and traffic light detection, lane assist, and emergency assist, where an inactive driver is sensed and the vehicle will come to a stop if the driver does not respond to system messaging. The A8 owner's manual dedicates forty-two pages to the vehicle's automation systems.

Additional systems that Audi has incorporated include a turn assist function, which monitors traffic in an oncoming lane when a turn signal is activated and the vehicle is driving below 10 mph. This is an extension of AEB to a turning situation.[9]

The ACC function allows for "stop and go" functionality, whereby the driver can set the distance to be maintained between the vehicle in front of the driver and maintain this distance, including a full stop and restart. This allows for greater use of ACC during slow or stopped traffic.

A trailer manoeuvre assist is also available that provides direction to the driver backing up as to which way to steer in order to move the trailer in a particular direction. Similar to BMW, Audi also provides for a collision-avoidance assist where, if the system detects a possible collision incident, it will provide guidance to the driver as to computed solutions to avoid a crash, although the driver must execute the manoeuvre.

8 *2019 Audi A8—Owner's Manual* (13 December 2018) at 138, online: *Audi* https://ownersmanuals2.com/audi/a8-s8-2019-owners-manual-73362.

9 "Driver Assistance Systems" (17 February 2017), online: *Audi MediaCenter* www.audi-mediacenter.com/en/technology-lexicon-7180/driver-assistance-systems-7184.

Audi currently has no plans to allow Traffic Jam Pilot in the North American market due to the complex regulatory framework. The driver attentiveness issue inherent in Level 3 technology, whereby the driver may be required to take back control if the system's ODD is exceeded, has left lawmakers at a loss and the issue of civil liability attaching to the manufacturer as an impediment to wider adoption.

E. KIA DRIVE WiSE

Kia states that its DRIVE WiSE system is designed to provide safety, convenience, and efficiency through the use of advanced driver assistance system (ADAS) technologies. Current technologies integrated into the Kia DRIVE WiSE system include ACC, FCW, AEB, and lane assist. Parking assist technologies are also integrated. The brand seeks to promote recognition of dangers with timely and intuitive warnings to drivers to allow better understanding of the driving environment while promoting optimization of routes. These functions all perform at SAE Level 2.

F. HYUNDAI SMARTSENSE

Hyundai has piloted an SAE Level 4 vehicle in South Korea but has not moved beyond the initial concept with this level of automation.

Its SmartSense technology uses many SAE Level 2 automation systems, including ACC (referred to as Smart Cruise Control), lane keeping, a blind-spot collision warning system, and FCW. Additional driving assist systems include Leading Vehicle Departure Alert, which notifies the driver when a stopped vehicle in traffic in front begins moving, and Highway Auto Curve Slowdown, which automatically slows the vehicle on curves while the cruise control is activated.

G. FORD/ARGO AI

Ford has partnered with Argo AI to develop an autonomous vehicle. Current road testing is occurring at numerous cities across the United States. Ford is not only developing autonomous vehicle technologies but is also working toward different applications of certain business structures, including ride-sharing apps and delivery services using the autonomous vehicles it is piloting.

Ford is using LiDAR and camera sensors and the data they generate to create high-resolution 3D maps. Its goal is to use these maps and the data generated from multiple vehicles to increase the reliability of the data obtained.

Ford and Argo are already testing in cities with a variety of differences, which is important to long-term development, particularly in locations such as Detroit, which experience a wide range of weather.

H. NISSAN PROPILOT ASSIST

Nissan fully acknowledges that its technology is designed as an SAE Level 2 automation only. It includes ACC, FCW, AEB, and lane assist technologies. ProPilot Assist specifically requires drivers to keep their hands on the wheel at all times or the technology will disengage.

I. HONDA

Honda has partnered with GM to develop the concept car model called Origin. It is specifically designed as an SAE Level 5 automated vehicle. It is not designed for purchase but rather to be used in conjunction with GM's Cruise ride-sharing app.

Honda is targeting Level 4 automation for private use in 2025.

J. MERCEDES-BENZ DRIVE PILOT

Mercedes-Benz is working to develop an SAE Level 3 system called DRIVE PILOT. It is designed for use on fully access-controlled highways, such as 400-series highways or freeways. The company notes that it already has many autonomous features, including AEB, lane assist, vehicle-to-everything (V2X) communication, and ACC.

The DRIVE PILOT system continuously monitors drivers to ensure that they remain available to resume control if required. The system will function during dynamic matters to a safe default if the driver is not able to resume control quickly enough.

Mercedes-Benz is designing the ODD for the DRIVE PILOT system to require machine-detectable lane markings; the absence of tunnels, tollbooths, or traffic-control devices; and legal regulatory approval in the jurisdiction. The plan is to use a geofence to limit the operation of the vehicle to locations where high-definition mapping has been done. Environmental factors, such as weather, will also limit availability. The company plans to continually increase the locations where the system can function.

Sensing equipment will include radar, LiDAR, camera, road-moisture sensors, ultrasonic sensors, and microphones.[10] Design parameters include dealing with crash-imminent scenarios such as sudden braking by the lead vehicle, sudden merging by another vehicle, or sudden appearance of an obstacle. The company recognizes that "there are physical limits to what the technology can do to avoid certain sudden events, just as there are physical limits to what the best of drivers can do to avoid crashes during sudden events."[11]

Design consideration has been given to the possibility of a crash while the DRIVE PILOT system is engaged. The system will attempt to transition to the user to allow the driver to take control, but if the driver is unable to for some reason, then the system will attempt to maintain steering control and bring the vehicle to a controlled stop. If steering control is no longer possible, then a full braking manoeuvre is executed to reduce the risk of secondary impact with other vehicles, obstacles, or pedestrians. The vehicle will automatically activate hazard lights, summon emergency assistance, turn on cabin lights, and provide information to first responders, including personal information of the occupants if available and the schematics of the vehicle to facilitate rescue.

---

10 "Introducing DRIVE PILOT: An Automated Driving System for the Highway" at 20, online (pdf): *Daimler* www.daimler.com/documents/innovation/other/2019-02-20-vssa-mercedes-benz-drive-pilot-a.pdf.

11 *Ibid* at 21.

Mercedes-Benz discusses the importance of consumer education and training to encourage adoption of automation.[12] This is planned through hands-on training, printed materials, and digital media. It is recognized that customers will have varying technical backgrounds and that technology such as this will be new to almost all consumers.

K. TOYOTA/LEXUS HIGHWAY TEAMMATE

Lexus and Toyota, its parent company, have developed the Highway Teammate system. Currently designed as an SAE Level 2 automation, the companies have said that they expect in the future to allow upgrades to SAE Level 3 as software and regulatory legislation come into force. Toyota has previously indicated a wariness about SAE Level 3 due to the requirement for hand-off between the system and the driver, indicating a preference for moving directly to SAE Level 4 if possible. Toyota had planned on showcasing SAE Level 4 vehicles in Tokyo during the 2020 Summer Olympics, but the COVID-19 pandemic delayed such plans.

Highway Teammate is expected to add to the SAE Level 2 technologies, such as ACC and AEB, by allowing the ability to handle highway lane changes, merging, and diverging through further use of side-detecting sensor suites used in systems, such as lane assist. Full details on the system have yet to be released.

L. WAYMO (FORMERLY GOOGLE SELF-DRIVING CAR PROJECT)

Billed as "the world's most experienced driver," Waymo's driver system has been put through millions of kilometres of driving in the real world as well as billions of miles in simulations. The system design includes the company building detailed 3D maps of the area in which it will be allowed to operate, including "information such as road profiles, curbs

12 See online: www.daimler.com/documents/innovation/other/vssa-mercedes-benz-and-bosch.pdf & www.mercedes-benz.com/en/innovation/autonomous/mercedes-benz-futureinsight-human-first.

and sidewalks, lane markers, crosswalks, traffic lights, stop signs, and other road features."[13]

Sensors are designed to detect and identify a number of objects, including pedestrians, cyclists, vehicles, roadwork, and other obstructions, as well as to read traffic controls. Waymo states that its sensors can see up to 300 metres. The sensor suite includes LiDAR, radar, GPS, a camera system, and supplemental sensors, which include audio microphones to detect sirens. Waymo vehicles are designed to act at an SAE Level 4 state of automation.

Rather than being an automobile manufacturer, Waymo's roots are in software development as an offspring of its parent company, Alphabet (which also owns Google). The company stresses that its predictive software allows its vehicle to determine the most likely paths of objects and react accordingly. The sensor suite provides data that the computing system perceives, predicts, and plans around. Perception includes identifying the objects detected, prediction includes identifying the likely behaviour of a similar object, and planning includes implementing a decision to ensure safe operation in relation to both the goal of continued travel and the object.[14] Specific design considerations have been implemented with first responders in mind so that Waymo's vehicles can detect and react by yielding and pulling over when first responders need to overtake them.

Waymo is currently testing autonomous passenger vehicles, a rideshare/taxi feature, and freight applications with Class 8 trucks (tractor-trailers and eighteen-wheelers).

M. ADVANCED TECHNOLOGIES GROUP (UBER)

Similar to Waymo, Advanced Technologies Group (ATG) began not in vehicle manufacture but in software. Its specific goal is not to manufacture a vehicle capable of autonomous function but to be able to take an already manufactured vehicle and modify the vehicle through the installation of

13 "Technology," online: *Waymo* https://waymo.com/tech/.

14 "Waymo Safety Report: On the Road to Fully Self-Driving" at 8, online (pdf): *Waymo* https://storage.googleapis.com/sdc-prod/v1/safety-report/Safety%20Report%20 2018.pdf.

sensors and software to support its self-driving system. Although the company's stated goal is not to produce such a vehicle itself, ATG has partnered with automotive manufacturers, including Toyota and Volvo, to integrate their systems at the manufacturing level.

By creating autonomous vehicles, ATG hopes to eliminate the need for human drivers in the use of its Uber app. This would allow the company to become, in essence, the world's largest taxi operator. Regulatory issues with Uber already abound regarding whether drivers are akin to taxi drivers or something else. ATG hopes to create a more efficient, safer, and cheaper way for people to travel.

Radar, LiDAR, seven cameras, GPS, and wireless data all contribute to the sensor suite on ATG's vehicles.[15]

15 For further information on the ATG system, see also *Collision Between Vehicle Controlled by Developmental Automated Driving System and Pedestrian, Tempe, Arizona, March 18, 2018*, NTSB/HAR-19/03, PB2019-101402 (reissued 26 June 2020), online (pdf): *National Transportation Safety Board* www.ntsb.gov/investigations/AccidentReports/Reports/HAR1903.pdf. The report is further reviewed in Appendix 1.

chapter 3

LEGISLATIVE AND POLICY REVIEW

In a federation such as Canada, the division of powers is an interesting place to begin the analysis of how statutory law will have to adapt to the changes created by autonomous vehicles. Provinces have had the authority to deal with local matters, such as driving and traffic, yet the federal government controls criminalization of actions. Driving crosses both spheres in the criminal and quasi-criminal realms. Civil matters are a provincial head of power, yet vehicle safety is regulated at the federal level, setting requirements for manufacturers across the country. Canada also cedes control over certain things, such as vehicle emission standards, to other authorities. A nation of its size cannot have the final say on issues that will affect manufacturers around the world but will have the ability to play a role in shaping the laws that will regulate such matters for years into the future.

A. FEDERAL REGULATORY LAWS

1) *Motor Vehicle Safety Act*, SC 1993, c 16

This is the federal Act that governs safety equipment and importation requirements for motor vehicles. It allows the federal transport minister to regulate safety standards and to require remediation if a safety concern is identified. It bars the import or use of vehicles that do not meet the requisite safety requirements. At section 9, it allows for an exemption from standards for a period to be specified for vehicles that "promote the development of (a) new safety features that are equivalent to or superior to those that conform to prescribed standards; or (b) new kinds of vehicles, technologies, vehicle systems or components."

Sections 13(1) and 13.1 of the Act allow for the adoption of regulations already in use in another country and the creation of short-term regulatory changes while full regulation is being considered. This power may be applied to autonomous vehicles by adopting laws already on the books in other jurisdictions.

Transport Canada, which is responsible for investigating and managing safety recalls and remedy of non-compliance, is the federal authority that will have a significant impact on shaping regulations for the design of and required functions for autonomous vehicles.

2) Testing Highly Automated Vehicles in Canada: Guidelines for Trial Organizations

Transport Canada

These guidelines[1] set up a number of recommendations but do not carry punishments for non-compliance, although failure to comply with them may be considered in determining an appropriate standard of care in a civil or criminal proceeding. The guidelines encourage sufficient testing in closed-course environments or on-road testing in another jurisdiction or some other form of validation mechanism, such as computer simulation prior to trialling on public roads. "Tests should consider the various environmental, road, and traffic conditions that can reasonably be expected to be encountered within the geographical area and timeframe for the planned trial."[2]

---

1 Minister of Transport & the Canadian Council for Motor Transport Administrators, "Testing Highly Automated Vehicles in Canada: Guidelines for Trial Organizations" (2018), online (pdf): *Transport Canada* https://tc.canada.ca/sites/default/files/migrated/19_ah_01_automated_vehicles_layout_en_r13.pdf.

2 *Ibid* at 11.

Labelling of trial vehicles is reviewed and referred to provincial or territorial transport agencies to determine what is appropriate. The guidelines encourage notifying regional or municipal officials, including local law enforcement and emergency response personnel, of any trials to occur within their jurisdiction and providing these officials with the information required for safe interactions with the automated vehicle.[3]

Data recording is highlighted as being especially important with autonomous vehicles. Vehicles should be able to transition safely between automated and non-automated modes, provide warning to the driver of the same, and provide for sufficient time to transition safely or bring the vehicle to a safe, minimal-risk condition and should have a mechanism to alert the driver of the failure of the autonomous system.

With specific regard to SAE Level 4 or 5 driverless vehicles, additional considerations are recommended. These include prior testing to perform all driving tasks, including object and event detection and response (OEDR) within the operational design domain (ODD); remote monitoring, including the ability to communicate with passengers; an alert to those monitoring should the automated system disengage or experience failure; and a fallback to achieve a minimal-risk condition.[4]

Transport Canada encourages testers to make a self-declaration of vehicle safety, including:

- Specifying the ODD of the trial vehicle and confirming that the trial vehicle is able to perform all the necessary [dynamic driving tasks (DDT)] within its ODD and will only be tested within its ODD;
- Specifying an appropriate DDT fallback, in the event of system malfunctions or failures while the vehicle is in operation, that can bring the vehicle to a minimal risk condition;
- Ensuring drivers or remote drivers are adequately trained and will remain attentive during the trial operations, incorporating measures to manage fatigue and to prevent driver distraction;

---

3 *Ibid.*

4 *Ibid* at 12.

- Ensuring the [automated driving system (ADS)] is equipped to facilitate safe human–machine interactions; this includes clear and effective communication with passengers and other road users;
- Ensuring a safe transition between automated and non-automated modes (where applicable), including the transfer of the DDT from the ADS to the driver or remote driver (if applicable), and vice versa;
- Addressing the safe operation of the trial vehicle in adverse weather conditions;
- Safely managing interactions with other road users, including vulnerable road users such as pedestrians and cyclists and protection of onboard users;
- Ensuring software and hardware updates to the ADS during the trial period will be safely managed and that provincial and territorial road transport agencies are notified of any changes; and
- Assessing and ensuring any cybersecurity risks associated with the trial are adequately addressed.[5]

Transparency is encouraged by the reporting of unplanned automation errors that result in serious incidents—for example, crashes; contravention of a traffic law, which compromises safety; or any other scenario where safety is compromised—and that such reports be shared with Transport Canada. Collaboration and information sharing also are encouraged, including allowing trials that are open to the general public to be observed in person by Transport Canada and provincial or territorial transport agencies.[6]

3) Canada's Safety Framework for Automated and Connected Vehicles

Transport Canada, February 2019 (most recent)

This document[7] sets out the federal policy direction for autonomous and connected vehicles. Its primary focus is safety. Research, testing, and data

5 *Ibid* at 13.

6 *Ibid* at 15.

7 "Canada's Safety Framework for Automated and Connected Vehicles" (2019), online (pdf): *Transport Canada* https://tc.canada.ca/sites/default/files/migrated/tc_safety_framework_for_acv_s.pdf.

collection are noted as foundational for continued development. The ability to adopt foreign regulations as in sections 13 and 13.1 of the *Motor Vehicle Safety Act* (MVSA) is considered in relation to autonomous vehicles. Consideration of the impact of the Canadian Motor Vehicle Safety Standards (CMVSS) to autonomous vehicles is given, especially as vehicles are developed that do not contemplate a human driver. Something as simple as the requirement for a brake pedal may be a hurdle to the testing or use of fully autonomous vehicles.

New powers, created in 2018, that allow for administrative monetary penalties and consent agreements with enforceable terms give Transport Canada a range of tools when working with manufacturers to ensure that safety standards are met. Transport Canada's Motor Vehicle Test Centre in Blainville, Quebec, has been modernized to allow for increased testing of advanced driver assistance system (ADAS) functions.

4) Safety Assessment for Automated Driving Systems in Canada

Transport Canada, January 2019

Transport Canada provides developers with an assessment tool for determining the safety of the technologies they wish to implement, recognizing that there is no existing regulation or standard for many autonomous driving technologies.[8] Thirteen points are identified as important for identification and assessment:

1) Level of automation and intended use
2) ODD
3) OEDR
4) International standards and best practices
5) Testing and validation, including pre-deployment testing and consideration of risk
6) Safety systems
7) Human–machine interface and accessibility of controls

8 "Safety Assessment for Automated Driving Systems in Canada" (2018), online (pdf): *Transport Canada* https://tc.canada.ca/sites/default/files/migrated/tc_safety_assessment_for_ads_s.pdf.

8) Public education and awareness
9) User protections during collisions or system failures
10) Cybersecurity
11) System updates and after-market repairs or modifications
12) User privacy
13) Collaboration with government agencies and law enforcement

Although not mandatory, consideration of the above topics is highly recommended by Transport Canada. An assessment writer's guide forms part of the report as Annex A, which is reproduced in Appendix 3 of this book.

5) Senate Report and Government Response

The Standing Senate Committee on Transport and Communications provided its report, *Driving Change: Technology and the Future of the Automated Vehicle*,[9] in January 2018 and outlined sixteen recommendations. The government's response in July 2018[10] addressed the recommendations. It identified the creation of an automated- and connected-vehicles working group and the importance of working with provincial and US partners in the development of regulation and cross-border functionality. Technical requirements related to cybersecurity and frequency bandwidth were acknowledged. Disruption beyond the transportation environment was noted, and the government stated that it recognized both the pitfalls and the opportunities offered to the economy by autonomous vehicles.

---

9 "Driving Change: Technology and the Future of the Automated Vehicle," Report of the Standing Senate Committee on Transport and Communications (January 2018), online (pdf): *Senate of Canada* https://sencanada.ca/content/sen/committee/421/TRCM/Reports/COM_RPT_TRCM_AutomatedVehicles_e.pdf.

10 "Government Response to the Ninth Report of the Standing Senate Committee on Transport and Communications, *Driving Change: Technology and the Future of the Automated Vehicle*" (July 2018), online (pdf): *Senate of Canada* https://sencanada.ca/content/sen/committee/421/TRCM/reports/MinisterGarneau_GovResp_b.pdf.

6) Canadian Jurisdictional Guidelines for the Safe Testing and Deployment of Highly Automated Vehicles

Canadian Council of Motor Transport Administrators, Automated Vehicles Working Group, June 2018

The Canadian Council of Motor Transport Administrators (CCMTA) seeks to promote consistency across Canadian jurisdictions in the regulation of autonomous vehicles. It addresses the federal and provincial powers discussed above, along with municipal roles that include roadway bylaw enforcement, traffic and parking enforcement, infrastructure adaptation, and managing passenger transportation (for example, taxi licences).

This paper[11] provides a number of recommendations for jurisdictions as well as manufacturers. It encourages jurisdictions responsible for regulation to create standing committees to deal with autonomous vehicles to work toward removing unnecessary barriers to safe testing and deployment. It suggests that consideration be given to the topic of registration and issuing permits at both the testing and full permitting levels, including recognition of permitting from other jurisdictions. Defining driver and passenger roles, as well as new kinds of training for highly automated vehicles, will be required. Recognizing that different skills will need to be tested for licensing drivers for the use of automated vehicles is needed. Whether this should be a different class of licence, a limitation, or an endorsement should be contemplated. Jurisdictions are encouraged to determine how careless- and distracted-driving laws should apply to autonomous vehicles. Legal responsibility for each vehicle operating on public roads should be identified so that parties know who will be responsible for what.

---

11 "Canadian Jurisdictional Guidelines for the Safe Testing and Deployment of Highly Automated Vehicles (Automated Driving System Levels 3-4-5)" (June 2018), online (pdf): *Canadian Council of Motor Transport Administrators* https://ccmta.ca/images/publications/pdf/CCMTA-AVGuidelines-sm.pdf. See 83–93 for the full list of recommendations.

B. PROVINCIAL REGULATORY LAWS

1) British Columbia

British Columbia has progressed to the point of producing a thought paper via its Office of the Chief Information Officer.[12] The thought paper identifies concerns that legislators will need to consider, specifically around cybersecurity, the requirement for increased bandwidth due to "enormous data volumes," and that the benefits are likely to outweigh the challenges.

British Columbia's single automotive insurance company, Insurance Corporation of British Columbia (ICBC), has issued a statement[13] that driverless vehicles are not currently legal in British Columbia, so vehicles operating in such modes would not be insured for their operation. This statement was made in response to a Tesla 3 using the summon function in a parking lot. At the other end of the spectrum, ICBC provides a 10 percent discount to vehicles equipped with autonomous emergency braking technology.[14] Although legislation dealing with driverless cars has not been created, automated technology is encouraged when supervised by a driver. Testing of an electronic autonomous shuttle under the Alberta approval model has also been undertaken at locations in British Columbia.

2) Alberta

Alberta has made no specific changes to its regulatory framework but is specifically allowing autonomous vehicles to be trialled on a case-by-case basis in the province. Companies will need to seek exemptions from the appropriate traffic safety laws. Approval of an application is at the sole discretion of the Registrar of Motor Vehicles. Currently, the electronic

---

12 British Columbia, Office of the Chief Information Officer, "Information Security Thought Paper: Autonomous Vehicles," online (pdf): *Government of British Columbia* www2.gov.bc.ca/assets/gov/british-columbians-our-governments/services-policies-for-government/information-management-technology/information-security/information-security-awareness/thought_paper_-_autonomous_vehicles.pdf.

13 Lyle Adriano, "ICBC Says Autonomous Cars Are Not Allowed" Insurance Business Canada (8 November 2019), online: www.insurancebusinessmag.com/ca/news/auto-motor/icbc-says-autonomous-cars-are-not-allowed-191011.aspx.

14 "Autoplan Insurance," online: *Insurance Corporation of British Columbia* www.icbc.com/insurance/costs/Pages/Discounts-and-savings.aspx?expand=div1.

autonomous shuttle (ELA) program operated by Pacific Western Transportation has obtained the required exemptions and has demonstrated their vehicle in various parts of Edmonton and Calgary.

Applications for vehicle safety exemption permits can be made online.[15]

3) Ontario

Ontario has taken significant steps toward regulating autonomous vehicles. A ten-year pilot program, launched in 2016, allows autonomous vehicles manufactured from inception to SAE Level 3 technology to be operated without the need to be registered as a pilot participant. After-market installation of SAE Level 3 technology is not exempted and will still be required to comply with the requirements of the pilot program. The program requires all vehicles to continue to have a human driver able to take control of the vehicle if required unless an exception is obtained through the program.

The pilot program requires the participant to be the owner of the vehicle being tested as well as one of the following: (1) an auto manufacturer as defined in the federal MVSA; (2) a technology company; (3) an academic or research institution; or (4) a manufacturer of parts, systems, equipment, or components for automated driving systems.[16] Participation in the program has a number of requirements, including the following:

1) The Ministry of Transportation of Ontario (MTO) must be notified of all vehicles participating.
2) The MTO must be notified of any collisions within 10 days of the occurrence, including the vehicles and people involved, locations, injuries, and damage.
3) Participants must provide an annual report with information about unplanned or non-scheduled disengagements of the system, testing environments, geography/terrain covered, weather conditions, number of kilometres driven, hours tested, and speeds driven.

---

15 "Vehicle Equipment Exemption Permits," online: *Government of Alberta* www.alberta.ca/vehicle-safety-exemption-permits.aspx.

16 "Ontario's Automated Vehicle Pilot Program" (2009) online: *Ontario Ministry of Transportation* www.mto.gov.on.ca/english/vehicles/automated-vehicles.shtml.

4) Touchpoint conversations with the MTO must occur every six months.
5) Specifications must be provided to the MTO regarding actions, design choices, and measures taken to ensure that cybersecurity has been accounted for, including how it might affect road safety.
6) There must be $5-million liability coverage or, if there are eight or more passengers, $8-million liability coverage.

Additional conditions for SAE Level 4 or 5 vehicles in a driverless mode require the following:

1) Notification of the municipality in which the vehicle is to be tested
2) A declaration regarding satisfactory results from prior testing, such as closed-course testing
3) Information regarding the operational design parameters
4) Direct oversight of the vehicle to allow it to be brought to a stop either through a trained passenger or a remote-control override
5) Visible signage to alert other drivers, as in Figure 3.1

FIGURE 3.1. ONTARIO SELF-DRIVING VEHICLE SIGN

The full application may be viewed online.[17]

Consideration will need to be given to inconsistencies between these pilot programs and current legislation. For example, it is considered stunt driving in Ontario to operate a motor vehicle "while the driver is not sitting in the driver's seat."[18] Thus, even the use of a summon feature, as part of a developed automated vehicle, would be caught under this provision absent approval through the pilot project. Ontario Regulation 306/15,[19] made under the *Highway Traffic Act* Pilot Project—

17 "Central Forms Repository," online: *Government of Ontario* www.forms.ssb.gov.on.ca/mbs/ssb/forms/ssbforms.nsf/FormDetail?OpenForm&ACT=RDR&TAB=PROFILE&SRCH=&ENV=WWE&TIT=023-5084&NO=023-5084E.

18 O Reg 455/07: Races, Contests and Stunts under *Highway Traffic Act*, RSO 1990, c H.8, s 3 at 6.

19 O Reg 306/15: Pilot Project—Automated Vehicles, filed 13 October 2015 under *Highway Traffic Act*, RSO 1990, c H.8.

Automated Vehicles, enacts the autonomous vehicle pilot program and is reproduced in Appendix 2 of this book.

Automated vehicles include passenger or commercial vehicles or street cars but specifically exclude motorcycles or motor-assisted bicycles. The pilot project applies to vehicles at SAE Level 3, 4, or 5. A separate program also exists for the trialling of "cooperative truck platooning," a system for trucking vehicles to follow closer to one another.

The Ontario Cooperative Truck Platooning Pilot Program is a pilot project in anticipation of commercial vehicles operating at SAE Level 1 or 2 with ADASs aiding drivers in groups, or platoons, of up to three vehicles operating at a minimum of 20 metres or 1.7 seconds following distance. The current program is limited in its geography to less than 300 kilometres of roadway throughout the province and is subject to a number of restrictions, including signage to warn other drivers of the use of the technology in the vehicle (see Figure 3.2).[20]

FIGURE 3.2. ONTARIO PLATOONING VEHICLE SIGN

Ontario has also created the Autonomous Vehicle Innovation Network (AVIN) to promote Ontario taking a leadership role in the development of autonomous vehicle technology in its borders. It focuses on a central hub and five distinct programs:

1) Autonomous research and development, which promote study
2) WinterTech, which specifically seeks review of technology adapted to a winter climate
3) Talent Development, which acts to create training and bandwidth to train a workforce to support this industry

20 "Ontario Cooperative Truck Platooning Pilot Program Conditions" (2018), online: *Ontario Ministry of Transportation* www.mto.gov.on.ca/english/trucks/cooperative-truck-platooning-conditions.shtml.

4) Demonstration Zone, which exists to showcase technology to the public
5) Regional technology development sites, which work with six educational institutions across Ontario as Centres of Excellence

When developing policy, AVIN will be the likely resource the provincial legislature will look to for information regarding automation.

4) Quebec

In 2018, Quebec amended its *Highway Safety Code*[21] and made specific amendments to deal with autonomous vehicles.

In defining "autonomous vehicle," the *Code* specified that the term includes any vehicle operating at SAE Level 3, 4, or 5.

Autonomous vehicles are dealt with specifically in section 492.8:

> No person may put an autonomous vehicle into operation on public highways, on highways under the administration of or maintained by the Ministère des Ressources naturelles et de la Faune, on private roads open to public vehicular traffic or on land occupied by shopping centres or other land where public traffic is allowed.
>
> The first paragraph does not apply to autonomous vehicles at driving automation level 3 of the SAE International's Standard J3016 whose sale is allowed in Canada.

This specifically bars autonomous vehicles except those that operate at SAE Level 3 and meet the requirements for sale as in the federal MVSA. Whether this limits such vehicles to those that come manufactured at SAE Level 3, as Ontario permits, or allows for those that have the technology installed after manufacture is not entirely clear.

Section 633.1 of the *Highway Safety Code* provides for the creation of a pilot project relating to autonomous vehicles and gives the minister power to provide an exemption from certain requirements under Quebec's

---

21 *Highway Safety Code*, CQLR c C-24.2.

Automobile Insurance Act.[22] Such pilot programs are authorized for five years but are allowed to be extended for a further two years.

Currently, the *Autonomous Bus and Minibus Pilot Project*[23] is the only authorized pilot project. It authorizes the testing of autonomous buses and minibuses, along with the collection of anonymized data for evaluation of the vehicles.

Participation in the project requires an application that includes the following:

1) The testing project
2) Objectives pursued
3) Vehicles intended to be used and the number of such vehicles
4) The area in which the testing is to be undertaken, including a description of the route proposed
5) Information ensuring compatibility with the location
6) Safety measures proposed
7) Duration of the project
8) Training to be given to the driver/occupant
9) Written authorization from the vehicle manufacturer to conduct testing
10) Notification to the police, civil protection, and first-responder authorities in the area where it is to be tested
11) No transportation of passengers in the first two weeks of operation

The program requires that a malfunction or loss of use of command or control equipment must cause the immediate stoppage of the vehicle. A driver must be able to immediately take over driving in an emergency. If an issue arises, the vehicle must not be able to resume autonomous function until necessary corrections are made. Notification to the Société de l'assurance automobile du Québec (Société) must occur if there is any accident causing damage or injury, any event involving the safety of road users, or a problem that poses a risk to road users. The minimum insurance coverage required is $1 million. The vehicles involved in the pilot

22 *Automobile Insurance Act*, CQLR c A-25.

23 *Autonomous Bus and Minibus Pilot Project*, CQLR C-24.2, r 37.01.

program are exempt from safety standards, but a program designed to ensure that the vehicle is in good working order must be maintained. Each year, information must be provided to the Société regarding the following:

1) The testing results obtained
2) The duration of the testing for each route
3) The total number of kilometres travelled per automated and manual driving mode
4) The dates of onboard software updates and a summary of the attendant effects on the testing
5) The total number of automated driving mode disengagements and the main reasons for them
6) A summary of traffic accidents
7) The number of mechanical or technological incidents with a description of each and the corrective action taken
8) The number of times the emergency stop was applied
9) The number of complaints received, the subject of the complaints, and the measures taken to remedy the situation
10) Any other element considered essential to the monitoring and evaluation of the testing project

FIGURE 3.3. QUEBEC AUTONOMOUS BUS LANE SIGN

Certain projects are specifically approved in the regulation. Reserved lanes are contemplated during the pilot project and must be signed, as shown in Figure 3.3.

Section 143 of the *Act Respecting Remunerated Passenger Transportation by Automobile*,[24] which came into force on 10 October 2020, authorizes the creation of pilot projects respecting the use of autonomous vehicles in taxi and ride-sharing situations.

24 *Act Respecting Remunerated Passenger Transportation by Automobile*, CQLR c T-11.2.

5) Nova Scotia

Nova Scotia has passed Bill 80, *An Act Respecting Highways and Traffic Safety*, although it is not yet in force.[25] It updates Nova Scotia's traffic law and includes references to autonomous vehicles. It gives the power to control autonomous vehicles and the features and conditions of their use by regulation.

Section 153 of the Act provides:

> A person who is authorized under this Act to drive the vehicle must be positioned at the controls of the vehicle and, at all times while a vehicle is being driven on a highway, the person must be able to personally drive the vehicle, irrespective of whether the vehicle is capable of operating autonomously or in an autonomous mode.

The requirement that the driver be "positioned at the controls of the vehicle" would prevent the use of vehicle-summoning features or automatic parking in a driverless mode.

Section 182 of the Act provides:

> (1) A person driving a vehicle or other conveyance shall drive with due care and attention and with reasonable consideration for other traffic on the highway.
>
> (2) For greater certainty, this Section applies irrespective of whether the vehicle being driven is capable of or is in fact being driven in an autonomous mode.

This specifically reminds drivers of their responsibility to operate with due care and attention even when operating in an autonomous function. What level of care or attention is required will need to be interpreted in conjunction with the level of automation and reasonable expectation of a driver.

Currently, no regulations have been promulgated under this Act. The regulations will be an important document to assess when available. In the meantime, Nova Scotia has taken significant steps toward recognizing the increasing effect that autonomous vehicles will have on driving.

---

25 2nd Sess, 63rd Leg, Nova Scotia, 2018 (assented to 11 October 2018), c 29.

6) Saskatchewan, Manitoba, Newfoundland and Labrador, New Brunswick, Prince Edward Island, Yukon, Northwest Territories, Nunavut

Currently, these provinces and territories do not have published policies or legislation relating specifically to the regulation of autonomous vehicles. Existing laws nonetheless apply to all vehicles, which would include autonomous examples. Certainly, technology to SAE Level 2 is well covered by existing laws.

C. INTERNATIONAL REGULATORY LAW

1) 1949 United Nations *Convention on Road Traffic*

Although provincial and national laws in Canada will have the greatest significance in the promulgation of autonomous vehicles, it is important to remember that Canada is a signatory to international treaties dealing with driving.

The United Nations *Convention on Road Traffic*[26] deals most acutely with cross-border travel of vehicles and international driving permits. As a signatory to this document, Canadian drivers can drive vehicles in other countries, and citizens of the signatory states can operate vehicles in Canada without needing to apply for a local driver's licence or permit. As well, this convention allows for vehicles to cross between member states and continue to be operated.

Although Canada shares only one land border, with the United States, the impact of autonomous vehicles may be more acute in areas such as Europe. If autonomous vehicles become the norm and technologies such as vehicle-to-everything become integral to the driving experience, it may be a requirement that terms in the convention are modified. Particular safety concerns may arise—for example, if a driver accustomed to driving in an environment with a high proportion of autonomous vehicles travels to a location where automation is not used, or vice versa. Even

26 *Convention on Road Traffic*, 19 September 1949, 125 UNTS 22 (entered into force 26 March 1952).

vehicles that are controlled by a human driver will continue to gain new technological requirements. Member countries such as Canada can add requirements for safety equipment in addition to the minimums required in the convention, but the risk remains that if American jurisdictions do not follow similar requirements an increased danger will result from vehicles operating over the Canadian-American border. The United Nations Economic Commission for Europe (UNECE) continues to consider these very issues. Transport Canada has been involved in these discussions.

chapter 4

CRIMINAL AND QUASI-CRIMINAL LIABILITY

The *Criminal Code* of Canada[1] defines offences of a criminal nature in Canada, whereas regulatory matters dealing with highway traffic law are assigned to the provinces. This chapter reviews the offences criminalized in the *Code* and how automated vehicles are likely to affect their application.

A. DANGEROUS DRIVING

Dangerous driving requires an operation of a conveyance in a way that is a marked departure from that of a normal driver. What will be considered a "normal driver" will be affected by the implementation of autonomous systems in vehicles as stated in the *Criminal Code*:

> 320.13(1) Everyone commits an offence who operates a conveyance in a manner that, having regard to all of the circumstances, is dangerous to the public.

1 *Criminal Code*, RSC 1985, c C-46 [*Code*].

1) *R v Beatty*, 2008 SCC 5

This case is the starting point for dangerous driving. The accused, for no apparent reason, suddenly crossed the solid centre line into the path of another vehicle, which caused the death of all three occupants in the other vehicle. The Supreme Court of Canada reiterated the test for dangerous driving as whether the actions of the accused are a "marked departure" from that of a "reasonably prudent driver." What a "reasonably prudent driver" is and how they are expected to act is interpreted in relation to the current societal expectations for drivers. What was reasonable as a driving behaviour years ago may not be considered as such for all time. Slight alterations from prudence are expected in the inherently dangerous act of driving but criminality only attaches for marked departures. As stated in *R v Beatty*, "A mere departure from the standard expected of a reasonably prudent person will meet the threshold for civil negligence, but will not suffice to ground liability for penal negligence. The distinction between a mere departure and a marked departure from the norm is a question of degree."[2]

The Court went on to note that the test for *mens rea* is important in dangerous driving cases. The modified subjective/objective test is applied in such a case. It is not merely whether a reasonable person would have appreciated the risks but whether the reasonable person, placed in the position of the accused, would have appreciated it. Defences such as incapacity or mistake of fact can apply. In assessing the *mens rea*, and by implication the "reasonably prudent person," the Court reviewed and adopted points from its earlier decision in *R v Hundal*.[3] It found that "because driving can only be undertaken by those who have a license, as a general rule, the law can take it as a given that those who drive are mentally and physically capable of doing so and that they are familiar with the requisite standard of care."[4] The Court continued by stating that *mens rea* can be inferred "from the voluntary act of driving,"[5] and "criminal fault can be based on the voluntary undertaking of the activity, the presumed

---

2 *R v Beatty*, 2008 SCC 5 at para 7 [*Beatty*].

3 *R v Hundal*, [1993] 1 SCR 867.

4 *Beatty*, above note 2 at para 30.

5 *Ibid* at para 31.

capacity to properly do so, and the failure to meet the requisite standard of care."[6]

The criminal standard for driving is not perfection. Perfection is too high a standard, and departure from perfection is not deserving of criminalization:

> Because driving, in large part, is automatic and reflexive, some departures from the standard expected of a reasonably prudent person will inevitably be the product. . . . Even the most able and prudent driver will from time to time suffer from momentary lapses of attention. . . . Such automatic and reflexive conduct may even pose a danger to other users of the highway.[7]

It is not the personal characteristics of the accused that are imported into the subjective/objective test but rather the context of the events surrounding the incident.[8] Drivers are measured against the hypothetical reasonably prudent driver in the context of what the driver knew and was facing, not the context of who the driver was, such as a young, inexperienced driver. The conduct of the driver and the manner in which they operate their motor vehicle is the test to determine the *actus reus* of dangerous driving. It is important not to focus on the consequences, such as an accident or a death, but to remain intent on the actions of the accused and the risk they posed, not whether such a risk was actualized into harm.

2) *R v Roy*, 2012 SCC 26

The Supreme Court of Canada revisited the issue of dangerous driving in the criminal context in this case. The accused pulled out his motorhome from a stop sign into the path of another vehicle. The passenger in the accused's vehicle died. The Court reiterated the ratio from *Beatty* that the "marked departure" standard is what separates civil liability, regulatory liability, and criminal liability.[9] The Court entered an acquittal as the action

6 *Ibid* at para 32.
7 *Ibid* at para 34.
8 *Ibid* at para 39.
9 *R v Roy*, 2012 SCC 26 at para 31.

of the accused, pulling out in front of another vehicle, was "consistent with simple misjudgment of speed and distance in difficult conditions and poor visibility."[10]

The issue of intent and *mens rea* with dangerous driving and autonomous vehicles will not need to be examined as time goes on, technology changes, experience is gained with new technology, and drivers adapt to these changes. The question of what a person in a particular situation thinks and how they are expected to react while operating an autonomous vehicle will change as experience levels of drivers dealing with autonomous vehicles change. While a driver at the turn of the last century may have seen horse and buggies sharing the roadway every day, drivers in the present are less likely to have the same level of experience with that sort of situation. The level and degree of automation will have a direct impact on what is expected.

Driving is a highly regulated activity. One goal of regulation is to inject a degree of predictability among drivers. This is the reasoning behind the "rules of the road" that most provinces have. Drivers can expect other drivers to react in a particular way in a particular situation. These basic algorithms are what allow thousands of vehicles to interact on a daily basis. Should a non-standard situation present itself, the human driver can make the best decision based on the information presented. This is the basis of the modified subjective/objective test. When an automated system is injected into the fray, it takes away some of this human decision making. In most situations, this is acceptable and even better than human decision making. The objective portion of the test promotes the standardization of reaction to common events on the roadway and mutual understanding among drivers, enhancing predictability, although there will always be drivers and situations that are less predictable.

As automation becomes more common and moves beyond the semi-autonomous vehicles that currently exist, it is conceivable that a driver not relying on automation will be considered the deviant. There could come a time when turning off the autonomous functions of a vehicle, in and of itself, could be seen as dangerous. Should we move toward fully

10 *Ibid* at para 55.

autonomous driving, a person who decides to override their vehicle's autonomous functions and rely on human decision making may someday be presumed dangerous. In current vehicle autonomy, the human factor is an absolute necessity as the programming has not yet reached a level of being able to react to anomalous or evolving situations. As programming and vehicle interaction improve, the human may become the weak point in the system.

Dangerous driving typically focuses on a driver. This is because it requires the operation of the motor vehicle involved as a precondition of the offence. This is different from criminal negligence (discussed below), which sometimes sees outside individuals, such as a mechanic or commercial owner, also charged following a tragic accident. Although the current situations surrounding dangerous driving do not include individuals other than the driver, there are some circumstances where an outside individual could be considered a possible defendant. Passengers who reach over and grab the wheel, outside of the driver's ability to stop them, have been prosecuted.[11] This minimal interaction with the fittings of the vehicle has nonetheless been considered operation.

A driver is always in care or control. However, a passenger can also be in care or control if they exert some control over the vehicle, like if they grab the wheel. The ability to exert some actual control is sufficient, such as a passenger grabbing the wheel. The somewhat philosophical question with real-world impact will be whether a programmer could be guilty. In both fully autonomous and semi-autonomous modes of operation, the driver relies on the computer to take over for them. In many ways, this is akin to a driver asking a passenger to "hold the wheel."[12] The difference, of course, and where this analogy fails, is that it would be unreasonable for a driver to divert their attention and rely on a passenger. Depending on the level of automation, it should be expected that drivers will divert their attention to other tasks. This is one of the main reasons that individuals will seek out autonomous vehicles.

---

11 See *Bélanger v The Queen*, [1970] SCR 567; *R v Scott*, 2007 NBPC 18.

12 *R v RSW*, [1995] OJ No 2872 (CJ Prov Ct), where two individuals were both found guilty of dangerous driving while sharing driving duties.

Until vehicles are fully autonomous, human interaction will be required; however, it will be up to courts to determine whether the actions taken by a driver were reasonable in the circumstances. Something may be expected but not reasonable. Something may be reasonable but not expected. In considering this issue, courts will need to focus on the aforementioned reasonably prudent driver. As this driver must be considered in the subjectively modified objective standard, how people react to autonomous vehicles will be key in assessing liability. Extraneous sources, including manufacturer instructions, may be required in determining what the expected standard of care is for a particular kind of car, in a particular situation, with a particular level of automation.

Criminal law exists to punish morally blameworthy acts. Civil law seeks to redress wrongs that do not rise to this level of negative intent. For this reason, criminal law does not recognize contributory negligence in the same way that civil law does. Two bad acts do not cancel each other or provide a defence in criminal law, but they may provide some offset for civil wrongdoing where each side harmed the other. The continuum of redress in driving law has been recognized to run from civil damages to regulatory action (such as careless driving) to dangerous driving and on to criminal negligence. The actual harm done is often similar; bad accidents resulting in death can exist across the continuum, but the intent and degree of departure from expected conduct are the differences.

There is ongoing debate as to what a reasonably prudent driver is. This is important as the interpretation of this phrase is the starting point for many criminal and quasi-criminal driving offences. The reasonably prudent driver is not necessarily the average driver. Average drivers may not always act in reasonably prudent ways. This can cause difficulties for triers of fact in determining criminal guilt. Juries may resort to referencing their own driving experience when determining such matters. Anyone who drives on a regular basis can think of times when often-seen events are "normal" but not necessarily reasonable or prudent. Drivers typically speed up to get through yellow lights; it would be rare not to find someone speeding on any particular road; many people still text and drive. These are not uncommon and, to many, may be normal driving. Depending on the situation, they could be reasonable and, in some cases, such as keeping with the flow and speed of traffic on a highway, may also be prudent and the safest course of action. Some actions may go further and, either on their own or in concert with the driving conditions or other actions, may constitute some degree of variation from what a reasonable and prudent driver would do. Criminal sanction is not for mere departure but requires more. This makes sense as society should not impose criminal sanction for matters that are not morally blameworthy. It would be hard to justify an action that the vast majority of the population engages in as a departure significant enough to justify intervention by the criminal justice system. Conversely, just because the majority would choose a particular action does not mean that it is morally acceptable and certainly not that it is morally praiseworthy. As a result, defining the reasonably prudent driver is often difficult and forms the basis of significant appellate authority, which continues to struggle with this very issue. Each counsel may have a different argument, each juror or judge a different view, and this is okay. What is important is the adaptability and capability for evolution of such terms.

In the realm of autonomous vehicles, the reasonably prudent driver will be further affected as society becomes more accustomed to autonomous vehicles. Given current states of automation, it is likely that the vast majority of people remain cautious and untrusting with regard to giving up varying degrees of control over their motor vehicle. Although some levels of automation are becoming more common, such as automated braking or lane assist, fully committing to outside control remains elusive. However, as this technology evolves and becomes more common, it will be less likely that failure to use such technology will be accepted as justification for an incident. Consider a person operating a vehicle equipped with automatic braking. This program uses sensors in the vehicle to detect obstructions at a particular distance in front of the vehicle. This distance typically varies depending on the speed of the vehicle. If an object is identified in the distance, the vehicle automatically applies the brakes and slows the vehicle. Will an individual who has a vehicle with this option but knowingly turns it off because they lack trust in the system be excused in any way should an accident, such as rear-ending another vehicle on the roadway, occur? The act of disengaging safety technology is in some ways akin to not performing proper maintenance on a vehicle.

Courts will struggle with individuals who may have turned off such technology out of valid concerns, such as the inability of the technology to adapt to icy conditions. In some ways, this may lead to some shifting of onus, be it acknowledged or unconscious, to individuals having to explain the failure to use installed automation. Over time, governments may require certain technologies. The failure to have functioning automation as required by regulation can play a part in assessment of reasonableness whether a person's actions are dangerous.[13] As the concept of the reasonably prudent driver evolves and the "new normal" of automation becomes more broadly accepted, the use or lack of use of such automation may form the basis for differing criminal liability.

Dangerous operation requires consideration of the manner of operation "having regard to all of the circumstances." The offence previously included reference to the use of the place at which the operation occurred and the amount of traffic. Although these specific factors have been removed, the importance of a contextual analysis of all circumstances is required. The reliance on the automated systems and whether this was appropriate will be important factors to consider.

The question of reasonable action may also apply to the question of an individual who buys a car specifically without this technology. Vintage cars often lack newer safety technology. Although some form of retrofitting of such vehicles may be mandated when autonomous vehicles become the norm, in the intervening years with semi-autonomous vehicles, issues as simple as cost or personal choice may keep some vehicles from incorporating new safety technologies. The assessment of the reasonably prudent driver will require a contextual review of the individual and the events of each case. Certainly, an individual who knows their vehicle lacks automated braking technology must keep absolute control. Does the inverse hold true where an individual relies on such technology, but an accident occurs nonetheless? A reasonably prudent driver may, or may not, rely on such features depending on the circumstances. This will undoubtedly

---

13 *R v Tayfel*, 2009 MBCA 124, where failing to have a functioning autopilot played into the assessment of the dangerous operation of an aircraft [*Tayfel*]. Consider *R v Blanchard*, 1994 CanLII 5251 (YK TC), and that statutory regulations can and should be used in assessing carelessness along with establishing minimum standards of care.

shift as higher levels of autonomy appear. In the meantime, drivers will be expected to be fully engaged as drivers until technology advances to a point where they can shift their focus to non-driving tasks. For now, degrees of autonomy exist to supplement a fully attentive driver, not to allow a shift of focus away from driving.

B. IMPAIRED DRIVING

An autonomous vehicle cannot become impaired by alcohol or a drug. As long as human input is required, there is risk in the human interaction. This discussion regarding autonomous vehicles and their impact on driving while impaired focuses on the issue of operation, which now subsumes the idea of care or control.

According to section 320.11 of the *Code*, *operate* means:

> (a) in respect of a motor vehicle, to drive it or to have care or control of it;
>
> (b) in respect of a vessel or aircraft, to navigate it, to assist in its navigation or to have care or control of it; and
>
> (c) in respect of railway equipment, to participate in the direct control of its motion, or to have care or control of it as a member of the equipment's crew, as a person who acts in lieu of a member of the equipment's crew by remote control, or otherwise.

1) *R v Boudreault*, 2012 SCC 56

In this case, the Supreme Court of Canada found that there must be a realistic risk of danger and not simply a theoretical risk of danger. The Court reviewed the idea of an "alternate plan" (that is, that a person had a plan other than to operate a conveyance while impaired), but cautioned that it must be objectively concrete and reliable and implemented by the accused, stating that "[a] plan may seem watertight, but the accused's level of impairment, demeanour or actions may demonstrate that there was nevertheless a realistic risk that the plan would be abandoned before its implementation."[14] The Supreme Court found that

14 *R v Boudreault*, 2012 SCC 56 at para 52.

> [i]n the absence of a contemporaneous intention to drive, a realistic risk of danger may arise in at least three ways. First, an inebriated person who initially does not intend to drive may later, while still impaired, change his or her mind and proceed to do so; second, an inebriated person behind the wheel may unintentionally set the vehicle in motion and third, through negligence, bad judgment or otherwise, a stationary or inoperable vehicle may endanger persons or property.[15]

Degrees of autonomy will affect whether a person remains in care or control of a vehicle. The first two concerns raised in *Boudreault* can easily occur in currently available autonomous vehicles. Virtually all autonomous vehicles allow a human driver to take over the operation of the vehicle. This recognizes the current state of the technology and the need to allow human intervention in a dynamic situation for which the vehicle is unprepared. Similarly, because this option exists, a driver may unintentionally take control of the vehicle. In some vehicles, the override to an autonomous state is as simple as touching the steering wheel. For this reason, current levels of automation do not eliminate the risk that an impaired individual in the driver's seat presents. The risk may be more difficult to prove as vehicles become more autonomous and individuals determine ways to set the vehicle on course without occupying the driver's seat, thus eliminating the presumption of care or control. We can imagine a police officer in the not-too-distant future pulling over a vehicle and finding two inebriated people in the back seat with the car driving itself. Who to charge may be difficult in such a situation, but this hurdle will be simply one more step required in establishing care or control.

It is easy to imagine a technology that prevents the concerns in the first two branches of *Boudreault.* A vehicle that prevents the occupant from taking control and relies on other fail-safe technology, such as slowing to a stop and refusing to move when faced with a dynamic situation, could be programmed to prevent impaired driving. Certainly, in some trials of ride-sharing or taxi services, the elimination of a human driver is a key economic factor in the development and adoption of autonomous driving technology. It may be that some individuals will prefer such a vehicle someday to

15 *Ibid* at para 42.

eliminate the risk they may see themselves as posing should they choose to consume alcohol or cannabis before requiring a ride home. The question to be asked will be whether technology can eliminate the "impairment" of a person through sufficient automation. This is equivalent to taking away the "operation" or care or control from the impaired individual and giving it to the autonomous functions, which will not be impaired. Determining what steps must be taken by an impaired driver to take control of the vehicle, and the likelihood that the driver would, will need to be considered in assessing the realistic risk posed by such a person. Consideration should also be given to the liability of an owner who sends an impaired person home in their automated vehicle and whether that person may be criminally negligent or liable as a party to the impaired person's actions.

Contrast the above situations with one where an impaired person uses a summoning feature on the vehicle. The person orders the vehicle to operate but not to control the steering, speed, or any other motion of the vehicle. The person is certainly ordering the vehicle to be put into motion but is insulated from the decision-making process that gives rise to the danger from which the law serves to protect society. Just as an impaired person may order a taxi to drive, including where to, the intervening control by the presumably sober taxi driver insulates the impaired person from criminal liability by limiting the control they exercise over the functionality of the vehicle. The level of automated function will need to be carefully reviewed to determine the degree of care or control a person exercises over an autonomous vehicle.

Technology may evolve to a point where the vehicle recognizes some degree of impairment, be it from a source such as alcohol or a drug, or through non-criminal but nonetheless concerning sources of impairment, such as fatigue or a medical issue, and the vehicle can then take over driving and override the human. This sort of technology already exists in limited degrees in aeronautics, and the balance between trust in the human and trust in the machine is constantly being reweighed. Whether technology should evolve to take away the operation of the vehicle or evolves to eliminate the impairment by supplementing an individual's usual ability to drive is a philosophical debate; both are flip sides of the same coin. Autonomous vehicles prevent impaired driving, thus reducing the carnage on our roadways. This may be the ultimate impetus toward the adoption of automated vehicles.

C. FAILURE TO STOP AFTER AN ACCIDENT

There are good reasons why we want drivers to remain at the scene of an accident. Where other parties may be injured or need help, this duty to remain and aid is important to prevent worse outcomes. By criminalizing leaving the scene, drivers are not in a better position to flee if they think they may have committed a crime, like impaired driving, and so harm to victims in an accident is limited. As stated in the *Code*:

> 320.16(1) Everyone commits an offence who operates a conveyance and who at the time of operating the conveyance knows that, or is reckless as to whether, the conveyance has been involved in an accident with a person or another conveyance and who fails, without reasonable excuse, to stop the conveyance, give their name and address and, if any person has been injured or appears to require assistance, offer assistance.

Amendments that came into force in December 2018 eliminated a previous requirement that the offence of failing to stop be "with intent to escape civil or criminal liability." In *R v McColl*, the Alberta Court of Appeal considered the issue of single-motor vehicle accidents where a passenger is injured, and the majority found that "[t]he original enactment makes it plain that Parliament's intention was to punish drivers leaving an accident scene without tendering assistance to an injured person."[16] The 2018 amendments would bring the dissenting opinion in line with the majority.

The impact of autonomous vehicles on charges of failing to stop after an accident is affected in multiple ways. The first consideration will be whether the occupant is a driver. Depending on the level of automation, there will be argument regarding whether the person actually operated the conveyance. This issue may be dealt with through statutory revisions that define operation in finer detail as automated vehicles become more commonplace, or it may be dealt with through reference to adaptation

16 *R v McColl*, 2008 ABCA 287 at para 22.

of the common law. Just as a passenger is not under a criminal duty to report an accident, an occupant of a Level 5 automated vehicle has no more control over the vehicle than a passenger in a taxi. That said, this particular charge exists to discourage people involved in accidents from fleeing the scene:

> The offence of failing to remain under s. 233(2) [as it then was] of the *Code* imposes a duty on the person having the care of a motor vehicle which has been involved in an accident, whether or not fault is attributable to him in respect of the accident, to remain and discharge the duties imposed upon him in such circumstances.[17]

The offence requires a person to know, or be reckless, as to whether the vehicle was involved in an accident. As the level of automation increases, the level of attention paid by the driver will decrease. This is one of the eventual goals of automation: to allow drivers to focus their attention elsewhere. Automation at lower levels does not affect this. We cannot rely on the fact that cruise control was engaged to justify not knowing that an accident occurred. However, a driver who falls asleep in a vehicle with a high level of automation and who wakes up in a vehicle that has not stopped may not know that an accident occurred. Although systems will undoubtedly be designed to react to more serious collisions, it would not be unthinkable for an extremely short event, such as a child running into the side of a vehicle while chasing a ball from a playground, being ignored as the collision might occur so quickly, and impact the vehicle in such a small manner that the vehicle could continue on its way. For this reason, the question of whether the driver even knew there was an accident will be at issue in such trials. As with any hit-and-run investigation, the first step will be to identify the vehicle. Once this is accomplished, investigators will have to move to collect data from onboard systems. Design consideration will need to be given to the storage of sensor data both internally to the vehicle and with the potential for backup elsewhere, such as with the manufacturer or in storage on a cloud. Information on what

17 *R v Naugle*, 2011 NSCA 33 at para 33, quoting with approval from *R v Gummer* (1983), 1 OAC 141, [1983] OJ No 181 at para 13.

the vehicle noted, if anything, and how and why it reacted as it did will be important. Whether the driver was notified in some way or had to take manual control of the vehicle will be relevant considerations for the court. This sort of consideration may shift blame from the occupant to the manufacturer, both criminally and civilly.

The next deliberation for the court will be whether the driver had the ability to stop. Automation at a high level may not permit the occupant to stop the vehicle. The vehicle may determine that it is unsafe to stop. Other circumstances, such as maintaining traffic flow and avoiding impact to other drivers, may be built into the systems of vehicles as they become more automated. Even in situations where the vehicle has the capacity to stop, the driver may lack the knowledge to do so. Lower levels of automation, where driver input is considered a possible required intervention, such as those at SAE Levels 0 to 3, will not provide any defence as the ability to stop is integral to any operator no matter how simple or complicated the vehicle. At Levels 4 and 5, where automation is such that drivers may no longer be active in the decisions regarding operation of the vehicle, it may come down to expectations of licensing. A Level 4 vehicle presumes the driver's ability to take control of the vehicle, although the vehicle may override the driver's ability to do so until a status has been reached that the vehicle systems deem safe. If this ability to take over is present, whether licensing requirements remain may be important in interpreting whether a person has a legal obligation to stop the vehicle. If a driver's licence is still required for a Level 4 vehicle, then the driver will likely be required to take action. Should the vehicle systems not allow the driver to stop within a set time, or at all, then this will be something the driver can point to along with what attempts they took to stop. At Level 5, the occupant is no longer a driver and has no ability to take control of the vehicle. We can imagine a system with an emergency stop button, but how the vehicle eventually reacts will be up to its programming. In such a situation, will the manufacturer or programmer be criminally liable? These issues may shift an evidentiary burden to the defendant to point to some evidence of this sort of possibility as a reasonable excuse for not stopping.

The dangerous but highly regulated action of driving carries with it the societal interest in individuals stopping to help each other at an accident. We do not impose this requirement on bystanders, but we do on anyone involved in the accident. In *R v Slessor*, the Ontario Court of Appeal released a three-way opinion, with Gale CJ finding that only one person in a car would have care or control unless the passenger exercised control over the driver.[18] Justice Laskin held that the offence only applied to the person in care or control at the time of the accident, and Schroeder J held that the passenger/owner would be liable for the offence if they were in the vehicle at the time of the accident. The interpretation in *Slessor* led to an acquittal, but when applied to an automated vehicle it would seem to suggest conviction for the passenger/owner. Courts will need to wrestle with the issue of whether an occupant in a fully automated vehicle is more akin to a bystander or an active participant. There are certainly strong moral reasons for helping others when an accident occurs, and both Parliament and the courts may still seek to encourage this strong societal interest, either through criminal sanction or by shifting it to a regulatory or civil sphere.

The issue of failing to report an accident may eventually become moot. The action of reporting the accident to police, providing contact information, and calling emergency assistance may be automated as well. Already systems such as OnStar have the ability to note that an accident has occurred, and a live person can then interact with the occupants of the vehicle. Police and emergency vehicles are sometimes even dispatched over the protestations of the individual involved. OnStar has led to more than one impaired driving conviction as a result of police attending even though the driver asked them not to be called.[19] An automated system that communicates the contact information of those involved in an accident is one natural progression. Enabling the system to contact emergency services may be another. The intent to make sure aid is provided to injured parties may be dealt with in this way or through locking of the vehicle's mobility after an accident until police have cleared the scene.

18 *R v Slessor*, [1970] 1 OR 664, 1969 CanLII 248 (CA).

19 See, for example, *R v Flight*, 2014 ABCA 185; *R v Morris*, 2010 ONCJ 40.

D. FLIGHT FROM A PEACE OFFICER

Due to the highly regulated nature of driving, there are many situations where police need to stop a vehicle. They do this to ensure proper licensing and insurance. They so this to check the fitness of the vehicle. Where a driver refuses to comply with an officer's requests, it can lead to dangerous situations. As a result, it is a criminal offence to not stop when police require it. As stated in the *Code*:

> 320.17 Everyone commits an offence who operates a motor vehicle or vessel while being pursued by a peace officer and who fails, without reasonable excuse, to stop the motor vehicle or vessel as soon as is reasonable in the circumstances.

Failing to stop or fleeing from police raises obvious dangers to the public. Other users of the roadway, pedestrians, and any property within reach of the roadway are at risk. A vehicle becomes, in essence, a one-tonne bullet careening down a highway, usually at high speed.

The driver of a motor vehicle at lower levels will not be affected as they will continue to be required to monitor the environment around them, including noting police following them and signalling with their lights and/or sirens. Drivers will still have the ability to override the system and bring the vehicle to a stop. At higher levels, it may take longer for the driver to become aware of police direction to stop, such as if they are asleep in a Level 4 automated vehicle, but the ability to stop the vehicle will remain. At Level 5, the driver may lack the ability or knowledge to stop the vehicle if being signalled by police to do so. Much of the danger of the flight from police is addressed as a result of the automated system continuing to drive in the safe manner in which it was programmed.

Again, this point may become moot. Manufacturers may eventually be mandated to allow for an override of some sort to be programmed to allow police to take control of a vehicle. This would allow the vehicle to make way for an emergency vehicle or be stopped by police if certain parameters are met. A kill switch that stops any vehicle may be an eventual loss of control that will be built into vehicles to preserve safety. At that point, flight from police in a conveyance may no longer be possible.

E. CRIMINAL NEGLIGENCE

Driving is specifically considered through offences like dangerous operation. However, all actions must comply with a minimum standard of care toward other people. This includes while driving. While the standard for driving is criminalized at a lower standard in dangerous driving, it can also be dealt with through general criminal negligence where the actions fall below this minimum standard of care. As stated in the *Code*:

> 219(1) Every one is criminally negligent who
>
> (a) in doing anything, or
>
> (b) in omitting to do anything that it is his duty to do,
>
> shows wanton or reckless disregard for the lives or safety of other persons.

Much of the discussion surrounding dangerous driving is equally applicable to matters involving criminal negligence, and a review of Section A, above in this chapter will be helpful when dealing with matters involving criminal negligence.

Criminal negligence requires bodily harm or death in order to be an offence. Actions that meet the intent criteria for criminal negligence but do not result in the consequential harm to another's physical well-being are not criminalized. That being said, where a vehicle is used in the criminally negligent behaviour, the criteria for dangerous driving is also proven. Both criminal negligence and dangerous driving require a lapse from the expected conduct of a typical driver. The difference is one of degree. Dangerous driving requires a marked departure, whereas criminal negligence is a marked and substantial departure.[20]

It would seem, then, that dangerous driving is typically a lesser and included offence to criminal negligence involving a motor vehicle. Where this becomes less clear is when the criminal negligence occurs by an individual who is not operating the conveyance at the time of the accident. Although care or control is now subsumed into operation by definition in the *Criminal Code* (covered in Section B, above in this chapter), it will be a

20 *R v Sharp* (1984), 12 CCC (3d) 428 (Ont CA) [*Sharp*].

step further to determine whether a person whose only interaction with the vehicle is programming its computer is acting in any way that puts them in a form of control over the operation of the vehicle. Since the computer controls the vehicle's actions, courts may find that the programmer is actually in care or control of the vehicle. If this is a bridge too far, then the prosecution may face some difficult decisions in trying to weigh if actions that did not cause bodily harm or death rise to the level of criminal negligence or if they are merely dangerous. If a programmer is not in care or control, then they cannot hold fault for dangerous operation of a motor vehicle. Since this is a test of degrees of departure from the norm, it will be difficult for courts and counsel to assess which way such cases should be prosecuted until actual cases come forward and rise to an appellate level.

Differing levels of automation may affect the assessment of negligent behaviour. Using cruise control as an example of automation, no one would suggest that a driver could rely on the use of cruise control as a reason to turn attention away from the roadway.[21] In fact, improper use of automation can lead to liability.[22] With greater levels of automation, however, the degree to which a person is expected to be attentive will change. As automation reaches a point where the system is in control the vast majority of the time, will the driver be required to maintain the same constant vigilance that is currently expected? A sudden shutdown of an automated system may evolve to be considered in the same vein as a sudden mechanical malfunction. In *R v Sharp*, a sudden mechanical malfunction was held to be an acceptable excuse for driving that otherwise seemed criminally negligent.[23] A digital malfunction may someday be similarly viewed. The manufacturer's guidelines, the limitations on technology, and the degree of trust society shifts away from drivers to automated systems will be important features for a jury to consider in criminal negligence cases.

---

21 See *R v Tabanao*, [2020] OJ No 2591 (Sup Ct J) (criminal negligence); *R v Buchanan*, [2002] OJ No 2593 (Sup Ct J) (found guilty of the lesser and included offence of dangerous driving) [*Buchanan*].

22 See *State v Tuttle*, 2007 Neb App LEXIS 22, 2007 WL 461136, where use of cruise control in inclement weather grounded liability.

23 *Sharp*, above note 20.

As risk increases, the subjective and objective assessments of the *mens rea* requirement converge.[24] A reasonable foreseeability of the harm occasioned is relevant in determining legal causation in criminal negligence matters.[25] With the many unknowns of automated vehicles, the issue of foreseeability of risk will be difficult to assess in the early days. What the risks are and how a reasonably prudent driver might react to particular situations will need to be assessed on an ongoing continuum. Since such situations will be novel, it will be difficult to assess decisions without similar situations to compare them to. When the criminal test adverts to actions that do not have comparators, a focus on the recommendations and expected standards in the design, programming, and manufacture of automated vehicles will be needed. An education of the trier of fact will be required relating to automated vehicles as a class and to the particular automated systems themselves, their use, and their requirements.

In *R v Lilgert*,[26] the accused, Karl Lilgert, was the fourth officer in charge of the ferry *Queen of the North* as it travelled from Prince Rupert to Port Hardy in British Columbia. The vessel was being operated by way of its autopilot at the time of the accident. The autopilot in question controlled the bearing and speed of the vessel. It had alarm features that would allow for notification if the vessel left its designed course, left a geofenced area, or approached an identified hazard. None of these alarms was set up or enabled at the time of the crash.[27] The ferry's autopilot maintained the vessel's course at a full speed of 17 knots directly into Gil Island, striking the island and sinking. This led to the death of two passengers aboard the *Queen of the North*. The court found that

> Mr. Lilgert's responsibility included the duty to oversee all operations on the bridge and to abide by the collision regulations and the ordinary practice of seamanship. This included maintaining a safe lookout

---

24 *R v Anderson*, [1990] 1 SCR 265.

25 *R v Canhoto* (1999), 140 CCC (3d) 321 (Ont CA).

26 *R v Lilgert*, 2013 BCSC 1329, aff'd 2014 BCCA 493, leave to appeal to the SCC refused, 2015 CanLII 26235.

27 "Marine Investigation Report M06W0052" (2008) at 18, online (pdf): *Transportation Safety Board of Canada* www.tsb.gc.ca/eng/rapports-reports/marine/2006/m06w0052/m06w0052.pdf.

> through sight, hearing, and navigational aids; maintaining a safe speed to take proper and effective action to avoid collision and stop, having regard to prevailing circumstances and conditions; and ascertaining risk of collision.[28]

Lilgert's failure to take steps to navigate the ferry was found to be criminally negligent. His actions were more than bad judgment, mere recklessness, or momentary inattentiveness. His actions, or rather his lack of action, in allowing the autopilot to operate without proper supervision were criminally liable. This demonstrates that in cases where supervision of autonomous systems is required, a person will be held liable for failing to do so.[29]

Fully realized Level 5 automated driving will presumably take the driving experience out of the hands of the driver, rendering the person merely an occupant. If a person is no longer actively controlling the actions of the conveyance, there is still the issue of whether passive interaction that does not connote any active care or control might still rise to a criminally negligent standard. A driver who falls asleep is not in control of their acts, so their driving is not dangerous, whereas a driver who sets out driving knowing, or where they ought to know, that they might fall asleep does meet the test for dangerous driving.[30] Applying this to the automated vehicle concept, even a driver who is not in control of the vehicle may be operating the vehicle dangerously if they set out on a course or conduct that they knew could create the danger eventually occasioned. Consider whether an owner will have the ability to control any parameters in a self-driving car. Vehicles are not always used merely for speedy transport, so some may want a vehicle that can take them on a leisurely drive at a slower speed. Conversely, some people may want their vehicle to go as fast as possible. Although vehicles may be programmed to follow speed limits, it is not beyond consideration that a person may unlock the ability of their vehicle to exceed a speed limit. Although the occupant may not be driving at the time of an accident, a vehicle with an unlocked speed parameter may create a potentially dangerous situation. This may even be

---

28 *Lilgert*, above note 26 at para 11.

29 See also *Ching Sheng Fishery Co v United States*, 1996 US Dist LEXIS 4287, 1996 AMC 1313.

30 *R v Jiang*, [2007] BCJ No 928 (CA); see also *Buchanan*, above note 21.

of more concern depending on whether vehicles are programmed to rely on other vehicles maintaining certain speeds. Unlocked parameters such as this need to be assessed much as issues such as speed are now. Although speed alone is rarely sufficient to ground a charge of dangerous driving or criminal negligence, extreme speed can.[31]

Criminal negligence involving designers, programmers, or manufacturers is discussed in Section H, below in this chapter, dealing with being a party to an offence.

F. MISCHIEF TO DATA

Autonomous vehicles rely on the integrity of their computers and the data in them. Interference with this data may lead to criminal sanction. As stated in the *Code*:

> 342.1(1) Everyone is guilty of an indictable offence and liable to imprisonment for a term of not more than 10 years, or is guilty of an offence punishable on summary conviction who, fraudulently and without colour of right, . . .
>
> (c) uses or causes to be used, directly or indirectly, a computer system with intent to commit an offence . . . under section 430 in relation to computer data or a computer system. . . .
>
> 430(1.1) Everyone commits mischief who willfully
>
> (a) destroys or alters computer data;
>
> (b) renders computer data meaningless, useless or ineffective;
>
> (c) obstructs, interrupts or interferes with the lawful use of computer data; or
>
> (d) obstructs, interrupts or interferes with a person in the lawful use of computer data or denies access to computer data to a person who is entitled to access to it.
>
> (2) Every one who commits mischief that causes actual danger to life is guilty of an indictable offence and liable to imprisonment for life.
>
> . . .

31 *R v Richards*, [2003] OJ No 1042 (CA).

(5) Every one who commits mischief in relation to computer data

(a) is guilty of an indictable offence and liable to imprisonment for a term not exceeding ten years; or

(b) is guilty of an offence punishable on summary conviction.

(5.1) Everyone who wilfully does an act or wilfully omits to do an act that it is their duty to do, if that act or omission is likely to constitute mischief causing actual danger to life, or to constitute mischief in relation to property or computer data,

(a) is guilty of an indictable offence and liable to imprisonment for a term not exceeding five years; or

(b) is guilty of an offence punishable on summary conviction.

The *Code*'s sections on mischief relating to data reflect the best attempts by Parliament to recognize and deal with an emerging issue. Section 430(1.1) provides for a number of ways in which interference with data can constitute mischief. If danger to life is caused, then the penalty can reach life in prison. Mischief to data *simpliciter* is a hybrid offence with a maximum penalty of ten years. This is important as it leaves the door open to a conditional sentence should a person be found guilty of such an offence. Section 430(5.1) deals with a situation where an act is likely to cause mischief to data, even if such mischief never occurs. This is rare in criminal law, where the risk-taking behaviour is criminalized even if the disruption never occurs. For this section, *wilfulness* is defined in section 429 and includes intended and reckless action. It also provides a defence of legal justification or with colour of right as long as the item damaged is solely owned and the act is not done with an intent to defraud such as if a person destroyed data in their own vehicle.

The prosecution must lead some evidence that the interference with data occurred—that is, was done wilfully—and that the accused "did not have actual permission or authority to do the act in question."[32] In many cases, the difficult issue will be proving that data has been destroyed or altered, in what way, and to what effect. As a result, resort to the provisions surrounding the attempt may need to be made.

32 *R v Livingston*, 2017 ONCJ 747 at para 16 [*Livingston*].

Computer data is defined in section 342.1 as "representations, including signs, signals or symbols, that are in a form suitable for processing in a computer system." The offence under section 342.1(1)(c) of fraudulently using a computer system to commit mischief to computer data requires some dishonest activity in the use of the system. Fraudulent or improper use can be inferred in any unauthorized use as "voluntary use for prohibited purposes clearly constitutes a dishonest act."[33] The definition of *computer system* in section 342.1 should be applied so that the use of one computer to access another without authorization, such as hacking a vehicle's onboard computer, would be unauthorized and fraudulent when the reasoning in *R c Parent*, quoted above, is applied. Authorization to use a personal computer is no defence if the accused uses that computer to access another that they do not have permission to access.

Theft or obtaining of data without consent is not currently an offence.[34] There must be some malice that goes beyond mere copying of the data to interfere with its lawful use, or it must fit one of the other requirements in section 430(1.1). An argument could be made that the unauthorized obtaining of data from an automated vehicle could interfere with the lawful enjoyment of the property as per section 430(1)(c), but this would require a court to ignore the more specific definition in section 430(1.1).

There are a few reasons why a person may wish to hack a vehicle. These could include theft of data or exploiting the data gateways that are opened by allowing a more vulnerable car computer system to access the data in a phone, such as banking information. Hacking can allow for a takeover of the vehicle, including for theft, for ransom, or to harm a person. Some hacking may be done without the intent to harm but with real risks and harm occurring. For more information on vehicle hacks, see Appendix 1 and Checkoway et al's "Comprehensive Experimental Analyses of Automotive Attack Surfaces."[35]

---

33 *R c Parent*, 2012 QCCA 1653 at para 36.

34 See *R v Maurer*, 2014 SKPC 118 at para 21, quoting *R v Stewart*, [1988] 1 SCR 963 at para 33: "To the extent that protection is warranted for confidential information it should be granted through legislative enactment and not through judicial extension of the concept of property or of the scope of the theft provision under the *Criminal Code*."

35 Stephen Checkoway et al, "Comprehensive Experimental Analyses of Automotive Attack Surfaces" in *SEC '11: Proceedings of the 20th USENIX Conference on Security*

G. TAKING A MOTOR VEHICLE OR VESSEL OR FOUND THEREIN WITHOUT CONSENT

A person need not commit theft to be guilty of taking a vehicle, or taking control of it, without the owner's consent:

> 335(1) Subject to subsection (1.1), every one who, without the consent of the owner, takes a motor vehicle or vessel with intent to drive, use, navigate or operate it or cause it to be driven, used, navigated or operated, or is an occupant of a motor vehicle or vessel knowing that it was taken without the consent of the owner, is guilty of an offence punishable on summary conviction.

This offence is different from pure theft. The two offences often occur in similar fact patterns, but an accused may be guilty of both offences. Parliament's intent in creating this offence "was to create a new and separate offence in order to provide a penalty in certain fact situations in which it was difficult or impossible to establish the offence of theft."[36] This offence can be committed not just by the person who takes the vehicle but also by any other occupant who knows the vehicle has been taken without consent. This offence may become more relevant with the growth of automated vehicles and the risk of hacking. A person who remotely takes control of a vehicle is taking control in a way that may not amount to a theft but does cause the vehicle to be driven, used, navigated, or operated without the consent of the owner. Where a vehicle may be temporarily controlled but not taken in such a way as to amount to theft, this section may apply and allow a more comprehensible prosecution. The prosecution will need to show how the vehicle was taken over, which will require some form of expert evidence, likely including data analysis.

H. PARTIES TO AN OFFENCE

A person can face criminal sanction not only for what they do but what they may help others do.

(2011), online (pdf): *Center for Automotive Embedded Systems Security* www.autosec.org/pubs/cars-usenixsec2011.pdf.

36 *Lafrance v R*, [1975] 2 SCR 201 at 213.

> 21(1) Every one is a party to an offence who
> (a) actually commits it;
> (b) does or omits to do anything for the purpose of aiding any person to commit it; or
> (c) abets any person in committing it. . . .
>
> 22.1 In respect of an offence that requires the prosecution to prove negligence, an organization is a party to the offence if
> (a) acting within the scope of their authority
> (i) one of its representatives is a party to the offence, or
> (ii) two or more of its representatives engage in conduct, whether by act or omission, such that, if it had been the conduct of only one representative, that representative would have been a party to the offence; and
> (b) the senior officer who is responsible for the aspect of the organization's activities that is relevant to the offence departs—or the senior officers, collectively, depart—markedly from the standard of care that, in the circumstances, could reasonably be expected to prevent a representative of the organization from being a party to the offence.

Although the commission of an offence is easy to grasp, being a party to an offence is less understood by most people. Automated vehicles at most levels will rely on preprogrammed systems to some degree. The greater the automation, the greater the level of responsibility that shifts to the programmer and the manufacturer. The issue that needs to be considered is whether the programmer and the manufacturer could be criminally liable for acts or omissions that result in another offence, such as dangerous driving or criminal negligence. Certainly, third-party actors who have a duty of care can be held liable where their failure to meet that duty of care leads to the offence. The owner of a trucking business who "breached his owner operator duties and obligations set by provincial legislation and regulations" can be a party to an offence of dangerous operation through aiding and abetting.[37]

37 *R v Fummerton*, 2017 ONSC 3866 at para 5 [*Fummerton*].

The owner of an autonomous vehicle who allows a person to occupy the vehicle in a state of increased risk, such as an unlicensed or impaired driver, may be a party to an offence. Sufficient controls will need to be in place to prevent such a person from taking control of the vehicle or an owner may be guilty in their own right of criminal negligence or as a party to an offence by abetting the commission of it. Assessing *mens rea* in such a case will require an assessment of the accused and whether they both intended to assist in the conduct and knew sufficient details of the assisted conduct.[38] The reasonable foreseeability of the harm is relevant in determining causation as well.[39] Knowledge, including imputed knowledge, of the control features of an autonomous vehicle will be significantly relevant. Whether an owner knew, or ought to have known, that manual control could be exercised in some way will aid in such an assessment.

Driving carries certain risks, but the societal benefit outweighs any potential risks when a person drives in accordance with the standards of this highly regulated activity. The risks of driving are assumed by the parties involved. This normally applies to the driver but also to companies and management in situations involving commercial vehicles as well.[40] As a result of this party liability, designers, programmers, and manufacturers will have to ensure that their actions do not give rise to liability. Although companies that are "owner/operators" of trucking firms are highly regulated through provincial legislation, as well as application of section 217.1 of the *Criminal Code*, the regulation surrounding automated vehicles is still being written. How that regulation eventually takes form will affect the duties imposed on these parties and the liability that may accrue to them.

Although it would be almost unthinkable that a company would intentionally design an automated vehicle with flaws that would lead to an accident, there is the possibility of criminal negligence. Programmers and companies will need to impose strict controls in the review of all automated vehicles to ensure that their actions are not such that a danger could arise through negligent design. The standard expected

38 See *R v MR*, [2011] OJ No 1017 (CA), where a flagman in a street race was held liable.

39 *R v Shilon*, [2006] OJ No 4896 (CA), leave to appeal to the SCC refused [2007] 2 SCR vi.

40 *Fummerton*, above note 37 at para 48.

of manufacturers will undoubtedly be high, but a marked departure, let alone a marked and substantial departure, will remain a high burden to prove. A real-world example of this sort of concern can be illustrated in the Toyota unintended acceleration investigation performed by the National Highway Traffic Safety Administration (NHTSA) and NASA. (This report is reviewed in Appendix 1.) Although the results of the study did not necessarily put blame on the Toyota Motor Company, the investigation itself was enough for Toyota to enter into a deferred prosecution agreement, costing the company $1.2 billion.[41] The concerns over possible negligence can lead to a corporation acting to protect itself. A system design that departs substantially from the standard of care expected of similar manufacturers could give rise to a corporate criminal responsibility.

The operation of the motor vehicle at some levels of automation is controlled by the program and not by the driver/occupant. As a result, the computer system has care and control of the vehicle. Another method of proving liability may arise in a constructive manner where programmers are seen as being virtually or digitally present. Physical presence in a digital age may become less important in such cases. Certainly, a person taking control of a vehicle remotely is nonetheless in care and control of the vehicle. A person interfering with the programming intentionally would be similarly controlling the vehicle by setting into motion the consequences of the interference with the proper operation of the system that controls the vehicle. The next logical step would be to find that the person responsible for the program that controls the vehicle will be held to some standard of care. The test for criminal negligence then only needs a degree of departure significant enough to warrant criminal sanction. Companies will be wary of such a set of circumstances arising. The airline industry has abandoned billions of dollars of airplanes due to issues with the automated systems in the Boeing 737 MAX. The automobile industry will need to take steps to ensure that its product does not end up in much the same way.

---

41 US, Department of Justice, Office of Public Affairs, News Release, "Justice Department Announces Criminal Charge Against Toyota Motor Corporation and Deferred Prosecution Agreement with $1.2 Billion Financial Penalty" (19 March 2014), online: www.justice.gov/opa/pr/justice-department-announces-criminal-charge-against-toyota-motor-corporation-and-deferred.

The further effect of party liability will lie not in whether the person committed a crime but what an appropriate sentence may be: "[G]uiltier minds tend to deserve or require greater punishment."[42] A person who is guilty as a result of "passive negligence" holds a lesser moral culpability than someone who is wilfully committing a harmful act.[43] As a result, this may be reflected in differing sentences rather than different findings of guilt, although a higher moral culpability shifts matters across the spectrum from civil to regulatory to criminal liability. The negligent programmer will necessarily be in a different position than the intentionally malevolent hacker.

I. ATTEMPTED OFFENCES

Even where an offence is not complete, where a person takes sufficient steps toward committing an offence, criminality may attach to the action. As stated in the *Code*:

> 24(1) Every one who, having an intent to commit an offence, does or omits to do anything for the purpose of carrying out the intention is guilty of an attempt to commit the offence whether or not it was possible under the circumstances to commit the offence.

Attempted offences require actual intent and purpose and not just recklessness. The case of *R v Livingston* provides guidance as follows:

> 84. Although s. 429(1) provides that the completed offence can be made out with recklessness, recklessness does not suffice for liability grounded in attempt. That is because s. 24 of the *Criminal Code*, the provision creating the offence of attempt, requires an intent to commit the offence and a purpose of carrying out that intention:
>
>> Every one who, *having an intent to commit an offence*, does or omits to do anything *for the purpose of carrying out the intention* is guilty of an attempt to commit the offence. . . . (emphasis added).

---

42 *R v Collingwood Prime Realty Holding Corp*, 2020 ONSC 2953 at para 50.

43 *Ibid* at paras 47–51.

> 85. This interpretation finds support in appellate decisions such as *R. v Ancio*, 1984 CanLII 69 (SCC), *R. v Janetas* (sub nom *R. v P.J.*) 2003 CanLII 57385 (ON CA) at para 30 and *R. v Sarrazin*, 2010 ONCA 577 at para 48. These cases hold that to be found guilty of attempt, the accused must have had the actual intent to commit the completed offence and that proof of recklessness is not sufficient.
>
> 86. The cases also make clear that an attempt to do the factually impossible is an attempt that encounters an intervening obstacle, and as a result cannot be completed. *United States v Dynar*, 1997 CanLII 359 (SCC) and other authorities, make it clear that such an act is still an attempt for the purposes of section 24(1). The section states that a person can be guilty of attempt "whether or not it was possible under the circumstances to commit the offence." What matters is whether the accused had the intent to commit the crime and went beyond mere preparation to do so.[44]

Since preparation to commit an offence does not rise to the level of criminality, a prosecution will not succeed until a person takes steps to commit the offence.

Interference with data need not occur as an attempt is sufficient. It may not be possible for a vehicle to be hacked, but the attempt is nonetheless a crime. An attempt at the impossible is still a criminal attempt.[45] As well, section 430(5.1) of the *Code* allows for a distinct offence where the attempt is likely to cause mischief to data even if the mischief does not occur. Therefore, an attempt to act in a way that is likely, although not certain, to destroy, alter, or obstruct data will be sufficient to ground an offence.

Another aspect of criminal law that should be considered is in issues of dangerous driving and criminal negligence. Where actions are taken that give rise to criminal negligence but do not occasion bodily harm or death, the actions may yet give rise to a conviction for an attempt. The analysis of the existing *mens rea* will be key in making such a determination. Applying the idea of attempt to driving law is currently a rarity. Many

---

44 *R v Livingston*, 2018 ONCJ 25 at paras 84–86.

45 *United States of America v Dynar*, [1997] 2 SCR 462, reference in *Livingston, ibid.*

of the most serious offences involving vehicles become apparent to police as a result of their consequences or direct observations. The person who merely attempts to drive dangerously or attempts to drive while impaired rarely comes to the attention of authorities and even more rarely faces charges. This does not mean that this area of law is not valid but merely less common.

J. PRIVACY ISSUES IN CRIMINAL LAW

Autonomous vehicles raise a number of privacy issues to a degree beyond the current state of the law. Although many vehicles have a device similar in many ways to the "black box" in an aircraft, the devices typically have limited data recorded on them. This changes significantly as automation increases. A vehicle that is more greatly automated tends to rely on a larger sensing and data-processing system than does a vehicle that relies on the human driver to make decisions. The greater the decisions made by the vehicle, the greater the data input required to make such decisions safely. To allow greater analysis of decisions made and the ability of vehicles to adapt and learn in some manner, the data is often stored. This data may then be transmitted to a manufacturer, stored locally in the vehicle, or both.

Section 8 of the *Canadian Charter of Rights and Freedoms* provides that "[e]veryone has the right to be secure against unreasonable search or seizure."[46] This right rests in the privacy interest that a person may have in something. If there is no privacy interest, then there is no right to be protected. The terms that a person agrees to upon purchasing an autonomous vehicle and what privacy right they may waive in an end-user license agreement (EULA) may affect a court's eventual determination of what, if any, privacy interest a person has in the data collected by their vehicle. Valid consent acts as a waiver to any section 8 right.[47] The first step is to understand what data is collected and how and what sort of privacy interest this may give rise to.

---

46 Part I of the *Constitution Act, 1982*, being Schedule B to the *Canada Act 1982* (UK), 1982, c 11.

47 *R v Reeves*, 2018 SCC 56 at para 13 [*Reeves*], referencing *R v Dyment*, [1988] 2 SCR 417.

1) What Is an Event Data Recorder?

Currently, the majority of vehicles on the road contain an event data recorder (EDR). This device records data about a vehicle just before or during a crash. The data is recorded with the intent that it can be retrieved and aid in the reconstruction of a crash. Although these devices exist in the majority of vehicles, many people do not know that they exist within their vehicles. Most EDRs work by recording certain data parameters in a continuous loop. They will record this data (usually only for a few seconds), prior to a particular event, usually a crash recognized by the system due to an extreme change in velocity. The NHTSA mandates that EDRs record the following data:

- Delta-V, longitudinal 0 to 250 ms, every 10 ms
- Maximum delta-V, longitudinal 0 to 300 ms
- Time, maximum delta-V, 0 to 300 ms
- Speed, vehicle indicated (5 s, 2 samples per second)
- Engine throttle, % full (or accelerator pedal, % full) (5 s, 2 samples per second)
- Service brake, on/off (5 s, 2 samples per second)
- Ignition cycle, at time of crash
- Ignition cycle, at time of download
- Safety belt status, driver
- Frontal airbag warning lamp, on/off
- Frontal airbag deployment, time to deploy (driver/passenger/stages)
- Multi-event, number of events
- Time from "event 1" to "event 2"
- Complete file recorded (yes/no)[48]

After being downloaded, data is often provided in chart form, as shown in tables 4.1 and 4.2 (the data has been created for these examples). Of interest is that although the data that must be recorded on an EDR is mandated, the installation of an EDR is not required. The results recorded on an EDR are interpretations of sensor data. For example, the speed may be recorded as a function of multiplying the rotation of the tires per minute by the expected

48 *Data Elements*, 49 CFR § 563.7 (2008).

size of the tires. Should someone have undersized or oversized tires installed on a vehicle, then the interpretation of the data would change.[49]

TABLE 4.1 EDR DATA DOWNLOAD

Seconds Before Algorithm Enable	Vehicle Speed (kph)	Engine Speed (rpm)	Percent Throttle	Brake Pedal Circuit Status
–5	100	4,300	45	OFF
–4	102	4,355	48	OFF
–3	102∂	4,378	48	OFF
–2	99	4,289	44	OFF
–1	74	2,500	0	ON

TABLE 4.2 EDR DELTA-V DATA DOWNLOAD

Time (ms)	Δ V (kph)	Time (ms)	Δ V (kph)	Time (ms)	Δ V (kph)
10	0.31	60	11.78	110	34.60
20	1.86	70	18.21	120	36.20
30	3.41	80	29.16	130	37.85
40	5.27	90	31.20	140	N/A
50	8.37	100	33.40	150	N/A

Rules surrounding EDRs require manufacturers to include information in the owner's manual for a vehicle to make the owner aware of the existence of the EDR and what its functions and capabilities are. Manufacturers are required to allow the retrieval of data from an EDR through commercially available tools. This requirement exists to enable crash investigators to access the data in an easier way and to keep the data from being protected through software that is not available to state agencies such as the police. As of model year 2010, approximately 92 percent of light vehicles had EDRs installed.[50] In the years since 2010, a smaller

49 Consider the impact of data from an EDR versus an outside source—a battle of credibility could ensue. For an example of this, see *Perron v Seiler* (2000), 31 MVR 190, [2000] WASCA 145.

50 77 Fed Reg 74146 (2012), quoted from "Collision Between a Car Operating with Automated Vehicle Control Systems and a Tractor-Semitrailer Truck Near Williston, Florida, May 7, 2016," NTSB/HAR-17/02, PB2017-102600 (reissued 12 October 2017), online

proportion of manufactured vehicles have had EDRs installed. This is as a result of manufacturers having a greater proprietary interest in obtaining and maintaining vehicles that they manufacture. Although most manufacturers have some version of a computing module in the vehicle that captures similar data to an EDR, and many collect even more data, since these devices are not classed as EDRs they do not comply with EDR requirements. For example, the Electronic Control Unit (ECU) in Tesla vehicles captures the data we would expect from an EDR but also additional data, which includes sensor data and images taken by the vehicle's onboard cameras. Some of this data is then communicated via Wi-Fi or other internet connectivity to Tesla to allow it to analyze data and provide updates to the vehicle, including software. The data is readable only with the aid of a Tesla proprietary program, so police rely on Tesla, as the manufacturer, to retrieve and interpret data from an ECU by cooperation rather than by requirement.

2) Privacy Interest

Since section 8 litigation relies on a privacy interest being asserted, it is important to understand how such interests may arise. A person must have a reasonable expectation of privacy in what is being searched.[51] Section 8 of the *Charter* protects people, not places.[52] A person can assert a privacy interest that is personal, territorial, or informational.[53] Data collected by a vehicle may be personal in nature, may be contained in property controlled by an individual (territorial), and certainly would be informational. As a result, the interest can arise in some or all of the three manners.

The United States, at the federal level, has enacted the *Driver Privacy Act of 2015*.[54] It requires that the owner or lessee of a motor vehicle own

(pdf): *National Transportation Safety Board* www.ntsb.gov/investigations/AccidentReports/Reports/HAR1702.pdf. The report is discussed in Appendix 1.

51 *Reeves*, above note 47 at para 12.

52 *R v Gomboc*, 2010 SCC 55 at para 17, referencing *Hunter v Southam Inc*, [1984] 2 SCR 145.

53 *Gomboc*, *ibid* at para 19, referencing *R v Tessling*, 2004 SCC 67.

54 *Driver Privacy Act of 2015*, US, Bill S.766, 114th Cong, 2015.

the data collected by an EDR. To access the data, police must meet one of five exceptions:

1) Obtain a warrant
2) Obtain consent
3) Be conducting an investigation or inspection authorized by federal law
4) Require the data to facilitate medical care as a result of a crash
5) Be conducting traffic safety research as long as no personal information is disclosed

In Canada, a person would need to assert their privacy interest in the data. Depending on the nature of the data recorded, significant personal information may exist. This may include photos of where an individual has been, what they have been doing, Global Positioning System (GPS) coordinates with time stamps, and access to other electronic devices, thereby opening a significant gateway. Personal privacy is not likely to be engaged in such a case as the data will rarely have an impact on the individual asserting the privacy interest. More likely, a person may assert territorial privacy depending on where the data is obtained from. A person has the right to control their own property, including the physical storage device on which the data is written. For example, a territorial claim will not likely be successful for data that is communicated off-site to a manufacturer.

Most likely, an individual will assert an informational privacy interest. There is a high reasonable expectation of privacy in computers generally.[55] This is especially true with computers and other electronic devices that provide a gateway to other information. These devices are no longer akin to filing cabinets merely acting as a receptacle for information but instead often act as paths to more information. As vehicles become more interconnected, interest in protection of this access grows. The greater the amount of data of a specific kind that is recorded, the greater the connectivity to other areas of a person's life and the larger extent to which access to that information pervades a person's life. It is no surprise, then, that there will be a reasonable expectation of privacy. The difference between a typical EDR and the type found in more advanced vehicles, which capture

55 See *R v Morelli*, 2010 SCC 8, and *R v Cole*, 2012 SCC 53.

a significantly greater amount of information, may tip the balance in the breadth of the privacy interest.

Given the Supreme Court's decision in *Reeves*,[56] it is clear that a third party who shares an interest in a device cannot consent to the search of such a device without the consent of all owners. Applying this to the issue of EDR and other motor vehicle data issues, it would seem unlikely that a manufacturer who collects data through downloads or Wi-Fi would be able to provide data to police without prior judicial authorization. This may be affected by the terms of an EULA and any waivers, so it will be important to obtain such documentation when considering such an argument. Certainly, the minority judgment of Wagner CJ and Karakatsanis J in *R v Mills*[57] puts the choice of medium used to communicate electronic information at issue in determining whether another party makes a copy of data and whether an expectation of privacy then arises.

Certainly, when determining whether an expectation of privacy arises, electronic communications are a difficult area of law. Consider the decision in *R v Patterson*:

> Mr. Patterson's claim to a reasonable expectation of privacy in his Facebook records dies here. No reasonable person would expect that communications such as these would remain private. . . . The communications were conducted over Facebook messenger, a medium which seemingly keeps an indelible record of supposedly private communications. All of the messaging took place over the Internet with snippets and artefacts of the conversation being captured on devices, servers and systems at every juncture of the communication. A reasonable Internet user might hope that such communications would remain private but no one with even a modicum of understanding of information technology would expect it.[58]

Courts will have to struggle with the evolving concept of electronic communication generally, but this will be felt more acutely in the case of autonomous vehicles. The collection of data in an autonomous vehicle is a given. How it is stored and shared may not be so clear-cut. EULAs

56 *Reeves*, above note 47.

57 *R v Mills*, 2019 SCC 22, Wagner CJ and Karakatsanis J dissenting.

58 *R v Patterson*, 2018 ONSC 4467 at para 21.

and evolving societal understanding of what data is collected, stored, and disseminated will affect whether any expectation of privacy is reasonable. As well, if a person does not know that the information is being recorded, then a different route may be required to establish a reasonable expectation of privacy. Privacy as a concept is evolving in the modern age as people become more connected at a rapid pace. Actions that are routinely completed by people on their phones each day would have been considered Orwellian a generation ago. The willing adoption of such technology reflects a societal change in the view of what is a reasonable expectation of privacy. The highly regulated nature of driving will affect the privacy interest as well.

3) Warrants for Data Recorders

Initially at least, data recorded by an autonomous vehicle will be quite similar to the data recorded on an EDR. This information will likely grow as the degree of automation grows, and the law surrounding EDRs will need to expand as well. Although EDR cases will provide a starting point for cases involving autonomous vehicles, the law will need to be adapted to the circumstances of each offence, the offender, the vehicle they use, and what data it may record.

4) *People v Xinos*, 192 Cal App 4th 637 (2011)

The California Court of Appeal (6th District) found that the warrantless seizure of EDR data was a breach of the accused's Fourth Amendment right. The court recognized the highly regulated nature of driving, including that some jurisdictions, such as the state of New York, require annual inspections of motor vehicles. It distinguished EDR data from such inspections in two ways, recognizing that California lacked such a requirement but also pointing to the significant difference between regulatory inspections and the pointed investigative technique after an accident.[59] The court found that

59 *People v Xinos*, 192 Cal App 4th 637 at 656 (2011).

> [t]he precision data recorded by the [sensing and diagnostic module (SDM)] was generated by [the defendant's] own vehicle for its systems operations. While a person's driving on public roads is observable, that highly precise, digital data is not being exposed to public view or being conveyed to anyone else. But we do not agree with [the] defendant that a manufacturer-installed SDM is a "closed container" separate from the vehicle itself. It is clearly an internal component of the vehicle itself, which is protected by the Fourth Amendment. We conclude that a motorist's subjective and reasonable expectation of privacy with regard to her or his own vehicle encompasses the digital data held in the vehicle's SDM.[60]

The court went on to consider other factors, such as probable cause, lawful seizure of criminal evidence, and harmless error, that could also justify the search but found that none of them applied to justify the seizure.

5) *R v Hamilton*, 2014 ONSC 447

This case involved the downloading or "imaging" of the data contained in the EDR of a vehicle involved in a fatal accident. Police had reasonable and probable grounds to charge the accused prior to the seizure of this data. It was not seized under exigent circumstances, nor was it seized incidental to arrest. The court found that the officer trespassed into the privacy of the accused by entering the vehicle and downloading the data. The court also found that the officer's "conduct went well beyond the kind of state intrusion which reasonable motorists would regard as incidental to the exercise of the privilege of operating a motor vehicle on a public highway."[61] Moreover, the information was of a sort that should be protected as it is information that "society accepts should remain out of the state's hands because of what it reveals about the person involved, the reasons why it was collected, and the circumstances in which it was intended to be used."[62] The court recognized the qualitatively different nature of the information contained in the EDR. Although some of the information might be "in the public view,"

60 *Ibid* at 659.

61 *R v Hamilton*, 2014 ONSC 447 at para 51.

62 *Ibid* at para 54.

such as general observations as to the speed or actions of the vehicle, the exceptional level of detail distinguishes this information from what an outside independent observer could record. The court found that as the owner of the vehicle involved in the accident, the accused also owned the data located in the EDR. This issue may play a greater role in autonomous vehicles that may be shared between parties or owned by a third party. As well, data that is not merely contained in the vehicle but also uploaded to other parties may affect whether the privacy interest remains the same. The court rejected the argument that the provincial *Highway Traffic Act*[63] authorized the search of the EDR. In doing so, the court found that section 82(2) of the Ontario Act exists for the purpose of bringing a motor vehicle into compliance with safety regulations and not to allow inspection and evidence gathering from a vehicle that is no longer operable.[64] In assessing section 24(2) of the *Charter* and the *Grant* analysis,[65] the court found that the search was not particularly egregious. The lesser seriousness of the breach favoured inclusion. The court found that the impact on the accused was moderate having considered the fact that the officer likely could have applied for and been granted a warrant and the lack of intrusion on the dignity or integrity of the accused's person. Society's interest in an adjudication of the case on its merits favoured inclusion as the evidence was real, not conscripted, and reliable. As a result, the evidence was not excluded.

6) *R v Glenfield*, 2015 ONSC 1304

This case dealt with the police downloading the data from an EDR without consent and without a warrant. The court recognized that there was a privacy interest in the data and that absent consent or prior judicial authorization, the police did breach the section 8 right of the accused. However, the court did eventually find that the evidence was nonetheless admissible under section 24(2) of the *Charter*. Due to the warrantless nature of the search, the onus was on the Crown to justify the search. Similar to *Hamilton* above, the court found that there was a reasonable expectation of

63 *Highway Traffic Act*, RSO 1990, c H.8.
64 *Hamilton*, above note 61 at para 87.
65 *R v Grant*, 2009 SCC 32 [*Grant*].

privacy in the EDR of a vehicle. Obtaining the data required the physical trespass into the vehicle, damaged as it was. It allowed the state to access information that it would not otherwise be privy to. The court specifically quoted from *R v Duarte*[66] and noted concern with the state obtaining electronic information from a person. The Court found both territorial and informational privacy interests and that the Crown had not justified the warrantless search.

Turning to section 24(2) of the *Charter*, the court applied the *Grant* analysis.[67] In considering the seriousness of the breach, the court determined that the lack of police training was not relevant in determining this issue. The officer did not know, at the time of seizure, that the data would be used in any particular prosecution. No policy surrounding obtaining warrants for EDR data existed, but such policies had been developed in the intervening time between the incident and the *Charter* application. Considering next the impact on the *Charter*-protected interest of the accused, the court determined that the impact was minimal. Much of this analysis turned on the limited data that was obtained—namely, information surrounding the five seconds prior to collision, including speed, brake activation, and accelerator position. The finite scope of the data and the fact that some information, such as evidence of speed, may be apparent to the wider world without needing to resort to the EDR, restricted the impact of the breach. It would be easy to imagine a greater impact being found in cases involving more significant data in an autonomous vehicle. The final factor of society's interest in the adjudication of the case on its merits was dealt with quickly, with the court noting that the exclusion would not "gut" the Crown's case. The court noted the seriousness of the offence, which resulted in the death of an eleven-year-old boy. In balancing the factors, the court decided in favour of inclusion.

7) *R v Fedan*, 2016 BCCA 26

At trial, the court found in this case that since the accused had no knowledge of the existence of the EDR, there could be no subjective privacy interest.

66 *R v Duarte*, [1990] SCR 30.

67 *Grant*, above note 65.

The trial court considered *Hamilton*, above, but found it a flawed analogy that the EDR was an "onboard computer." This is important when considering application of such reasoning to autonomous vehicles, where data collected will be more akin to that found in an onboard computer. The British Columbia Court of Appeal found that the accused lacked any territorial privacy interest in the EDR as a result of the vehicle having been lawfully seized pursuant to section 489(2) of the *Criminal Code*. The court found that the data contained in the EDR provided no personal information:

> The captured information pertained only to the use of the vehicle in a five-second window of time before a deployment or near-deployment event. It did not capture any information that revealed intimate details of Mr. Fedan's biographical core, and in particular about who was driving the car. Further evidence had to be obtained to connect the driving of his vehicle to Mr. Fedan himself. In my view, Mr. Fedan's informational privacy interests were not engaged by the downloading of the SDM data.[68]

The Court of Appeal went on to differentiate the data located in an EDR and that of a personal computer: "[I]t contained no intimate details of the driver's biographical core, lifestyle or personal choices, or information that could be said to directly compromise his 'dignity, integrity and autonomy.'"[69] A contextual analysis of what data may be contained and how it may relate to the accused will be required as data captured becomes more substantial. As internal computers in a vehicle become more expansive in the data they capture, the analysis will shift. If the computer becomes more like a cellphone, then it will be treated as such. As long as the data remains limited, the privacy interest will remain limited. The reasons behind hacking reflect this increase in data contained in vehicle computers.

8) *R v Anstie*, 2019 ONSC 976

The accused was operating a rented vehicle in this case when he was involved in an accident. Police applied for a warrant for the accused's blood, which had been drawn at the hospital after the accident. The

68 *R v Fedan*, 2016 BCCA 26 at para 81 [*Fedan*].
69 *Ibid* at para 82.

information to obtain the warrant relied, in part, on data downloaded from the EDR in the rented vehicle that the accused operated. The court recognized the different privacy interest in a rental vehicle, pointing to the rental agreement, which "stipulates that the Renter consents to any Event Data Recorder or similar device, being retrieved and the data used by the owners of the vehicle."[70] The court found that the nature of the data was such that it did not give rise to a reasonable expectation of privacy. This, coupled with the rental agreement, persuaded the court that there was no section 8 breach.

The importance of the particular wording of the rental agreement is thus heightened. We could consider the wording in an EULA, which might make the data the property of the manufacturer collecting it rather than the owner of the motor vehicle itself. Further complications may arise where data could be co-owned, requiring the consent of the co-owners to share it with state authorities. Different data may be subject to different interests depending on ownership defined in an EULA. This case highlights the importance of a considered analysis of documentation that most vehicle owners never review, including the owner's manual and the paperwork signed at ownership. Further consideration to the issue of second-hand purchase and resale will also arise. If data does come into the hands of someone other than the operator of the motor vehicle, such as a manufacturer; can an EULA authorize disclosure if the operator was not privy to the EULA, such as if the vehicle was not purchased from the manufacturer? In many jurisdictions, vehicles either cannot be or are not sold directly from manufacturers. In the case of an autonomous vehicle, where data may be communicated to a third party, it will be an important legal issue to determine if the EULA is valid. This will include assessing whether the owner is a party to the contract, whether the EULA runs with the vehicle and not merely with the owner, whether there was a meeting of the minds sufficient to ground the contract, and how all of this plays out in the subjective mind of the person before the court.

---

70 *R v Anstie*, 2019 ONSC 976 at para 22 [*Anstie*].

9) *R v Attard*, 2020 ONCJ 108

The Ontario Court of Justice in this case adopted much of the reasoning in *Hamilton* and *Glenfield.* It found that

> the specific nature of the data recorded in the EDR is different information that a member of the public could reasonably observe. We expect that a witness to a collision may observe; the movement of the vehicle(s) before impact, or provide an educated guess on speed, or whether there was any braking. However, the witness will never be able to provide engine speed, throttle position, the state of the driver's seatbelt switch, whether the passenger air bag was abled or disabled, the time between impact and airbag deployment, ignition cycle counts, engine RPM, brake oil pressure, cruise control, steering input, or longitudinal acceleration which is all recorded on the EDR.[71]

The court recognized the reduced level of expectation of privacy in a vehicle but nonetheless found a violation of the accused's section 8 rights. In assessing section 24(2) of the *Charter*, the court found that since the state of the law surrounding EDRs is no longer in the state of uncertainty that it was at the time the earlier decisions were made, the breach was more serious. The officer's testimony that he was aware of the jurisprudence requiring prior judicial authorization for the EDR was aggravating. The impact on the accused was considered moderate. The court recognized the extremely serious nature of the offence as cutting both ways. Society's interest is greater in more serious cases, but its interest in having a justice system beyond reproach, even in serious cases, is similarly increased. The court determined that exclusion of the evidence was required and distinguished *Fedan*[72] and *Anstie*[73] on their facts.

---

71 *R v Attard*, 2020 ONCJ 108 at para 59 [*Attard*].

72 *Fedan*, above note 68

73 *Anstie*, above note 70.

10) *R v Wawrykiewycz*, 2020 ONCA 269

In this case, the police conducted surveillance on a suspected drug dealer. The accused was operating his father's car and parked it in a public parking space. Police attended and swabbed the door handle, and analysis determined that the accused had handled cocaine. The Ontario Court of Appeal determined that the accused had a privacy interest in the vehicle. Even though he was not the owner of it, he nonetheless retained an interest in it due to using it and his ability to regulate access to it. The Court of Appeal deferred to the trial judge's ruling on section 24(2) of the *Charter* and admitted the evidence. This case is important in considering privacy interests where vehicles may be loaned to different people. Shared ownership could be considered in an analogous way.

11) *R v McNeill*, 2020 ONCA 313

In this case, the police obtained a warrant to seize and examine any cellphone found in a particular location that was associated with drug trafficking. In seizing cellphones found at that location, a cellphone for a person not identified as a target was seized and searched. The Ontario Court of Appeal found that the authorization to search any electronic device found in the location was sufficient and did not need to identify the particular owner. Consider this in the case of a motor vehicle's internal computer. The police will not need to identify the particular owner in order to obtain the data. This may be of the greatest importance when seizing data that is not stored directly in the vehicle but downloaded somewhere off-site. Since the issuing justice is allowed to consider the specific privacy interests of an unknown class of persons, this could be applied to data stored on a car manufacturer's server. This may also allow police to seize a vehicle's computer components along with any cellular devices when considering a dangerous driving case. Authorizing justices will need to be cognizant of the scope of devices of which they are authorizing search and seizure when considering all electronic devices found in a location such as a vehicle. They will also have to consider the privacy rights of the group of people who may have used the vehicle, not just the particular individual who was driving the car at the time of an accident. This will become more important as computers in vehicles collect more and more data in the future.

12) *United States v Jones*, 565 US 400, 132 S Ct 945 (2012)

In considering the use of GPS data and determining privacy interests, Alito J noted that "in the pre-computer age ... surveillance for any extended period of time was difficult and costly and therefore rarely undertaken.... Devices like the [GPS] used in the present case, however, make long-term monitoring relatively easy and cheap."[74] The degree with which technology allows for data to be collected and conclusions drawn has changed significantly. Although a person may not have a great privacy interest in attending a particular public location, knowing the frequency, time of day, and duration of visits a person makes to each location they attend is different. Justice Sotomayor's concurring decision considered as follows that:

> the existence of a reasonable societal expectation of privacy in the sum of one's public movements. I would ask whether people reasonably expect that their movements will be recorded and aggregated in a manner that enables the government to ascertain, more or less at will, their political and religious beliefs, sexual habits and so on.[75]

It is through this aggregation and analysis that the privacy interest may change. The ease with which data can be collected, collated, and assessed has changed. Although an individual's location at any particular point in time may not go to their biographical core in the manner considered in Canadian law, the aggregate information may.

---

74 See *United States v Jones*, 565 US 400, 132 S Ct 945 at 12 (2012) of Alito J's decision concurring in the majority result.

75 *Ibid* at 4 of Sotomayor J's decision concurring in the majority result.

13) Conclusions to Be Drawn Regarding *Charter*-Protected Interests

In considering these cases, a number of themes emerge. First, the data contained in current EDR systems is limited. It may or may not engage privacy interests. Courts differ significantly in the interpretation of what data may give rise to a privacy interest. Not all information that a person wishes to maintain privately gives rise to the reasonable expectation of privacy that would engage section 8 rights. As the kind of data contained in electronic records in a vehicle evolves, so too will the law need to evolve to keep up. For vehicles that record GPS, photo, or more significant biographical data, the courts will likely tend toward greater protections. Where the data is limited and anonymized, the courts will tend to consider that no privacy right is engaged.

As understanding of technology changes, so too will the remedies that are imposed. *Attard* recognized that although police had been operating in a situation of some uncertainty at the times of *Hamilton* and *Glenfield*, that uncertainty no longer exists. Police must recognize the state of the law as it develops. Although police training is not necessarily directly relevant to a breach or remedy, the knowledge of an officer, and thus the seriousness of their actions, is directly impacted when they breach a well-known or established right.

Agreements that can affect an individual's reasonable expectation of privacy will be extremely important. Police may need to have access to documents affecting privacy as the courts move forward in order to assess whether certain privacy interests are waived. As such agreements are typically proprietary, different manufacturers could take different stances with regard to the terms in such agreements. The area of consent in EULAs will be an emerging area of litigation as privacy interests in data recorded in a vehicle change. Although data being located outside a vehicle will decrease the territorial privacy interest an accused may assert, this may give rise to a continually increasing informational privacy interest as the data recorded increases. EDRs are not onboard computers, but some vehicles do have onboard computers. When those are linked to other technology, such as a cellphone, the information contained therein becomes more significant. Passwords, tracking movements, and a person's habits can be analyzed depending on the data collected.

Police already have the ability to obtain a warrant to track a person's movements by use of cellphone data (pinging) or by installing a tracking device on a person's vehicle. An increase in the networking capabilities of vehicles will lead to an investigative tool available to the state that provides information to a degree not yet seen. One-stop access to location, speed, travel routes, internal and external video and audio, and cellphone data, including on a live feed, would be possible. Police will need to develop new tools to limit access in certain situations to only what is needed or they will exceed their lawful powers. Courts will need to assess when each level of intrusion is justified when granting warrants and how overreach is dealt with when it occurs.

K. REGULATORY OFFENCES

Quasi-criminal regulatory offences, such as careless driving, may also occur with automated vehicles. Every jurisdiction across Canada has some form of regulatory offence for careless driving, such as section 130 of Ontario's *Highway Traffic Act*. The test for careless driving is whether a person drove without due care and attention. The charge deals with inadvertent negligence rather than the advertent negligence dealt with by criminal law. It deals with the absence of thought, care, and attention. Any degree of inadvertence is sufficient, and degree is not required as it would be in a criminal matter.[76] *Mens rea* is not a necessary burden of proof in such an offence.[77]

Careless driving is a constantly shifting standard depending on current conditions, including any conditions that ordinary drivers would take into consideration.[78] Normally, this includes considerations based on road conditions, weather, and traffic. The test is more than that of a civil level and deserving of punishment but does not rise to the level required for criminal sanction. The use of automated systems will be one

76 *R v Jacobsen* (1964), 48 WWR 272, 44 CR 24 (BC CA).
77 *R v McIver*, [1965] 2 OR 475 (CA), aff'd [1966] SCR 254.
78 *R v Beauchamp*, [1953] OR 422 (CA).

more factor for a court to consider. Although the past driving history and typical driving habits are not relevant to determine whether an individual drove carelessly on a particular occasion, the personal circumstances of an accused where they advert to an ongoing risk can be relevant.[79] An individual using an automated function in a conveyance must know how to use it properly. Failure to properly use the automated feature may be akin to taking an ongoing risk.

Momentary inadvertence on its own does not represent risk to the level of carelessness that should attract regulatory sanction.[80] However, momentary inadvertence, coupled with other circumstances, could give rise to regulatory or criminal fault.[81] The true question is, "What would be expected of a reasonably prudent driver?"[82] As societal experience with automated systems increases, what can be expected of a reasonable driver will shift. Certainly, the degree of automation and the level of attentiveness that it continues to demand of a driver will change the assessment in a particular case.

Vehicle maintenance will be an important consideration in regulatory offences involving automated vehicles. Owners and operators of vehicles are required to meet minimum safety criteria under provincial legislation. Failure to do so may rise to differing levels of negligence from the civil to the criminal but will be a contributing factor in making such an assessment.[83]

Licensing of drivers is a provincial head of power that may need to be considered as automated vehicles increase in number and sophistication. Although certain automated features require an active driver, as vehicles approach and exceed SAE Levels 4 and 5, a driver's licence may become increasingly irrelevant. Level 5 automated vehicles presuppose that the occupant not only will not, but cannot, take control of the vehicle's motion. At this level of automation, the person is an occupant, not a driver. The

79 *R v Wolff* (1966), 57 WWR 702 (Sask Mag Ct).

80 *R v Namink*, [1979] OJ No 317 (Co Ct); *R v Marceau* (1978), 2 MVR 202 (Que SC).

81 *R v Sloboda*, 2007 MBCA 49 at para 17. See also *Beatty*, above note 2, in considering a momentary lapse in attention in dangerous driving.

82 *Burlington (City) v Boyd*, 2019 ONCJ 584 at para 85.

83 *R v McDorman*, [1983] BCJ No 2511, aff'd (1984), 27 MVR 37 (BC Co Ct).

requirement that a person be licensed may no longer exist. Instead, the vehicle itself may require some form of licensing that communicates a competence evidenced by the vehicle itself. At Level 4 automation, the driver could theoretically take control, but the design presumes that the driving function will be performed by the system. At this level of automation, as long as the automated systems are engaged, a person may no longer need the knowledge currently required to obtain a driver's licence. A family car that is operated by one member of the family but is also used as an automated conveyance by the children may need to be considered. A limited class of licence to be "behind the wheel" in such a vehicle or to allow a person to drive as long as the automated systems are functioning may be considered in much the same way as a learner's permit. These licences may have restrictions or conditions, and whether driving actions breach those conditions may be relevant in determining whether those actions were careless.[84]

Even at higher levels of automation, emergency overrides that allow an occupant to stop a vehicle may exist. Stopping a vehicle is a function of operation in the same way that acceleration and steering are.[85] As a result, whether the system comes to an immediate stop or functions in some other way, such as pulling over or exiting the live lane of traffic before stopping, may be a design function that engineers will have to consider and occupants will need to understand before using an emergency stop.

The closest current example would be the emergency buttons on trains. Most trains now do not have a direct emergency stop; instead, pushing the button alerts the train staff. In the United Kingdom, rolling stock is required to have an emergency brake. The conductor receives an alarm and has three seconds to override the emergency stop if stopping would be unsafe. Improper use of the alarm chain is punishable by a fine of up to £1,000.[86] The New York City subway deals with use of the emergency cord in a non-emergency as a $100 fine.[87] Metrolinx, which operates

---

84 *R v Ashton*, [1985] OJ No 1795 (Dist Ct).

85 *R v Jacobs*, [1955] BCJ No 95 (CA).

86 Railway bylaws pursuant to s 219 of the *Transport Act 2000*, 2000, c 38, s 11(3).

87 Transit Adjudication Bureau, "Rules of Conduct and Fines," online: *Metropolitan Transportation Authority* https://new.mta.info/document/17001.

GO Transit in Ontario, provides that "[n]o person shall interfere with or activate the passenger assistance alarm devices on the Corporation's vehicles or property without reasonable cause."[88] The associated fine under Ontario's *Provincial Offences Act*[89] is $150. These lower fines in New York and Ontario reflect the fact that the emergency button does not stop the train but signals an alarm and a response by staff.

The action that an autonomous vehicle takes in response to an emergency stop function may affect the resulting penalty. If the function brought the vehicle to a complete stop immediately and caused an accident, then criminal liability may ensue in the same way that an intentional stopping to "brake check" a tailgating vehicle can lead to criminal liability.[90]

Driving requires a degree of alertness to ensure safety. Failing to meet this standard, by falling asleep in *R v McCullough*,[91] founded a conviction for careless driving. As automation rises, this level of required alertness should shift. It will be necessary for the court to know the degree of automation before a proper assessment can be made as to the proper standard of care to be applied to the driver.

The test for mechanical fitness is whether an owner and driver used reasonable care and skill to ensure that the vehicle is safe for operation on a highway. It is not an expectation of ensuring perfection of the mechanical nature of the vehicle at all times.[92] Nonetheless, in certain jurisdictions, permitting a vehicle that is in an unsafe condition to be operated can attract regulatory liability.[93] Additional penalties may apply for commercial vehicles. Further emphasis, including a wider array of penalties, may be necessary as occupants of the vehicle may no longer have the same

---

88 "By-Law No. 2," s 3.32, online (pdf): *GO Transit* www.gotransit.com/static_files/gotransit/assets/pdf/Policies/By-Law_No2.pdf.

89 *Provincial Offences Act*, RSO 1990, c P.33.

90 *R v Chalak*, 2020 ONCJ 97; *R v McKay*, 2014 ONCJ 540; *R v Blackburn*, 2004 CanLII 28908 (ON CA).

91 *R v McCullough*, [1999] AJ No 837 (Prov Ct).

92 *Morton (Next friend of) v Sykes*, [1951] OJ No 250 (HC).

93 See, for example, s 84(1) of Ontario's *Highway Traffic Act*: "No person shall drive or operate or *permit the driving or operation upon a highway* of a vehicle, a street car or vehicles that in combination are in a dangerous or unsafe condition" [emphasis added].

responsibilities in ensuring vehicle fitness where they are no longer the licensed driver. The owner may need to be deemed liable, in the definition of *operator*, for a wider selection of offences.

Automation in vehicles has not been mandated to this point. Although laws require many safety features, from seatbelts to mufflers to proper tires, none of these take control over the fittings of the vehicle out of the hands of the driver without the driver making the decision to do so. As automation increases and safety is enhanced by some of these features, automation may become mandatory. A century ago, electric lights seemed unthinkable; four decades ago, seatbelts were controversial; and in the last decade, mandatory backup cameras in cars have become standard. It is not unthinkable that such technologies will be mandated in newer vehicles, but there are few examples of technology being required to be retrofitted in older-model cars. Even unleaded gas did not make the vehicles themselves illegal but instead limited the availability of the outside factor, the leaded gasoline. If the National Transportation Safety Board and NHTSA recommendations regarding vehicle-to-vehicle (V2V) technology are adapted, governments will have to decide if they must be retrofitted in older vehicles. There is precedent that not installing the latest improvements or devices is not, in and of itself, negligent.[94] However, the courts left open whether the failure to install a reasonable safety device could be negligent if the lack of such a device affected the safety of the vehicle. At times, courts have been critical of failure to adopt new technology.[95]

The onus may be on all levels of government to assess whether such safety features are significant enough to require them. The cost and ease of installation of such devices may influence the eventual regulatory scheme. Changes to the legislation are not required in certain jurisdictions. Ontario could require such safety devices by regulation under section 102 of its *Highway Traffic Act*. Certainly, in aviation examples, a functioning

94 *Gascon v Belhumeur*, [1942] CCS No 68; *Winter v British Columbia Electric Railway Co*, [1908] BCJ No 75 (SC).

95 "A compelling case could be made that the overall lack of automation and safety equipment on C-Gimy was completely unacceptable. It was truly a 1960s Volkswagen—basic, reliable but unsafe": *R v 7506406 Canada Inc (Ornge)*, 2017 ONCJ 750 at para 81, discussing a helicopter crash.

autopilot may be required. The failure to follow a regulatory requirement for installation can be considered in assessing criminal liability.[96]

Operators of motor vehicles must adapt their driving technique to the conditions they face. These include external factors, such as the weather, but also factors under their control, such as the use of automation. The duty of courts will be to establish the standard of care required of a reasonably prudent person who has access to the technologies in the vehicle that they are driving. A person may rely on the safety features of a vehicle if such reliance is based on sound knowledge and expected intervention by the safety feature. When a person pushes the brake pedal, they expect the vehicle to slow. Liability requires the accused to be able to appreciate the risk their conduct gives rise to.[97] If the accused could not expect the system to fail to react, then culpability may not be proven.

Returning to the example of pressing the brake and expecting the vehicle to slow, this assumption may not be valid if the vehicle finds itself on ice but generally would hold true. The outside conditions can affect the reasonableness of the driver's actions and expectations. A driver is expected to modify their actions based on outside factors such as weather but cannot be blamed if factors were not apparent.[98] The reasonableness of reliance on automation will be much the same. Outside factors and the manufacturer's recommendations will form the basis for a standard of care. Departure from that standard and where that falls on a spectrum of blameworthiness will decide what sort of charge can be founded. Certainly, there are already cases where automated systems have acted outside of driver intervention, causing unintended and unwarranted braking by the automated emergency braking system.[99]

---

96 *Tayfel*, above note 13.

97 *R v Grosvenor (Alta QB)*, [1993] AJ No 744 (QB).

98 *R v Gareau*, 2018 ONCJ 565; *R v McNeil*, 2012 ONCJ 157.

99 See the ongoing Department of Transportation, NHTSA Investigation, PE 19-010 (9 September 2019), regarding the Nissan Rogue and Mazda's recall notice for 2019 and 2020 Model Year Mazda3s, online (pdf): *National Highway Traffic Safety Administration* https://static.nhtsa.gov/odi/inv/2019/INOA-PE19010-2831.PDF.

L. SELF-INCRIMINATION

Section 11(c) of the *Charter* provides that any person charged with an offence has the right "not to be compelled to be a witness in proceedings against that person in respect of the offence." Section 7 reads: "Everyone has the right to life, liberty and security of the person and the right not to be deprived thereof except in accordance with the principles of fundamental justice." This right includes the right against self-incrimination as part of the right to remain silent.

Automated data provision to government authorities will require an assessment of the rationale behind the collection of the data, including the privacy interests engaged, the right against self-incrimination, and the purpose to which the information is being put.

All provinces provide that a person involved in an accident must report the accident and provide certain information. The *Criminal Code* also imposes certain duties, already discussed, on a person involved in an accident to render aid and identify themselves. Generally, such statements are inadmissible in the trial of a person for a criminal charge. There are statutory exceptions, such as the use of such statements to form grounds to make a breath sample demand,[100] but such statements are generally not admissible for the proof of their content.[101]

Where a vehicle automatically provides data, the nature of the data will be key in determining the privacy interest and the impact on *Charter*-protected rights. Information that is routinely provided in a statutorily compelled reporting scheme, such as fisheries licence cases, is admissible as against a person in a regulatory offence.[102] The nature of the information and the activity plays into the assessment of what use can be made of the statement. Driving has been deemed a "necessity of life," which must be assessed differently than participating in a regulated industry such as

---

100 *Code*, above note 1, s 320.31(9): "A statement made by a person to a peace officer, including a statement compelled under a provincial Act, is admissible in evidence for the purpose of justifying a demand made under section 320.27 or 320.28."

101 *R v White*, [1999] 2 SCR 417. See also *R v Bingley*, 2015 ONCA 439.

102 *R v Fitzpatrick*, [1995] 4 SCR 154.

the fisheries.[103] The difference between a regular driver and a commercial driver may therefore also enter into the balancing.

Whether the data is provided under an agreement with a private relationship, such as customer or manufacturer, or if the data is statutorily compelled under a future law to promote driving safety will have an impact on whether a *Charter* interest is engaged. If legislation is promulgated that requires information to be provided, the use to which it can be put will be tested.

The content of the data will need to be assessed. Like EDR data, the breadth of the information and whether the information provided goes to the core biographical information of a person will affect the privacy interest. Furthermore, the use for which the data is obtained will matter. Specific provision in relation to a criminal investigation is more likely to trigger *Charter* protection than a regulatory requirement for data collected during a highly regulated activity. Both privacy rights and interest against self-incrimination will likely be advanced.

The use to which the data is put will need to be assessed. Collection of data for valid verification requirements is different than collection for penal investigation.[104] If the purpose of collection shifts, its use may infringe the *Charter*.

Legislators will need to take such issues into account when crafting legislation surrounding data collection in autonomous vehicles.

---

103 *White*, above note 101 at para 55.

104 *R v Jarvis*, 2002 SCC 73.

chapter 5

CIVIL LIABILITY

Jaye Hooper

A. LIABILITY IN TORT

The implementation of any new technology creates questions of liability for both the innovator and the user.[1] Until autonomous vehicles are in the general market and a body of caselaw is developed, forecasting the potential issues in civil liability is difficult. Governments view the automation of transportation as having such promise, from both an environmental and an urban development standpoint, that they are pushing the technology forward. Manufacturers are wary of potential avenues of litigation. Lawyers are creative and responsive to a changing environment.

Initial civil litigation will likely use arguments of product liability overlapped with motor vehicle litigation principles. However, these principles are problematic as motor vehicle accidents have one basic assumption: that a human being is operating the car. When you remove the judgment and action (or inaction) of a human being from the litigation, the result can be problematic for litigants attempting to prove negligence. The analysis becomes even more difficult when only partially automated controls are enacted.

1 Andrew Swanson, "'Somebody Grab the Wheel!': State Autonomous Vehicle Legislation and the Road to a National Regime" (2014) 97 *Marquette Law Review* 1085, online: https://scholarship.law.marquette.edu/mulr/vol97/iss4/8 [Swanson].

Human behaviour will also become an essential part of this new analysis. Early warning signs of boredom and distraction while individuals are still in the "driver's seat" of an automated vehicle have caused concern over the future of this technology. Avid, tech-savvy users have also misunderstood the limitations to the technology, with tragic outcomes. Who is at fault when these accidents occur? Should they simply be considered "user error," or should a manufacturer be responsible for understanding the tendencies of the occupants of these vehicles and their resultant vulnerabilities? These are the types of issues courts will have to grapple with as the technology becomes more readily available.

B. THE GOVERNMENTAL PUSH

In 2018, the report of the Standing Senate Committee on Transport and Communications described the current status of automated vehicles as follows:

> With the converging automotive and technology industries, modern vehicles already contain considerable levels of automation, including millions of lines of code. New players, including Tesla and Google, have shaken up the automotive industry, and taken major steps towards a driverless and connected future.[2]

We are approaching the end of an era for the traditional, individually owned, human-driven automobile. In the not-too-distant future, people will be able to summon a driverless taxi from their smartphone and may therefore decide to forego vehicle ownership in favour of these shared automated vehicles. Providing an optimistic view of this developing technology, the committee highlighted the following:

> This could herald the beginning of a new age of transportation, where, for instance, the nearly 1,700 road deaths and 117,000 injuries that

2 *Driving Change: Technology and the Future of the Automated Vehicle*, Report of the Standing Senate Committee on Transport and Communications (2018) at 3, online: *Senate of Canada* https://sencanada.ca/content/sen/committee/421/TRCM/Reports/COM_RPT_TRCM_AutomatedVehicles_e.pdf.

> occurred in 2015 because of human error become grim relics of a primitive past, and cars weave through the country's streets with a computer-run efficiency.[3]

Contrast this glowing forecast with the current limitations to this technology as summarized by the current Tesla Model 3's owner manual:

> *Limitations*
> Many factors can impact the performance of Autopilot components, causing them to be unable to function as intended. These include (but are not limited to):
>
> - Poor visibility (due to heavy rain, snow, fog, etc.).
> - Bright light (due to oncoming headlights, direct sunlight, etc.).
> - Damage or obstructions caused by mud, ice, snow, etc.
> - Interference or obstruction by object(s) mounted onto the vehicle (such as a bike rack).
> - Obstruction caused by applying excessive paint or adhesive products (such as wraps, stickers, rubber coating, etc.) onto the vehicle.
> - Narrow or winding roads.
> - A damaged or misaligned bumper.
> - Interference from other equipment that generates ultrasonic waves.
> - Extremely hot or cold temperatures.[4]

Many of the factors listed above are the same factors that lead to accidents in non-automated vehicles.

1) General Liability Concepts

There are five basic elements to every claim in negligence: (1) the defendant owes the plaintiff a duty of care; (2) the defendant's behaviour breached the standard of care; (3) the plaintiff suffered compensable damages; (4) the damages were caused in fact by the defendant's breach; and (5) the damages are not too remote in law. For product liability cases, the guiding principle began with a dead snail in a bottle of ginger beer in the central

---

3 *Ibid* at 9.

4 See Tesla 3 owner's manual, online: www.tesla.com/sites/default/files/model_3_owners_manual_north_america_en.pdf at page 81.

lowlands of Scotland. In making a finding against the manufacturer, Lord Atkin made the following classic statement:

> A manufacturer of products, which he sells in such a form as to show that he intends them to reach the ultimate consumer in the form in which they left him with no reasonable possibility of intermediate examination, and with the knowledge that the absence of reasonable care in the preparation or putting up of the products will result in an injury to the consumer's life or property, owes a duty to the consumer to take that reasonable care.[5]

This statement has been the starting point of product liability cases ever since. The rationale is that a manufacturer who brings itself into a relationship with a consumer, which may expose the consumer to danger if proper care is not observed, must exercise reasonable care to safeguard the consumer from that danger.[6]

As product liability cases developed, the courts looked for the following elements before finding that a consumer had a cause of action:

> (i) the defendant owed a legal duty of care to the plaintiff in respect of the product; (ii) the product was defective; (iii) the defendant was negligent in failing to meet the requisite standard of care; (iv) the defect caused the plaintiffs [*sic*] injuries; and (v) the plaintiff suffered damage as a result of the defendant's negligence.[7]

The nature of what constituted a "defect" expanded over time. It included more than simply a defect in the actual product; it could include a defect or absence in a warning of the product's danger or the failure to make the product as safe as possible.[8]

As explained by Huddart J of the British Columbia Court of Appeal in *Harrington v Dow Corning Corp*, typically the four steps in a product

---

5 *Donoghue v Stevenson*, [1932] AC 562 at 599 (HL), cited in *Mustapha v Culligan of Canada Ltd*, 2008 SCC 27 at para 6.

6 *Buchan v Ortho Pharmaceutical (Canada) Ltd* (1986), 54 OR (2d) 92 (CA) [*Buchan*].

7 *Ragoonanan Estate v Imperial Tobacco Canada Ltd* (2000), 51 OR (3d) 603 at para 84 (SC) [*Ragoonanan*], quoting Klar et al, *Remedies in Tort*, vol 3 (loose-leaf, Toronto: Carswell, 1987), ch 20 at 8.

8 *Kuiper v Cook (Canada) Inc*, 2018 ONSC 6487.

liability class action are (1) determining whether the product is defective or whether, "although non-defective, [the product] has a propensity to injure"; (2) determining what the manufacturer knew about the dangerousness of its product; (3) determining "the reasonableness of the warning (whether direct or by a learned intermediary) given the state of the art and the extent of the risks inherent in the product's use"; and (4) determining individual causation and damages.[9]

The first step, known as the general causation step, determines whether the product can cause harm. The second step is part of determining whether the manufacturer had a duty of care not to sell the product or to sell it only with an appropriate warning. The third step focuses on the adequacy of the warning. The fourth step determines individual causation and the quantification of the compensation for the consequent harm.[10]

It should be noted that the care that must be taken does not relate to the quality of the product but rather to safety. "Safe but shoddy" does not generally create liability.[11]

What is meant by "safe" when considering autonomous vehicles? Is it a relative concept to be compared to a traditional vehicle? Every forecast and every study predicts that an autonomous vehicle will be *safer* than a traditional automobile. Absent evidence of a direct manufacturing error or the failure to use proper software, if the metrics to be used are the industry standards of a standard automobile, it would likely be very difficult to prove a general lack of safety in the actual vehicle.

This may have also been true in advancement of automobiles throughout the 1900s, yet we have not had any shortage of litigation over the accidents that did occur. When automobile manufacturers began to produce vehicles that could attain a high rate of speed, the issue was not whether the vehicles themselves would prevent all accidents as accidents were expected. Absent a specific design defect that made a crash more likely, manufacturer liability in relation to design focused on the "crashworthiness" of the vehicle. Liability was based on the fact that collisions

---

9 *Harrington v Dow Corning Corp*, 2000 BCCA 605, aff'g [1996] 8 WWR 485 (BCSC), leave to appeal to the SCC refused, [2001] SCCA No 21 at paras 42–46.

10 *Ibid*.

11 *Thorpe v Honda Canada, Inc*, 2011 SKQB 72.

were expected in the ordinary course of the use of the vehicle; however, there were two different collisions to be considered. The first was the external collision of the vehicle with something else. The second was the collision of the occupants' bodies within the interior of the vehicle itself. The courts readily held that consumers had a reasonable expectation that the manufacturer had taken appropriate care not to expose the vehicle occupant to an unreasonable risk of injury by designing a vehicle that could withstand some level of external impact.[12] Whether consumers held a reasonable expectation that the vehicle would be designed in such a manner to reduce the risk of injury if the occupants' bodies struck the inside of the vehicle became a question in decisions such as *Gallant v Beitz; Nissan Automobile Co (Canada) Ltd, Third Party*[13] and *Baker v Suzuki Motors Co*.[14] In these early decisions, although not determinative of what defined "crashworthiness," the acceptance by the courts of a possible cause of action against car manufacturers for not designing a vehicle safe for its occupants following a collision was followed by steady improvements in seat design and internal airbags, thus improving public safety.

One of the most common myths concerning autonomous vehicles is that they are just on the horizon for the average consumer. That is simply not possible. All of the current driver assistance systems that are in use today operate for only short time periods and for extremely limited situations (automatic parking, emergency braking, lane warnings). Once the car drives itself *continuously* for minutes or hours, there is no room for error.[15]

2) Manufacturer's Liability

An automobile manufacturer owes a duty of care not only to the initial purchaser but to all subsequent users of the vehicle.[16]

12 *Ragoonanan*, above note 7 at para 91.

13 *Gallant v Beitz; Nissan Automobile Co (Canada) Ltd, Third Party* (1983), 42 OR (2d) 86 (SC) [*Gallant*].

14 *Baker v Suzuki Motors Co*, [1993] 8 WWR 1 (ABQB).

15 Alexander Hars, "Top Misconceptions of Autonomous Cars and Self-Driving Vehicles" (2016) 2016-09 *Thinking Outside the Box: Inventivio Innovation Briefs* at 9, online (pdf): *Inventivio* www.inventivio.com/innovationbriefs/2016-09/Top-misconceptions-of-self-driving-cars.pdf [Hars].

16 *Hans v Volvo Trucks North America Inc*, 2018 BCCA 410 at para 18 [*Hans* BCCA].

a) Negligent Design

Let us assume that, when considering the types of claims and potential liability in autonomous vehicles, we are not dealing with a vehicle with an obvious defect. If any car manufacturer produced such a vehicle, the finding of negligence would be practically irresistible.[17]

The manufacturer's duty of care not to design a product negligently is based on the theory that the manufacturer should be held responsible for the choices it makes that affect the safety of the product. The manufacturer has a duty to make "reasonable efforts to reduce any risk to life and limb that may be inherent in [its] design."[18] In *Nicholson et al v John Deere Ltd et al*, Smith J noted that a manufacturer does not have the right to manufacture an inherently dangerous article when a method exists of manufacturing the same article without the risk of harm.[19] Although this may be possible for the riding lawn mower in *Nicholson*, first invented in 1946, this creates a significant obstacle to a prospective plaintiff who may believe a corner was cut in the design and manufacturing process of cutting-edge technology.

First, there will be a paucity of expertise in the design of autonomous vehicles other than those experts who are *involved* in the cutting-edge nature of the design and development of these vehicles. We might assume that litigants can seek expertise from an expert who works for a different car manufacturer, but this presents an intellectual property issue. How can a manufacturer, in an expanding area of industry, be expected, in the face of bald allegations within a statement of claim of negligent design, to turn over its research and development or testing data to an "expert" who may be linked to a competitor?

We can also sympathize with plaintiff's counsel, who will have to embark on what is arguably a fishing expedition to try to determine what information on design and testing is even possibly producible. Autonomous vehicles are enabled by multiple hardware and software components. There are a variety of sensor technologies that assess and react to a

17 Stephen M Waddams, *Products Liability*, 4th ed (Toronto: Carswell, 2002) at 67 [Waddams].

18 *Gallant*, above note 13 at 90; see also *Rentway Canada Ltd v Laidlaw Transport Ltd*, [1989] OJ No 786, 1989 CarswellOnt 23 [*Rentway*].

19 *Nicholson et al v John Deere Ltd et al* (1986), 58 OR (2d) 53 (SC), var'd on other grounds (1989), 68 OR (2d) 191 at 60 (CA).

vehicle's environment at all times. The function of autonomous vehicles relies heavily on innovation. Inputs into sensors must be interpreted by software and then translated into action.[20]

One saving grace is the general acceptance of the recognition by the court that a manufacturer's negligence may have to be proven by inference:

> Since the injured plaintiff almost never has any direct proof of what has occurred in the manufacturer's plant, he usually must resort to circumstantial evidence. In the ordinary case this means that he must rely upon the doctrine of *res ipsa loquitur.* In order to bring himself within the doctrine, he must make it appear that the cause of the injury was something which lay within the responsibility of the defendant. In other words, he must introduce evidence to exclude the possibility that it was due to his own conduct, or that of intermediate handlers or any meddling third party.[[21]]

Professor Linden, now Mr. Justice Linden, in his book *Canadian Tort Law* (1977), considered the policy reasons supporting an inference of the manufacturer's negligence at pp 224–5:

> The policy reasons which fuelled the growth of *res ipsa loquitur* are not difficult to understand. The onus of proof resting on a plaintiff can be onerous, especially in those situations where he personally knows absolutely nothing about what happened. His plight is even more unenviable when a defendant does know or has access to the facts, but feigns ignorance.

Some contend that *res ipsa loquitur* should be available only where the defendant possesses actual knowledge of the occurrence and where the plaintiff lacks it. This cannot be. If this were the sole reason of *res ipsa*

---

20 Nikolaus Lang et al, "Can Self-Driving Cars Stop the Urban Mobility Meltdown?" (8 July 2020), online: *Boston Consulting Group* www.bcg.com/publications/2020/How-autonomous-vehicles-can-benefit-urban-mobility [Lang et al].

21 William L Prosser, *Law of Torts*, 3d ed (St Paul, MN: West Publishing, 1964) at 671, quoted in *Farro v Nutone Electrical Ltd (Ont CA)* (1990), 72 OR (2d) 637 at 7–8 (CA) [*Farro*].

> *loquitur*, it could be easily undermined by defendants who would all too often proclaim their ignorance of the events. Moreover, there would be insufficient incentive for defendants to investigate the facts. Rather, the courts must enumerate the various types of situations where defendants are normally apprised of the facts and where plaintiffs are not. An explanation should be demanded in these cases on pain of liability, even if the defendant pleads lack of knowledge.[22]

In *Products Liability*, Stephen Waddams explained it this way:

> Rarely can a plaintiff prove by direct evidence that a defect existed when the product containing it left the factory. The existence of a defect, and its presence in the product at the material time, has always been held to be provable by inference from circumstantial evidence. Such evidence usually shows that the plaintiff has not misused the product, and that it has failed in normal use. The ability of the plaintiff to succeed on such evidence is rightly regarded as an important part of the substantive law of products liability.[23]

The Nova Scotia Court of Appeal decision in *Johansson v General Motors of Canada Ltd*[24] provides an interesting example of the court grappling with the absence of concrete evidence as to a defect. Mrs Johansson's Chevrolet Lumina swerved off the road for no apparent reason. She suffered a serious brain injury. Years after the accident, General Motors issued a recall notice citing a steering "defect" in the Lumina. Mrs Johansson sued. The trial judge considered the Supreme Court of Canada's treatment of *res ipsa loquitur* in *Fontaine v British Columbia (Official Administrator)* and found that, absent a regulatory benchmark, or expert evidence, a plaintiff could not succeed in a claim.[25] He granted a non-suit in

---

22 Allen M Linden, *Canadian Tort Law* (Toronto: Butterworths, 1977) at 224–25 [Linden], quoted in *Farro*, *ibid* at 8.

23 Waddams, above note 17 at 63.

24 *Johansson v General Motors of Canada Ltd*, 2012 NSCA 120 [*Johansson*].

25 *Fontaine v British Columbia (Official Administrator)*, [1998] 1 SCR 424 [*Fontaine*]. Note that in *Fontaine*, the Supreme Court retired the maxim of *res ipsa loquitur* and found it no longer a separate component in negligence; however, the Court still allows for its use where the facts permit an inference of negligence and there is no other reasonable explanation for the accident.

favour of the defendants. The Nova Scotia Court of Appeal found that the trial judge had confused liability without negligence with the trier of fact's function of deciding whether to reasonably *infer* negligence:

> Drawing inferences is standard fare for juries. An inference is a finding deduced or induced from a premise without direct evidence of the inferred fact. It is a factual jump on the reasoning path. The judge ensures that the span is not so broad or irrational that a reasonable jury would stumble. Otherwise the system trusts the jury's common sense and agility to mind the gap and land softly. To resolve the non-suit motion simply because there is no direct evidence of GMC's standard of care for rack and pinion steering assemblies, is to emasculate the jury's function of assessing whether or not to reasonably infer the standard's particulars from appropriate evidence. In *Grant v Australian Knitting Mills Limited*, 1935 CanLII 428 (UK JCPC) [1936] A.C. 85 (H.L.), pp. 96 and 101, Lord Wright, in well-known extracts, discussed the process of inference from circumstantial evidence in a products liability case:
>
> > [The defendant's counsel] contended that the appellant's case involved arguing in a circle; his argument, he said, was that the garments must have caused the dermatitis because they contained excess sulphites and must have contained excess sulphites because they caused the disease: but nought, he said, added to nought still is no more than nought. This, however, does not do justice either to the process of reasoning by way of probable inference which has to do so much in human affairs, or to the nature of circumstantial evidence in law courts. Mathematical, or strict logical, demonstration is generally impossible: juries are in practice told that they must act on such reasonable balance of probabilities as would suffice to determine a reasonable man to take a decision in the grave affairs of life. Pieces of evidence, each by itself insufficient, may together constitute a significant whole, and justify by their combined effect a conclusion.
> >
> > . . .
> >
> > But when the position of the manufacturers is considered, different questions arise: there is no privity of contract between

> the appellant and the manufacturers: between them the liability, if any, must be in tort, and the gist of the cause of action is negligence. The facts set out in the foregoing show, in their Lordships' judgment, negligence in manufacture. According to the evidence, the method of manufacture was correct: the danger of excess sulphites being left was recognized and was guarded against: the process was intended to be fool proof. If excess sulphites were left in the garment, that could only be because someone was at fault. The appellant is not required to lay his finger on the exact person in all the chain who was responsible, or to specify what he did wrong. *Negligence is found as a matter of inference from the existence of the defects taken in connection with all the known circumstances*: even if the manufacturers could by apt evidence have rebutted that inference they have not done so. [emphasis added][26]

The plaintiff's burden of proving that a car manufacturer is responsible for the defective part or condition that ultimately caused the collision may be discharged by "excluding the possibility that some other person created the hazard after the product left the factory."[27]

Not all cases will need to rely upon the inference of liability. There may be direct evidence with respect to the defect even in the face of an apparent advancement of technology. In *Phillips et al v Ford Motor Co of Canada Ltd et al*,[28] the court was tasked with reviewing a purported advancement in the braking system of the Lincoln Continental. The Lincoln's 1965 model was the first year Ford used powered front-wheel disc brakes. It was sold to Mr Nathan Phillips that year, and he drove it daily until an ill-fated date in December 1967 when he and his wife used the Lincoln to run an errand and go to dinner. During the initial errand, Mr Phillips felt "something happen," and the brake pedal stuck. It "righted itself," according to Mr Phillips, and he didn't think more of it. Unfortunately,

---

26 *Johansson*, above note 24 at para 81.

27 *Hans v Volvo Trucks North America Inc*, 2016 BCSC 1155 at para 334 [*Hans* BCSC], aff'd by *Hans* BCCA, above note 16. See also *Smith v Inglis Ltd* (1978), 83 DLR (3d) 215 (NSCA) at para 8 [*Smith*]; *Johansson*, above note 24 at para 85; *Farro*, above note 21 at para 52.

28 *Phillips et al v Ford Motor Co of Canada Ltd et al* (1970), 2 OR 714 (SC) [*Phillips*].

on the couple's way to dinner, they approached an intersection where the light turned yellow. Mr Phillips attempted to apply the brakes only to once again realize that the pedal would not deploy. Panicked as he was quickly approaching the stopped vehicles ahead, Mr Phillips veered to the right onto the curb, where he struck a pedestrian.

The 1965 Lincoln Continental was considered to have a luxury braking system, and the term "feathering" was used at trial to describe the featherweight pressure needed for the brakes to be activated. The braking system was purportedly also designed with a "fail-safe" feature so that if there was a power failure in the system, the user could exert brute force on the pedal to lock up the rear wheels and bring the vehicle to a stop. Expert evidence estimated that ten times the pressure on the brakes was required if the power was lost. The court further accepted that Mr Phillips was not aware of what steps he had to take in this situation; however, the court found that given Mr Phillips's advanced age and limited strength, even if he had known what to do, he would not have the physical strength to press the brake down at ten times the pressure needed in the powered braking system. The court found that the "so-called fail-safe braking feature was inadequate and designed without a proper regard to the situations a motorist must be expected to encounter in traffic on power brake failure."[29] It did not help Ford's defence that nothing within the manual mentioned what to do if the power braking system failed.

The example in *Phillips* can be compared to the tragic fatal accident involving a self-driving Tesla that did not recognize a tractor-trailer turning left in front of it. The operator of that Tesla owned a technology consulting firm and was described posthumously as a "man who spent his life focused on innovation and the promise of technology and who believed strongly in Tesla's mission."[30]

A second fatal crash involving a Tesla occurred two years later. In March 2018, Wei Huang had enacted the vehicle's Autopilot with the adaptive cruise control distance set to the minimum. Under that setting, the car

---

29 *Ibid* at 14.

30 Bill Vlasic & Neal E Boudette, "Self-Driving Tesla Was Involved in Fatal Crash, U.S. Says" *New York Times* (30 June 2016), online: www.nytimes.com/2016/07/01/business/self-driving-tesla-fatal-crash-investigation.html.

is expected to stay in its lane and remain a fixed distance from the vehicle ahead. According to Tesla, the driver is expected to "keep both hands on the wheel and monitor the road, too."[31] Although the corporate website reminds Tesla drivers that Autopilot is a driver assistance tool, not a replacement for active driver supervision,[32] one can appreciate that sitting behind a wheel for long lengths of time where the vehicle has complete control over driving would lead to inattention. Interestingly, vulnerabilities within the Autopilot mode were highlighted by this crash. The Autopilot will fail to understand the absence of lane markers if they disappear, or the lanes split. The system may not see stationary objects and is designed to discard radar data about things that aren't moving to prevent false alarms.[33]

After a series of crashes in 2018, it became clear that drivers did not understand the limitations of these self-driving vehicles. One problem may be the name of the technology itself. Calling this technology "autopilot" creates the concept that the vehicle can pilot itself, yet this is only a Level 2 semi-autonomous system, which is described by the SAE as combining cruise control, lane-keeping assist, self-parking, and the ability to automatically change lanes.[34]

In January 2018, a Tesla Model S slammed into a stopped firetruck that had responded to an accident on the freeway in California because the driver did not appreciate that the sensors might not pick up on stopped vehicles. Fortunately, no one was hurt.[35] That accident was quickly followed by police stopping an individual who was driving under the influence but justified his alcohol consumption on the basis that the vehicle was in autopilot.[36]

---

31 Jack Stewart, "Tesla's Autopilot Was Involved in Another Deadly Car Crash" *Wired* (30 March 2018), online: www.wired.com/story/tesla-autopilot-self-driving-crash-california.

32 See online: www.tesla.com/en_CA/autopilot as of June 2021.

33 *Ibid.*

34 Press Release, "SAE International Releases Updated Visual Chart for Its 'Levels of Driving Automation' Standard for Self-Driving Vehicles" (11 December 2018), online: *SAE International* www.sae.org/news/press-room/2018/12/sae-international-releases-updated-visual-chart-for-its-%E2%80%9Clevels-of-driving-automation%E2%80%9D-standard-for-self-driving-vehicles.

35 Jack Stewart, "People Keep Confusing Their Teslas for Self-Driving Cars" *Wired* (24 January 2018), online: www.wired.com/story/tesla-autopilot-crash-dui.

36 *Ibid.*

Manufacturers have realized that keeping the driver's attention is a significant problem and have made attempts to maintain that attention in different ways; however, it remains an ongoing issue.

In addition, industry standards play a very significant role in determining whether the design of a product is safe. This obviously becomes problematic when products are being developed as the standards are in flux. Liability for negligent "development" requires evidence that a safer alternative would have resulted but for the defendants' negligence. As stated in *Baker v Suzuki Motors Co*: "[T]he absence of testing alone cannot be proof of negligence unless the tests, had they been done, would have enabled the manufacturer to design the motorcycle in such a way that the fire would not have occurred. Without this type of evidence, this allegation of negligence must fail."[37]

Consider the above discussion about the term *autopilot*. As autonomous vehicles are being developed, most, if not all, manufacturers use this term in their marketing and manuals. Yet what one manufacturer calls "autopilot" incorporates different types of assistive modalities than what another manufacturer calls "autopilot." No standards can be determined for the autopilot functions in vehicles without a standard on what "autopilot" entails. Manufacturers are quick to compare the autopilot function in their motor vehicles to that of airplanes. Although planes on autopilot also require the attention of professional pilots, the level of training far exceeds that of an automobile driver and includes simulations of the autopilot mode. Through their own testing, manufacturers are aware that consumers do not generally perform well at maintaining vigilance over long periods of time in a task that is not substantially interactive.[38] We could argue that this is increasingly so in younger generations, who have grown up on devices that provide ongoing stimulation.

Despite their knowledge of the human propensity for distraction, manufacturers are also quick to blame any crash on driver error. Tesla's

---

37 *Baker v Suzuki Motors Co*, [1993] 8 WWR 1 (ABQB) at para 75, as adopted in *Martin v Astrazeneca Pharmaceuticals Plc*, 2012 ONSC 2744 [*Martin*].

38 KC Webb, "Products Liability and Autonomous Vehicles: Who's Driving Whom?" (2016) 23 *University of Richmond Journal of Law & Technology* 9 at 26, online: https://jolt.richmond.edu/2017/05/13/volume23_issue4_webb.

CEO Elon Musk has blamed crashes to date on "driver overconfidence."[39] This comment by one of the industry leaders is in complete contrast to the scholarly articles suggesting that the benefits of autonomous vehicles include increased "productivity." A key selling feature of future technology suggests that drivers will be able to be "more productive" during their usual commute.[40] In fact, Google, a frontrunner in this area, stated that the goals of its autonomous vehicles are to prevent traffic accidents, free up people's time, and reduce carbon emissions.[41] How can this be a true potential future selling point when the driver must be attentive at all times? These corporate messages are likely confusing to those anxious to take advantage of this technology.

This was evident when two different crashes were compared. Tesla blamed the 2016 death of Joshua Brown on technology supplied by Mobileye, an Israeli company. The technology was found not to be able to discern a white transport-trailer against a blue sky. Consumers may not understand that radar outputs of detected objects are sometimes ignored by the vehicle's software to deal with the generation of "false positives." Without the radar ignoring certain objects, an overpass would be reported as an obstacle, causing the vehicle to stop in the middle of the highway.[42]

However, the lack of evidence of a breach of industry standards is but one factor to be considered by the trier of fact. It is for the trier of fact to decide whether, in the circumstances of a particular case, "evidence of industry practice on the one hand, or evidence surrounding the defect, on the other, should tip the scale."[43] Consider a product that technically meets all industry standards but has been subject to numerous consumer complaints to put the manufacturer on notice of a potential problem.

---

39 Andrew J Hawkins, "Tesla Didn't Fix an Autopilot Problem for Three Years, and Now Another Person Is Dead" *The Verge* (17 May 2019), online: www.theverge.com/2019/5/17/18629214/tesla-autopilot-crash-death-josh-brown-jeremy-banner [Hawkins].

40 See Swanson, above note 1 at 1088, and David King, "Putting the Reins on Autonomous Vehicle Liability: Why Horse Accidents Are the Best Common Law Analogy" (2018) 19 *North Carolina Journal of Law & Technology* 127 at 131, online (pdf): https://core.ac.uk/download/pdf/214582966.pdf.

41 Sebastien Thrun, "What We're Driving At" (9 October 2010), online (blog): *Google: Official Blog* http://googleblog.blogspot.com/2010/10/what-were-driving-at.html.

42 Stewart, above note 35.

43 *Johansson*, above note 24.

That is what a jury faced in *Stilwell v World Kitchen Inc*,[44] which focused on a crockpot that shattered while being washed, causing serious injury to the plaintiff. The evidence at trial was that the manufacturer had received 2,000 reports of injuries in relation to the crockpot.

In *Resurfice Corp v Hanke*,[45] the Supreme Court of Canada considered the allegation of a negligent design and the issues of foreseeability and causation. Mr Hanke was the operator of an ice-resurfacing machine. He was injured when he placed a hose intended for the water tank into the gasoline tank of the machine, therefore overfilling the gasoline tank and releasing vapours, which were subsequently ignited by an overhead heater. Mr Hanke sued the manufacturer and distributor of the machine for damages, alleging that the gasoline and water tanks were similar in appearance and were placed too close together so as to be easily confused. The trial judge dismissed the action, finding that a manufacturer could not reasonably foresee that an operator would mix up the two tanks, particularly given that the gasoline tank had a label on it that stated clearly "Gasoline Only." The trial judge further found that there was no negligent design in the two tanks that would have confused a reasonable operator.

The Court of Appeal reversed the trial judge's decision and ordered a new trial. The unanimous decision of the Supreme Court of Canada overturned the appeal and restored the trial judge's original dismissal of the action.

For innocent third parties injured by autonomous vehicles, the current finger pointing between manufacturers and humans may be answered through insurance. In 2018, the Insurance Bureau of Canada recommended the use of a single insurance policy covering both human error and automated technology malfunction.[46]

---

44 *Stilwell v World Kitchen Inc*, 2014 ONCA 770 [*Stilwell*].

45 *Resurfice Corp v Hanke*, 2007 SCC 7.

46 "The Future of Insurance: Automated Vehicles," online: *Insurance Bureau of Canada* www.ibc.ca/on/the-future/automated-vehicles [IBC, "The Future"].

b) Autonomous Vehicle Manufacturers and the Potential for Liability Freedom Under the "Risk-Utility" Analysis

When safety defects in the overall design have been alleged, a court may consider whether the risks of the design outweigh its utility. This "risk-utility analysis" weighs the "risks of the impugned design against the ease, cost, risk, and loss of utility of the proposed safer design."[47] Risk-utility analysis requires weighing any foreseeable risk against the foreseeable utility of the product based on the information available to the manufacturer at the time of distribution or implantation and without the benefit of hindsight. The ease or difficulty in avoiding the risk also needs to be assessed.[48]

In *Rentway v Laidlaw*,[49] Granger J compiled a list of factors to consider when balancing the risks inherent in the product, as designed, against its utility and cost—namely, (1) the utility of the product to the public as a whole and to the individual user; (2) the nature of the product—that is, the likelihood that it will cause injury; (3) the availability of a safer design; (4) the potential for designing and manufacturing the product so that it is safer but remains functional and reasonably priced; (5) the ability of the plaintiff to have avoided injury by careful use of the product; (6) the degree of awareness of the potential danger of the product that reasonably can be attributed to the plaintiff; and (7) the manufacturer's ability to spread any costs related to improving the safety of the design.[50]

In normal negligence cases, remedial measures taken after the loss will not be admissible at trial. However, if those remedial measures are such that they demonstrate that a safer product could be made relatively easily and cost-effectively, this may be admissible for the proof of that fact.[51] Consider therefore, technological developments that are ongoing in the improvement and capabilities of autonomous vehicles. What a manufacturer may claim is an "advancement" expected in the ongoing development of new technology may arguably be a remedial measure that

---

47 Dean F Edgell, *Product Liability Law in Canada* (Markham, ON: Butterworths, 2000) at 52.

48 *Brantford Engineering v Underground Specialties*, 2014 ONSC 4726.

49 *Rentway*, above note 18.

50 *Ibid* at 164, aff'd [1994] OJ No 50 (CA).

51 *Hans* BCSC, above note 27, aff'd by *Hans* BCCA, above note 16 at paras 7–8.

ought to have been considered before the technology was installed into the vehicle. Software updates can be done virtually, which may be missed by a potential plaintiff.

Manufacturers who are knee-deep in research and development costs may also remediate in a cost-efficient manner. For example, after the 2016 Tesla crash involving the unseen white tractor-trailer, Tesla ended its relationship with the software company that had developed the manner in which the camera's information was interpreted. They decided to develop the software in-house. Three years later, Jeremy Banner was killed in the same software glitch on a Florida highway when his Tesla collided with a tractor-trailer crossing its path. It appears to be only after the second accident that the decision was made to develop proper algorithms to train the camera output to detect trucks that are perpendicular as this had, previously, been deemed too "uncommon."[52]

Following several complaints after fatal and non-fatal accidents involving Tesla, the manufacturer's response was interesting. Rather than accept any responsibility for limitations to its technology, Tesla put the responsibility on the drivers. Tesla's CEO, Elon Musk, went so far as criticizing drivers as being "over-confident" in his company's technology.[53] This begs the question: If a driver has to be "fully attentive" when using an autopilot feature in a vehicle that costs more than a vehicle without these advanced self-driving features, why would a consumer purchase it in the first place? Proponents of autonomous vehicles push back on this question by focusing on the fact that self-driving cars are expected to improve traffic congestion, fuel use, parking, and mobility for the disabled.[54]

The US government, obviously concerned with consumer interest, announced a US$4 billion investment to "accelerate the development and adoption of safe vehicle automation through a real-world pilot project in January 2016. Eventually, part of that program required the autonomous vehicle to accept all responsibility for any accident, "regardless of whether

---

52 Hawkins, above note 37.

53 Andrew J Hawkins, "Tesla Didn't Fix an Autopilot Problem for Three Years, and Now Another Person Is Dead" *The Verge* (17 May 2019), online: www.theverge.com/2019/5/17/18629214/tesla-autopilot-crash-death-josh-brown-jeremy-banner.

54 King, above note 40 at 131.

a human occupies the car."[55] We have not gone this far in Canada, although the Insurance Bureau of Canada has called upon the federal government to enact legislation that would require the sharing of data between the manufacturers and vehicle owners to help determine the cause of collision.[56]

c) Duty to Warn

It is generally accepted that the duty to take reasonable care often creates a separate duty to the manufacturer of a duty to warn against dangers inherent in the product.[57] The warning must be clear, complete, and easily understood.[58]

"[A] manufacturer of a product has a duty . . . to warn consumers of dangers inherent in the use of [the] product of which [the manufacturer] has knowledge or ought to have knowledge."[59] Justice La Forest explained the rationale for a manufacturer's duty of care to warn in *Hollis v Dow Corning Corp* as follows:

> The rationale for the manufacturer's duty to warn can be traced to the "neighbour principle," which lies at the heart of the law of negligence, and was set down in its classic form by Lord Atkin in *Donoghue v Stevenson*, [1932] A.C. 562 (H.L.). When manufacturers place products into the flow of commerce, they create a relationship of reliance with consumers, who have far less knowledge than the manufacturers concerning the dangers inherent in the use of the products, and are therefore put at risk if the product is not safe. The duty to warn serves to correct the knowledge imbalance between manufacturers and consumers by alerting consumers to any dangers and allowing them to make informed decisions concerning the safe use of the product.[60]

---

55 Richard Adhikari, "Feds Put AI in the Driver's Seat" *TechNewsWorld* (11 February 2016), online: www.technewsworld.com/story/83102.html.

56 IBC, "The Future," above note 46.

57 John G Fleming, *The Law of Torts*, 6th ed (Sydney: Law Book Co, 1983) at 459, and Linden, above note 22 at 563ff.

58 *Buchan*, above note 6.

59 *Hollis v Dow Corning Corp*, [1995] 4 SCR 634 at para 20 [*Hollis*]; see also *Lambert v Lastoplex Chemicals*, [1972] SCR 569 at 574 [*Lambert*]; *Bow Valley Husky (Bermuda) Ltd v Saint John Shipbuilding Ltd*, [1997] 3 SCR 1210 at para 19.

60 *Hollis*, above note 59 at para 21.

The warnings must be reasonably communicated and detailed to give the consumer a full indication of each of the specific dangers that arise from the ordinary use of the product.[61]

The manufacturer's duty to alert consumers about dangers associated with the use of a product is a continuing duty, requiring manufacturers to warn not only of dangers known at the time of sale but also of dangers discovered after the product has been sold and delivered.[62]

The duty to warn is not only relevant to a discussion of how the product is used. It may be considered when determining if the purchaser would have proceeded with the initial purchase to begin with. Reconsider the shattered crockpot in *Stilwell*. The Ontario Court of Appeal found that the evidence allowed an inference that, had the purchaser been "adequately warned that the combination of an internal stress and an impact while caring for the product in the manner recommended by the manufacturer could cause catastrophic failure, exposing the user to risk of significant injuries,"[63] she would not have purchased the product initially.

The general principle to be applied in determining the degree of explicitness required in a warning was enunciated by the Supreme Court of Canada in *Lambert v Lastoplex Chemicals*.[64] In *Lambert*, the plaintiff purchased cans of a fast-drying lacquer sealer manufactured by Lastoplex Chemicals, which he intended to use to seal a parquet floor in his basement. In a separate area of the basement were two pilot lights: one in the natural gas heater and a second in a water heater. These heaters were in a separate room, but there was no door on the doorway in between.

While applying the sealer, the plaintiff saw a line of flame advancing toward him. He ran up the stairs, but an explosion resulted in severe burns to his body and considerable property damage. He and his wife brought a claim against the manufacturer, who defended the claim based on the warnings clearly applied to the product.

Although the warnings specifically referred to keeping the product away from open flames and pilot lights, Laskin CJ found:

61 *Ibid* at para 20.

62 *Ibid*; *Rivtow Marine Ltd v Washington Iron Works*, [1974] SCR 1189 at 1200 [*Rivtow*].

63 *Stilwell*, above note 44 at para 50.

64 *Lambert*, above note 59.

> [T]he cautions on the labels affixed to the container cans of Supremo W-200 lacked the explicitness which the degree of danger in its use in a gas-serviced residence demanded. A home owner preparing to use the lacquer sealer could not reasonably be expected to realize by reading the three cautions that the product when applied as directed gives off vapours to such a degree as likely to create a risk of fire from a spark or from a pilot light in another part of the basement area.[65]

Later in his reasons, Laskin CJ wrote:

> Where manufactured products are put on the market for ultimate purchase and use by the general public and carry danger (in this case, by reason of high inflammability), although put to the use for which they are intended, the manufacturer, knowing of their hazardous nature, has a duty to specify the attendant dangers, which it must be taken to appreciate in a detail not known to the ordinary consumer or user. A general warning, as for example, that the product is inflammable, will not suffice where the likelihood of fire may be increased according to the surroundings in which it may reasonably be expected that the product will be used. The required explicitness of the warning will, of course, vary with the danger likely to be encountered in the ordinary use of the product.[66]

The applicable principle of law according to which the positions of the parties in this case should be assessed may be stated as follows: where manufactured products are put on the market for ultimate purchase and use by the general public and carry danger (in this case, by reason of high inflammability), although put to the use for which they are intended, the manufacturer, knowing of their hazardous nature, has a duty to specify the attendant dangers, which it must be taken to appreciate in a detail not known to the ordinary consumer or user.

A warning must be communicated clearly and understandably in a manner calculated to inform the user of the nature of the risk and the extent of the danger; it should be in terms commensurate with the gravity of the potential hazard, and it should not be neutralized or negated by

65 *Ibid* at 575.
66 *Ibid* at 574–75.

collateral efforts on the part of the manufacturer. The nature and extent of any given warning will depend on what is reasonable having regard to all the facts and circumstances relevant to the product in question.[67]

A manufacturer must also consider what dangers may exist when the product is put not only to its intended use but also to a reasonably foreseeable use by an ultimate consumer, as stated in *Prosser and Keeton on Torts*:

> A manufacturer or other seller is subject to liability for failing either to warn or adequately to warn about a risk or hazard inherent in the way a product is designed that is related to the intended uses as well as the reasonably foreseeable uses that may be made of the products it sells.[68]

This premise was adopted in *Deshane v Deere & Co*:

> I take the law to be as stated by the Court of Appeals of New York in *Robinson v Reed-Prentice Division of Package Machinery Co.*, 403 N.E. 2d 440 (1980) at p. 444:
>
> > Well settled it is that a manufacturer is under a duty to use reasonable care in designing his product when "used in the manner for which the product was intended ... as well as an unintended yet reasonably foreseeable use."[69]

The duty to warn is a continuous one.[70] This means that a manufacturer must warn a consumer not only of dangers known at the time of sale but also of dangers discovered after the product has been sold and delivered:

> [T]he knowledge of the danger involved in the continued use of these cranes for the purpose for which they were designed carried with it a duty to warn those to whom the cranes had been supplied and this duty arose at the moment when the respondents or either of them became seized with the knowledge.[71]

---

67 *Hollis*, above note 59 at para 55.

68 William Lloyd Prosser et al, *Prosser and Keeton on Torts*, 5th ed (St Paul, MN: West Publishing, 1988) at 685 [Prosser et al].

69 *Deshane v Deere & Co* (1993), 15 OR (3d) 225 at 11 (CA).

70 *Buchan*, above note 6 at para 101.

71 *Rivtow*, above note 62 at 1200. See also *Hollis*, above note 59 at para 20.

One general limitation to the duty to warn relates to obvious dangers. There should be no liability for failing to warn someone of a risk, danger, or hazard that is already appreciated by the reasonable user. We can consider this limitation on the basis of causation: the failure to warn did not *cause* the harm. A user of a knife is presumed to understand that it will cut. An automobile, by its very nature, imposes dangers if not operated properly. In *Schulz v Leeside Developments Ltd*,[72] the British Columbia Court of Appeal found that the suppliers/renters of a V-hull fibreglass boat propelled by a fifty-horsepower outboard motor had no duty to warn a seemingly capable and careful eighteen-year-old person of the obvious danger of riding on the bow of the boat when it was travelling at full speed.

A manufacturer may discharge its duty to warn consumers by providing an adequate warning to a "learned intermediary." The duty of manufacturers of pharmaceuticals and medical devices is discharged if the manufacturer provides the physicians or surgeons, rather than the consumers, with an adequate warning of the potential dangers associated with the use of the drug or medical device.[73] Given that the consumer's trust and reliance are with the intermediary rather than the manufacturer, the ability for the manufacturer to escape liability in this instance is understandable. Unfortunately for car manufacturers, automotive advertising to establish reliance on a particular brand would effectively eliminate any argument of a learned intermediary. In 2018, global automotive advertising expenditure totalled US$35.5 billion.[74] Automotive advertising is focused on performance and safety. Those advertisements are not suggesting that a consumer look to a learned intermediary but rather are seeking reliance on the brand and reputation of the company.

A third limitation negating the duty to warn is on misuse or modification. Prosser in *Prosser and Keeton on Torts* explained this rationale:

> It is often said that there is no duty to guard against unforeseeable misuse. This probably means nothing more than concluding that a misuse

---

72 *Schulz v Leeside Developments Ltd* (1978), 90 DLR (3d) 98 (BCCA).

73 *Buchan*, above note 6 at paras 23 and 59; *Hollis*, above note 59 at paras 28–29.

74 "Auto Industry Still Heavily Invested in TV for Advertising" *Marketing Charts* (21 March 2019), online: www.marketingcharts.com/industries/automotive-industries-107807.

> may be so rare and unusual that a manufacturer must be regarded as not negligent as a matter of law in failing to warn against a damaging event produced in this manner.[75]

This argument of misuse will be rarely applied by courts as a complete defence; rather, courts will generally prefer to apportion liability between the negligent user and the manufacturer rather than exonerating the manufacturer. The Nova Scotia Court of Appeal used this apportionment approach in *Smith v Inglis Ltd.*[76] In that case, the user of a refrigerator had sued for electric shock. The evidence found that the shock had resulted from both a defect in the refrigerator's electrical system and the removal of a grounding prong from the refrigerator's electrical cord. The court held that it was foreseeable for a user with only two-pronged electrical outlets in their kitchen to remove the grounding prong in order to plug in the device.

Currently, many of the features in autonomous vehicles can also be disabled at any time by the user. Manufacturers will likely have to provide clear instructions to those users as to what the impact of turning off any one part of the autonomous feature will mean in the driving experience. Take the recent fatal Uber crash in Arizona, United States, in June 2018. Prior to the crash, Uber had disabled the system used to automatically apply brakes in potentially dangerous situations. The rationale was that Uber, as a driver service, needed to provide a smooth ride for its passengers. Automatic braking was seen to potentially cause "erratic vehicle behaviour."[77] By disabling this automated braking system, Uber relied upon the human backup driver to intervene; however, the system was not designed to alert the driver that the system had been disengaged. The Uber driver, apparently bored, sitting idly behind the wheel while the car drove itself, decided to stream a television show on her phone.[78]

---

75 Prosser et al, above note 68.

76 *Smith*, above note 27.

77 Daisuke Wakabayashi, "Emergency Braking Was Disabled When Self-Driving Uber Killed Woman, Report Says" *New York Times* (24 May 2018), online: www.nytimes.com/2018/05/24/technology/uber-autonomous-car-ntsb-investigation.html.

78 Heather Somerville & David Shepardson, "Uber Driver Was Streaming Hulu Show Just Before Self-Driving Car Crash: Police Report" *CNBC* (22 June 2018), online:

Although that driver is undoubtedly at fault, it is well known that drivers who are actually driving their vehicles are prone to distraction. Therefore, it is foreseeable that drivers sitting behind a wheel as simply a "backup" would be even more tempted to find something else to focus upon. In addition, cognitive science research on distracted driving suggests that even if the driver is paying some attention to the roadway, there is a delay in response time when an emergency arises as driver re-engagement is not instantaneous.[79]

Proponents of autonomous vehicles push against the publication of warnings throughout the driving experience as this would force car companies to talk out of both sides of their mouths—potentially confusing consumers and creating a further barrier to the creation of a market for the product. However, it is highly doubtful that a court will allow a manufacturer, for its own interest in building a brand, to fail to disclose warnings in a fledgling technology.

d) Duty of the Supplier/Distributor

Courts have not hesitated to find that companies that supply, distribute, sell, or import a product owe a similar duty of care to the ultimate consumer to ensure that the product is free of defects. The first case to set out this liability was *Watson v Buckley and Osborne, Garrett and Co Ltd (Ogee Ltd)*:

> I do not think it matters whether the man is a manufacturer or whether he is a distributor. It seems to me to be the same in the case of a person through whose hands there has passed a commodity which ultimately reaches a consumer to his detriment. Where that person has intentionally so excluded interference with, or examination of, the article by the consumer, then he has, of his own accord, brought himself into direct relationship with that consumer so as to be responsible to the consumer for any injury the consumer may sustain as a result of the distributor's negligence. The duty is there.

---

www.cnbc.com/2018/06/22/uber-driver-streamed-the-voice-before-self-driving-car-crash.html.

79 Webb, above note 38 at 26.

> I do not think that the distributor can escape liability for gross carelessness, where the consumer has been injured, by saying: "The initial mistake was made by someone for whose actions I am not responsible."[80]

In dealing specifically with motor vehicles, McNair J in *Andrews v Hopkinson* said:

> I see no reason why the motor dealer should not equally be held liable if he put into circulation in the hands of his customer a motor car which is in fact in a dangerous condition, when the defect rendering the condition dangerous is one which could and ought to have been discovered by reasonable diligence on his part.[81]

The rationale for holding the distributor liable was explained in *Ruegger v Shell Oil Company of Canada Ltd and Farrow*.[82] Mr Ruegger was a farmer growing crops of tomatoes, corn, pumpkins, and squash. He engaged the defendant Farrow to spray his corn to kill weeds. Farrow used a weed killer produced by the defendant Shell Oil, which came into contact with other crops grown by Ruegger, rendering them unmarketable. The weed killer product did not contain any warning with respect to its potential to ruin other types of crop. In defending against the breach of a duty to warn, Shell Oil argued that it did not really manufacture the weed killer in question but formulated it with ingredients purchased from other manufacturers. It claimed it was unaware of the potential of one of the ingredients to cause the harm inflicted on the crops. The court did not accept this:

> The Shell Oil Company cannot escape liability by pleading ignorance of the characteristics of Amine 80. I agree with the decision in *Laplant v DuPont*, 347 S.W. (2d) 231 that the manufacturer and distributor must be treated as an expert in the field and that it knew or ought to have known of the characteristic against which an adequate warning should have been given.[83]

---

80 *Watson v Buckley and Osborne, Garrett and Co Ltd (Ogee Ltd)*, [1940] 1 All ER 174, as quoted in *Phillips*, above note 28 at 32–33.

81 *Andrews v Hopkinson*, [1956] 3 All ER 422, as quoted in *Phillips*, above note 28 at 33.

82 *Ruegger v Shell Oil Company of Canada Ltd and Farrow* (1964), 1 OR 88 (SC).

83 *Ibid* at para 30.

The Supreme Court of Canada examined a distributor's duty to warn in *Rivtow*:

> [T]he knowledge of the danger involved in the continued use of these cranes for the purpose for which they were designed carried with it a duty to warn those to whom the cranes had been supplied and this duty arose at the moment when the respondents [Washington Iron Works, the manufacturer, and Walkem Machinery, the sole distributor in British Columbia] or either of them became seized with the knowledge. . . .[84]
>
> Walkem, which was not a party to [such negligence in design and manufacture], is equally liable with Washington for failing to warn the appellant [Rivtow, the user].[85]

Given that manufacturers are aware of general misconceptions in relation to autonomous vehicles, courts should require that extensive warnings be displayed throughout the driving experience. Burying a warning within a 500-page manual should not be sufficient. In addition, the warning may need to vary depending on whether the user is operating the vehicle within their usual routes or in a new area. Consumers envision simple control mechanisms operating their vehicle, such as "camera spots a child in the road, camera recognizes it is a child, vehicle comes to a stop before the child." In reality, autonomous vehicles rely on machine learning and pattern recognition through artificial intelligence. Images are not immediately recognized; they are learned. Probabilistic reasoning and guessing are developed through extensive testing. It is unclear, however, if consumer confidence will create a market for a vehicle that accurately "guesses." In a 2015 study of consumer confidence, only 50 percent of those asked said they would ride in an autonomous vehicle. That number was significantly reduced when the interviewees were asked if they were willing to put their child in the car.[86] Bryan Walker Smith, a fellow at Stanford University's Center for Automotive Research, put it this way:

---

84 *Rivtow*, above note 62 at 1200.

85 *Ibid* at 1208.

86 Adrienne Lafrance, "One Thing Baby Boomers and Millennials Agree On: Self-Driving Cars" *The Atlantic* (16 October 2015), online: www.theatlantic.com/technology/archive/2015/10/snake-people-cars/410923.

> It's the one headline, "machine kills child," rather than the 30,000 obituaries we have every year from humans killed on the roads. . . . It's the fear of robots. There's something scarier about a machine malfunctioning and taking away control from somebody. We saw that in the Toyota unintended acceleration cases, when people would describe their horror at feeling like they could lose control of their car.[87]

It is interesting that, currently, autonomous vehicles cannot be programmed to break the law. As a result, they are required to comply with all highway rules, including the speed limit. Although this is another means to reduce motor vehicle accidents, it also means that the autonomous vehicles may not blend in with traffic flow, creating potential hazards. For this reason, proponents of autonomous vehicles advocate developing them to strategically break the rules of the road so that they can exist fluidly within the current system of human drivers.[88]

3) Other Potential Parties in Tort

As governments are pushing manufacturers to advance autonomous vehicles on the basis of public safety and the environment, there could be potential exposure for municipalities that are not planning appropriately for these vehicles. City planners will need to build infrastructure with an understanding of the vulnerabilities of these vehicles. In a simulation of transportation conditions in five urban archetypes conducted by Boston Consulting Group, a key finding was that "[m]unicipal authorities must decide early whether [autonomous vehicles] are the right choice for their city, and plan accordingly."[89]

---

87 Claire Cain Miller, "When Driverless Cars Break the Law" *New York Times* (13 May 2014), online: http://nytimes.com/2014/05/14/upshot/when-driverless-cars-break-the-law.html.

88 Webb, above note 38 at 14.

89 Lang et al, above note 20.

Potential consumers of autonomous vehicles will expect, even demand, that they be able to operate these vehicles safely wherever they wish to travel and at the time they wish to travel.[90]

In *Blueprint for Autonomous Urbanism*, the National Association of City Transportation Officials (NACTO) offered a general guide to city planners to optimize the automated mobility revolution toward safe, efficient, and inclusive transportation networks.[91] Yet city projects are currently being built that were in the planning stages years ago, before autonomous vehicles were a serious consideration.

As products are advanced, there have been attempts to sue the entity that is approving the standards that have been put in place. In *More v Bauer Nike Hockey Inc*,[92] the plaintiff suffered a brain injury in a hockey game. He sued the manufacturer of his helmet as well as the entity that set standards and approved the helmet. The basis of the claim against the manufacturer was that it had not set stricter standards in the design and production of helmets. The British Columbia Court of Appeal overturned the trial judge's initial finding of a duty of care owed by the Canadian Standards Association (CSA) as it could extend the risk of liability to the CSA that might prevent it from operating, which "would result in harm . . . to manufacturers, and ultimately, consumers of goods that now benefit from the establishment and certification of minimum standards."[93]

Although many counsel of industrial plaintiffs will seek to include both the manufacturer of the autonomous vehicle and all of the manufacturers of the components that have alleged to have failed, this may not be necessary from a liability perspective. The duty of the manufacturer to take reasonable care in the manufacture of its product extends to component parts that may have been supplied by a submanufacturer or others that the manufacturer incorporates into the final product.[94]

---

90 Hars, above note 15.

91 "Blueprint for Autonomous Urbanism," 2d ed (2019), online (pdf): *National Association of City Transportation Officials* https://nacto.org/publication/bau2.

92 *More v Bauer Nike Hockey Inc*, 2011 BCCA 419.

93 *Ibid* at para 60.

94 *Farro*, above note 21; *Pennock v Aerostar International Inc*, 2012 BCSC 1422.

4) Liability for Maintaining Roads

Section 44 of the *Municipal Act, 2001*[95] requires municipalities to keep highways in a state of repair reasonable in these circumstances:

1. *Non-repair*: The plaintiff must prove on a balance of probabilities that the municipality failed to keep the road in question in a reasonable state of repair.
2. *Causation*: The plaintiff must prove the "non-repair" caused the accident.
3. *Statutory Defences*: Proof of "non-repair" and causation establish a *prima facie* case of liability against a municipality. The municipality then has the onus of establishing that at least one of the three defenses in s. 44(3) applies.
4. *Contributory Negligence*: A municipality that cannot establish any of the three defences in s. 44(3) will be found liable. The municipality can, however, show the plaintiff's driving caused or contributed to the plaintiff's injuries.[96]

In *Smith v Safranyos*,[97] the Ontario Court of Appeal upheld the trial judge's finding that the City of Hamilton was negligent in its design and maintenance of a particular intersection. The trial judge had found that the failure of the municipality to ensure a painted stop line at the intersection, combined with poor sightlines in the intersection's design, caused the subsequent motor vehicle accident. As future technologies, including vehicle-to-infrastructure (V2I) and vehicle-to-everything (V2X), become more common and relied upon, owners of infrastructure may hold duties to ensure their proper operation. One could imagine an autonomous vehicle relying on data being provided to it from a faulty sensor built into infrastructure—for example, traffic lights. Built-in redundancies—such as multiple sensors and error reporting—or regular inspections may be required to satisfy the statutory defences in section 44(3) for municipalities responsible for the other end of V2X technologies.

---

95 *Municipal Act, 2001*, SO 2001, c 25.

96 *Fordham v Dutton-Dunwich (Municipality)*, 2014 ONCA 891 at para 26 [citation omitted].

97 *Smith v Safranyos*, 2018 ONCA 760.

There does appear to be a "disconnect" between the push by federal and provincial governments for the advancement of autonomous vehicles and municipal planning. New infrastructure projects, however, do not appear to be factoring in the future presence of autonomous vehicles. Once autonomous vehicles become prevalent on roadways, we can foresee a possible positive duty of municipalities to ensure that any road deficiencies, roadwork, and road closures be continually updated to ensure that those vehicles have up-to-date information.

5) Invasion of Privacy/Intrusion upon Seclusion

The Ontario Court of Appeal recognized the tort of intrusion upon seclusion in the case of *Jones v Tsige*:

> The key features of this cause of action are, first, that the defendant's conduct must be intentional, within which I would . . . include reckless; second, that the defendant must have invaded, without lawful justification, the plaintiff's private affairs or concerns; and third, that a reasonable person would regard the invasion as highly offensive causing distress, humiliation or anguish. However, proof of harm to a recognized economic interest is not an element of the cause of action. I return below to the question of damages, but state here that I believe it important to emphasize that given the intangible nature of the interest protected, damages for intrusion upon seclusion will ordinarily be measured by a modest conventional sum.[98]

The Ontario Court of Appeal limited such actions to deliberate and significant invasions of personal privacy, providing a non-exhaustive list including: information pertaining to financial or health records, sexual practices or orientation, and employment or other private correspondence. The Ontario Court of Appeal stated that such disclosure, if viewed objectively, would be highly offensive.[99] The key point to the decision is that the information disclosed matters. Where only contact information and

---

98 *Jones v Tsige*, 2012 ONCA 32 at para 71.

99 *Ibid* at para 72.

information that is largely public knowledge, such as a birth or pregnancy, are obtained, there is no significant invasion of privacy.[100] Data of the type collected by an autonomous vehicle may not reach the standard of being significant personal information.

Although proven damages may be minimal, or even unproven, some intangible damages may be redressed. In a large class-action suit, these could add up quickly. The more egregious the actions of the record holder and the invasion of the privacy, the greater the damages.

C. LIABILITY IN CONTRACT

1) Contracts Generally

A contract creates rights and liabilities between the parties. Under the principle of privity of contract, only the parties who are part of the contract may sue if there is a breach. A breach of contract occurs when one party fails to live up to their obligations or commitments made under the contract.

Although the wording between the various acts may differ slightly, in general, provincial and federal legislation creates an implied warranty in every contract for sale or supply of a consumer product that it is (1) fit for its intended purpose and (2) of merchantable quality.

The length of time of this warranty is generally for "a reasonable time period" following the delivery of the product. "Reasonable time period" depends on the price paid and the terms of the contract. Given the cost of automobiles and the premium cost of autonomous vehicles, consumers are generally protected during the life of the vehicle.

Claims against the manufacturer or distributor under most consumer protection statutes are strict liability, meaning, once it is proven that the vehicle is not fit for its intended purpose or of merchantable quality, liability will follow.[101]

---

100 *Broutzas v Rouge Valley Health System*, 2018 ONSC 6315 at paras 151–53.

101 Waddams, above note 17 at 94.

a) Fit for Its Intended Purpose

The *Sale of Goods Act*[102] creates an implied condition that the product is "reasonably fit for the purpose" or intended use by the purchaser.

In *Fortin c Mazda Canada inc*, the Quebec Court of Appeal reversed the lower court's decision, ordering Mazda to pay damages for a latent defect.[103] In that case, Mazda3 vehicles from 2004 to 2007 were affected by a defective locking mechanism on the driver's side door that allowed the door to become unlocked and the vehicle to be stolen. The court rejected the argument that compliance with legal and industry standards somehow exonerated the manufacturer. Although the locking mechanism generally worked well, the court applied an objective standard that consumers would hold a legitimate belief that the vehicle's locking system would be capable of creating a reasonable obstacle against malicious intrusion.

Combining the duty to inform with consumer protection, the Quebec Court of Appeal went further in *Fortin* and found that, once Mazda became aware of the defect, any individual who purchased the Mazda3 without being informed of the defect and before it was corrected would be entitled to a reduction in the purchase price.

b) Of Merchantable Quality

The vehicle must be fit to sell. This means that if the latent defects discovered by the consumer reduce the value of the vehicle or eliminate its resale potential, this is actionable. Although not specifically pleaded, the class actions against Volkswagen for inducing customers to purchase diesel cars by misrepresenting their emissions would fall within both aspects of the *Sale of Goods Act*.[104] No one would expect that these vehicles could be resold following the disclosure of the software misstating the emissions by 40 percent.

---

102 *Sale of Goods Act*, RSO 1990, c S 1.

103 *Fortin c Mazda Canada inc*, 2016 QCCA 31, rev'g 2014 QCCS 2617 [*Fortin*].

104 See the Notice of Action in *Quenneville v Volkswagen Group Canada Inc*, Court file no: CV-15-22729-CP. Consumer protection legislation is referred to at para 17.

2) End-User Licence Agreements and Limitations Therein

Individuals purchasing vehicles are faced with a significant amount of paperwork upon purchase. In addition to the usual manuals, contracts, and agreements with a typical vehicle, self-driving vehicles may also have software agreements, often called end-user licence agreements (EULAs). To be enforceable, contracts require a meeting of the minds. These contracts may be in print or digital form and are common among the digital experiences of most people by now. These are the agreements many people scroll through and accept without spending much, if any, time reading them. These agreements can affect where, and for what amount, a person may sue. They can carry indemnity requirements. How, when, and in what format they are presented can affect their enforceability. Form and presentation matter.[105] Where "fine print" and legalese are avoided, the plain language will bind, even when a party did not read the contract.[106] Agreements will bind all parties unless a person can show that one of a few certain conditions exists:

> *Non Est Factum*—The signer, through no carelessness on his or her part, is mistaken as to the document's nature and character;
>
> Fraud or Misrepresentation—The signer is induced to sign the contract by fraud or misrepresentation;
>
> Objective Lack of *Consensus Ad Idem*—Where it is unreasonable for a person relying on the signed contract to believe that the signer really did assent to its terms;
>
> Unconscionable—was the contract formed in unconscionable circumstances;
>
> Public Policy—There is an overriding public policy that outweighs the very strong public interest in the enforcement of contracts.[107]

---

105 *Rudder v Microsoft Corp*, 1999 CanLII 14923 at para 16 (ON SC).

106 *Ibid* at para 14.

107 *Arif v Li*, 2016 ONSC 4579 at para 50 [citations omitted].

Preprinted forms and waivers are not a new invention. Arguments relating to preprinted forms have been litigated for decades.[108] A party must establish "(1) that in the circumstances a reasonable person would have known that she did not intend to agree to the release she signed; and (2) that in these circumstances the defendants failed to take reasonable steps to bring the content of the release to her attention."[109]

The Supreme Court of Canada recently considered unconscionability in *Uber Technologies v Heller*.[110] Heller had commenced an action against Uber for violations of employment standard legislation. Under Uber's standard service agreement, disputes were required to be mediated and arbitrated in the Netherlands. The cost of the administrative fees initiating the mediation and arbitration process were most of Heller's annual income. In affirming the Ontario Court of Appeal's finding that the clause requiring this litigation process unconscionable, the Supreme Court of Canada reaffirmed that "unconscionability is an equitable doctrine that is used to set aside 'unfair agreements [that] resulted from an inequality of bargaining power.'"[111] Unconscionability "requires both an inequality of bargaining power and a resulting improvident bargain."[112] Improvidence is an equitable concept that cannot be reduced to an exact science and must be assessed contextually.[113] Such assessments relating to the purchasers of motor vehicles will require an assessment as to the terms of the contract and the relationship between seller and buyer, especially with second-hand sales.

The sale of motor vehicles is also controlled by statute. For example, in Ontario, O Reg 332/08 requires as follows:

> *Disclosure and Marketing*
>
> 4.(1) A registrant shall be clear and truthful in describing the features, benefits and prices connected with the motor vehicles in which the

108 *Tilden Rent-A-Car Co v Clendenning*, 18 OR (2d) 601 at para 33 (CA).

109 *Karroll v Silver Star Mountain Resorts Ltd*, 1988 CanLII 3294 at para 24 (BC SC).

110 *Uber Technologies v Heller*, 2020 SCC 16 [*Uber*].

111 *Ibid* at para 54, quoting John D McCamus, *The Law of Contracts*, 2d ed (Toronto: Irwin Law, 2012) at 424.

112 *Uber*, above note 110 at para 65.

113 *Ibid* at paras 75–78.

> registrant trades and in explaining the products, services, programs and prices connected with those vehicles.
>
> (2) A registrant shall ensure that all representations, including advertising, made by or on behalf of the registrant in connection with trading in motor vehicles, are legal, decent, ethical and truthful.
>
> (3) Before entering into a contract with a customer who is not a registered motor vehicle dealer in respect of a trade in a motor vehicle, a registered motor vehicle dealer shall explain to the customer the terms of the contract between the customer and the dealer, including the financial and other obligations, if any, of the customer under the contract.[114]

Conditions in an EULA are likely to be enforced when fairly presented, even if the contracting party did not read them, absent the condition being unconscionable or against public policy. If the statutory requirements are followed, then this is even more certain.

D. CIVIL PROCEDURE

1) Pleadings

With regard to product liability, specific types of negligence exist. A claim must plead the elements of each type. In *Martin v Astrazeneca Pharmaceuticals Plc*, the importance of distinguishing the types of negligence in a claim was stated as follows:

> There is also a complete failure to provide particulars of each type of negligence. Rule 25.06(1) of the *Rules of Civil Procedure* requires that a statement of claim "contain a concise statement of the material facts on which the party relies for the claim." This rule directs the disclosure of the "material" facts, which include facts that establish the constituent elements of the claim. The material facts are to be stated with precision and clarity.
>
> This pleading offends rule 25.06(1) because it fails to acknowledge the differences between the various types of negligent activity. Instead

114 Code of Ethics and Operation of Committees under *Motor Vehicle Dealers Act, 2002*, SO 2002, c 30, Sched B.

> of precision and clarity, the pleading is muddled and vague. The defendants are entitled to know the material facts that the plaintiffs rely on to support each area of negligence. Generalized allegations of negligence are not sufficient: see *Khan v Canada (A.G.)*, [2009] O.J. No. 715 (S.C.J.) at para. 19, aff'd, 2009 ONCA 737, leave to appeal to S.C.C. refused, [2009] S.C.C.A. No. 516. As Strathy J. emphasized in *Cerqueira v Ontario*, 2010 ONSC 3954 at para. 12, "defendants are entitled to know the case they must meet. The court must be fair to the plaintiff, but it must also be fair to the defendants."[115]

Therefore, as an example, to plead a reasonable cause of action for a design defect, a plaintiff must identify the design defect that made the product dangerous to use or that made the product more dangerous to use than it would have been had other, safer design choices been made. The same can be said for the failure to warn. The defendant has the right to understand if the plaintiff is alleging the nature of the warning and when the plaintiff alleges that the warning ought to have been made.

The plaintiff's counsel should also take care to specify the particular allegations for each defendant rather than lumping all defendants together.

For breach of contract allegations, claims should ensure that material facts are outlined for each of the elements: the existence of the contract, the plaintiff's performance under the contract, and the defendant's breach of that contract and the resultant damages.

2) Class Actions

Canadian courts are not strangers to class-action litigation. As problems are located in technologies within autonomous vehicles and recalls are issued, any losses or injuries that result from the defects subject to the recall will more than likely find their way to a class action. The best example of this to date is *Hamilton v Toyota Motor Sales, USA, Inc*,[116] a class action commenced following the alleged unintentional acceleration of

---

115 *Martin*, above note 37 at paras 131–32.

116 *Hamilton v Toyota Motor Sales, USA, Inc*, 2014 ONSC 785.

the 2007 Toyota Camry. In 2009 and 2010, several proposed class actions related to Toyota and Lexus vehicles were initiated across Canada and in the United States. In this litigation, a settlement was achieved through a "malfunction theory," where there was no ability for the class to prove the precise defect but where sufficient proof of the effect of that defect had been proven (the unwanted acceleration).

The creativity of plaintiff counsel in class actions is highlighted by *Fortin*,[117] described above. In that class-action litigation, the members of the class were divided into two subclasses: the first involving vehicle owners whose vehicle had been stolen and the second involving owners who still had their vehicle but were inconvenienced by having to take their vehicle in for repair. Although the second subclass had a creative argument of inconvenience, the Quebec Court of Appeal dismissed it as being an inconsequential loss, similar to normal inconvenience suffered by all vehicle owners over the course of the ownership of their automobile.

117 *Fortin*, above note 103.

chapter 6

WHY MOVE TOWARD AUTONOMOUS VEHICLES?

A. SAFETY

Initially, automated vehicles will suffer from growing pains as vehicles are programmed and we learn how to use them. As well, they will suffer from an unexpected predicament. These vehicles follow the rules of the road—strictly. As a result of not bending or breaking the law, they react in ways that human drivers do not always expect.[1] For example, a person may try to merge illegally. A human driver may let the illegal merger occur and utter a curse under their breath. The automated vehicle may not expect or understand the merger and may maintain its lane. The fault lies with the illegally merging driver but nonetheless ends in a crash. For now, the inability of automation to appreciate the inventive stupidity of human decision making is a limiting factor.

Driver error is responsible for the vast majority of vehicle crashes. Some studies suggest that up to 94 percent of crashes are as a result of driver, and

---

1 See Brandon Schoettle & Michael Sivak, "A Preliminary Analysis of Real-World Crashes Involving Self-Driving Vehicles," UMTRI-2015-34 (October 2015), online (pdf): *University of Michigan Transportation Research Institute* www.umich.edu/~umtriswt/PDF/UMTRI-2015-34.pdf.

thus human, error.[2] Failing to recognize a risk, or failing to make the right decision to deal with such a risk, leads to human error. Human error also includes the failure to implement an appropriate reaction (for example, overcompensating) or non-performance (for example, falling asleep). By increasing the capabilities of vehicles to provide for better risk assessment through increased sensing technology and better communication from the vehicle to the driver, the failure to appreciate a hazard can be eliminated. In many situations, having the system take over at a critical juncture to react when the human driver does not, such as with automated braking and lane-keeping systems, eliminates significant risk. The vehicle system reacting to a dynamic situation may still face some risks regarding performance issues should the situation be so unpredictable that the system does not have time to comply. However, ongoing development and testing should help minimize those occurrences. With proper programming and lead times built into system decisions, the greater risk may be an impatient or frustrated human trying to take back control from a vehicle. Non-performance issues will be eliminated by constant monitoring by the system. In short, the implementation of automated systems has the potential to prevent a large number of motor vehicle crashes.

The remaining number of crashes is roughly equally distributed between vehicle defects, environmental issues, and unknown issues. Proper vehicle maintenance will always be an issue. However, automated vehicles may play some role in solving this issue as well. It is not unheard of for a vehicle to operate with a "check engine soon" light on. In the future, an automated vehicle may decide that there is a critical defect such that it locks out its own use or takes itself to a mechanic. Operational parameters, such as the type of tire installed on the vehicle, may need to be updated by the owner. A vehicle may adjust its driving in consideration of outside factors such as this. If the vehicle is told that a snow tire is installed, then it

---

2 "Critical Reasons for Crashes Investigated in the National Motor Vehicle Crash Causation Survey," DOT HS 812 115 (February 2015), online: *National Highway Traffic Safety Administration, Department of Transportation* https://crashstats.nhtsa.dot.gov/Api/Public/ViewPublication/812115#:~:text=Critical%20reason%20attributed%20to%20environment&text=In%20about%2050%20percent%20(%C2%B1,7.2%25)%20of%20the%20crashes.

may assess frictional coefficients in cold temperatures differently. Human error may still creep into some crashes, but this risk of human choice in adjusting parameters will be more advertent and thus more blameworthy.

Until technology progresses to the point where the system can operate faster than a human in all situations, impatience and human override will remain significant risks. Currently, autonomous vehicles are not permitted to break any law or regulation, including the posted speed limit. It is inconceivable that drivers will patiently sit behind the wheel of their automated vehicle while being steadily passed by other vehicles on the highway.

B. SHARED OWNERSHIP

The rise of ride-sharing apps, such as Uber and Lyft, has highlighted the demand for personalized transportation solutions. Taxis have existed almost as long as the automobile. Advancements in the area of technology have allowed greater use of vehicles and made every car owner a potential taxi driver. Significant regulatory risks go along with this. Taxi licences require a number of conditions to be met, such as specific insurance requirements and checks of the individual's driving history and criminal record depending on the jurisdiction. These requirements exist to promote safety but add cost to the operation. Ride-sharing apps skirt most of these issues by ignoring them, which has caused problems but has not seemed to dull the public's interest in lower-cost, personalized travel. The trade-off of security for convenience is especially interesting in the area of autonomous vehicles. Although some people may have concerns over purchasing or relying on an autonomous vehicle because of safety reasons, there is already a demographic that identifies convenience and cost as key drivers in its transportation choices and will be a targeted group for the implementation of autonomous vehicles.

The concept of ride sharing is now well developed. Most vehicles are not in use for the vast majority of the time,[3] and ride sharing provides an

3 Brandon Schoettle & Michael Sivak, "Potential Impact of Self-Driving Vehicles on Household Vehicle Demand and Usage," UMTRI-2015-3 (February 2015), online (pdf): *University of Michigan Transportation Research Institute* https://deepblue.lib.umich.edu/bitstream/handle/2027.42/110789/103157.pdf?sequence=1&isAllowed=y.

opportunity to use them more fully. The greater the number of vehicles in a shared or networked ownership arrangement, the greater the number of options for people. As shared ownership rises, people may plan their days differently. Disruption to the traditional workday of 9 a.m. to 5 p.m. may occur. Interestingly, the impact of the COVID-19 pandemic has accelerated such disruption in many ways. Policies, such as mandatory attendance at a physical office, that were once thought of as sacrosanct have been shown to be pliable. It is not suggested that rush hour will completely disappear, but distribution of work hours to limit physical presence in offices is already occurring and may be further hastened by shared ownership models. Reliance on ride sharing could also have an impact on people who need to book appointments or attend professional visits by limiting their access to transportation during peak times.[4] But this may be offset by the increased access to transportation that may not have previously been available for individuals who did not have a personal vehicle.

The greatest advantage of shared ownership models is the reduction in cost. Instead of buying a vehicle, the capital costs can be shared. Urban locations are most amenable to such a model as the higher concentration of people allows for the vehicle to limit time between passengers and minimize time spent empty. Compared to personal vehicle ownership, autonomous vehicles could operate in a manner best described as enhanced public transit. They could serve as a new layer in the transportation system, situated as more personalized and more readily available than traditional buses or subways but less costly. We can envision different levels of membership, including personal priority and use at one end and shared carpool options at the other.

The impact of shared ownership extends beyond the cost of ownership and the impact of accessibility. Concepts such as insurance will be disrupted significantly. Instead of the current model of insuring the primary driver, companies will have to determine risk across a group of people. Since the occupants are not controlling the vehicle, the actuarial assessment will need to account for other factors. Insurance models such

4 Dorothy J Glancy, "Privacy in Autonomous Vehicles" (2012) 52:4 *Santa Clara Law Review* 1171, online: https://digitalcommons.law.scu.edu/lawreview/vol52/iss4/3.

as those involving taxi fleets, cruise ships, and airlines may be useful foundations on which to build.[5] Many insurance companies already allow customers to obtain reductions in premiums if they agree to monitor their driving, especially in relation to speed and braking. Such monitoring will be made easier in connected vehicles, which will allow for a more individualized assessment as to risk. As well, how often a person uses the autonomous features of their vehicle may affect premiums.[6]

C. FEWER CARS IN THE DRIVEWAY, MORE CARS ON THE ROAD

Autonomous vehicles may reduce the number of vehicles on the road through shared ownership, including within a household. If a single family can plan for one person using the family vehicle at a particular time, and then the vehicle returns autonomously to pick up the second family member for another trip, fewer vehicles may need to be manufactured. This example, however, means that the vehicle is on the road for a greater amount of time, which could add to congestion. Two vehicles of a household may be driving at the same time, but they are never driving empty. In the autonomous vehicle model, the return function to pick up the next passenger means that the vehicle travels more kilometres.

The increased travel by vehicles in such scenarios may be offset by environmental savings. Fewer vehicles will need to be manufactured. Better coordination of autonomous vehicles should lead to fewer accidents and fewer traffic snarls. The environmental impact of eliminating a single traffic jam would offset a considerable amount of empty travel time. More efficient travel limits the amount of fuel and time spent driving. Vehicle platooning to create better aerodynamics and reduce drag, leading to more economical fuel use, will also create offsets. Proper planning in vehicle use

---

5 Michele Bertoncello & Dominik Wee, "Ten Ways Autonomous Driving Could Redefine the Automotive World" (1 June 2015), online: *McKinsey & Company* www.mckinsey.com/industries/automotive-and-assembly/our-insights/ten-ways-autonomous-driving-could-redefine-the-automotive-world#.

6 Alexandra Cutean, "Autonomous Vehicles and the Future of Work in Canada" (2017) at 24, online (pdf): *Information and Communications Technology Council* www.ictc-ctic.ca/wp-content/uploads/2018/01/ICTC_-Autonomous-Vehicles-and-The-Future-of-Work-in-Canada-1-1.pdf.

could also increase adoption of more environmentally friendly technology, such as electric vehicles, as charging between trips could be designed on a systematic level to eliminate concerns about the range of such vehicles.

Autonomous vehicles will eventually be able to communicate in such a way as to determine traffic patterns and react in the most efficient manner. This will allow greater use of existing infrastructure. More efficient use of roadways, perhaps at higher speeds, will limit travel time and the time on the roadway of each vehicle per trip.

The impact of autonomous vehicles on the concept of parking also needs to be considered. Shared ownership is most efficient when the vehicles are constantly in use, so rather than park, autonomous vehicles may "return to home"; they may loiter in the area; they may seek the closest parking spot, which is communicated through vehicle-to-everything (V2X) systems; or they may complete a driving task for another person. In each scenario, the impact on parking is different. Autonomous vehicles may not follow any one option but could act differently depending on the situation. However, each option affects the infrastructure needed to support driving.

D. SPEED

Autonomous vehicles presuppose processing power that allows for perception and consideration of data at a higher rate than human reaction. When coupled with V2X communication technology and the higher amount of data that the system can process, the consideration of variables should allow autonomous vehicles to travel at higher speeds. Speed limits are largely based on identified risks in certain areas and human reaction times to deal with those risks. For example, the greater risk of children entering a roadway near a school necessitates lower speed limits. Although there will always be situations that mandate lower speeds, the increased ability to perceive and react to dynamic situations may allow faster travel, especially on restricted-access highways.

Vehicle platooning will allow space on the road to be freed. The impact on the trucking industry alone may allow one or even no driver to handle multiple vehicles. This will allow increased fuel efficiency, as discussed above, but also will allow closer travel between all vehicles due to faster reaction times.

Further impact on the speed of travel can be realized through the reduction of traffic congestion that autonomous vehicles promise. Fewer collisions and traffic jams and the possible redistribution of traffic to a more efficient use of existing infrastructure mean that even travel at existing speed limits may be faster.

With greater speeds possible for connected autonomous vehicles, the implementation of reserved lanes for these vehicles to allow better realization of the benefits of the technology may be required. This is to keep human drivers from becoming a danger to autonomous vehicles. This may also impact adoption of autonomous vehicles in the same way carpool lanes encourage shared riding and could also have the added benefit of making people who wish to retain human control over their vehicle feel better about not interacting with autonomous vehicles operating at increased speeds.

E. COMFORT

One of the greatest arguments for the adoption of autonomous vehicles is comfort. With the elimination of the need for a dedicated driving position, vehicle interiors can be redesigned. For example, an interior structure more similar to a train, where occupants face each other, or a layout that includes built-in workstations could allow for efficient use of time during transit. Conversely, sparser interiors may allow greater passenger numbers, and room could be freed up with the removal of control structures such as steering wheels, pedals, and gear shifts. The impact on the safety of such designs will need to be considered to ensure that they continue to meet crash-readiness standards.

F. DANGERS

The progression through differing levels of autonomy may seem gradual, but the impact is significant. Although current technologies help the driver, the engagement of the driver is a key component—and remains an expectation—of the whole-system approach. Drivers' minds may wander for a few seconds—this has always been the case—and the current automated systems work to improve on the driver's own decision making. But as automated systems shift to taking over for longer periods of time, the attention span of the user will shift. A driver will not be able to monitor things on a continuous level for a significant span of time when most of their interactions are eliminated. The attention span of the user must be considered until automation reaches near full automation, as at SAE Level 4. In many ways, Levels 2 and 3 are the most dangerous as the degree of attention expected of the human user is altered significantly from traditional driving norms but is still very much required. The limit of such technology is not understood well enough by the driving public to ensure safe use.[7]

Humans feel loss of control acutely. When driving, the feeling of control is intimately linked with the act, and there is great reluctance to give up that control. Drivers feel they are safest when they are operating the vehicle. However, drivers overestimate their own driving ability.[8] Concerns relating to loss of control are based on the illusion of superiority created by our ungrounded self-confidence. These concerns have been voiced with almost every technological safety measure introduced. Even seatbelts were seen as taking away control.[9] Autonomous systems such as the anti-lock braking system (ABS), which has been standard in all vehicles in Canada since 2012, are already in place and have changed the degree of control a driver has over the vehicle. Such systems were not universally accepted upon their implementation but have become standard nonetheless. The ABS is specifically useful in considering the wider impacts

---

7 Consider this report (discussed in Appendix 1): "Collision Between a Car Operating with Automated Vehicle Control Systems and a Tractor-Semitrailer Truck Near Williston, Florida, May 7, 2016," NTSB/HAR-17/02, PB2017-102600 (reissued 12 October 2017), online (pdf): *National Transportation Safety Board* www.ntsb.gov/investigations/AccidentReports/Reports/HAR1702.pdf.

8 Alexander Hars, "Top Misconceptions of Autonomous Cars and Self-Driving Vehicles" (2016) 2016-09 *Thinking Outside the Box: Inventivio Innovation Briefs* at 9, online (pdf): *Inventivio* www.inventivio.com/innovationbriefs/2016-09/Top-misconceptions-of-self-driving-cars.pdf.

9 John Zazula, "June 22, 1987: Albertans Prepare for Seatbelt Law" *CBC News* (23 June 2016), online: www.cbc.ca/news/canada/edmonton/june-22-1987-albertans-prepare-for-seatbelt-law-1.3649730.

of technology, where the benefit of closed-track testing is not as clearly realized under real-world conditions.[10] Few vehicles operate by direct control. Acceleration, braking, and gear shifts all operate through fly-by-wire electronic interfaces in modern vehicles, with even steering moving to such technology in certain production models. Pilots were initially wary of such technology in aviation, but such worries have been overcome. The same concerns will likely take time to be overcome in drivers. But just as no one can imagine a car without seatbelts, these advancements will similarly become standard over time.

Autonomous vehicles, especially those at SAE Levels 4 and 5, are expected to operate in almost any situation where a human can. Although autonomous vehicles will have an operational design domain (ODD), which limits the situations in which they can operate, they must be designed to recognize and react to a plethora of situations. Expecting perfection is unrealistic. Even humans get themselves into situations beyond their abilities. The difference is that autonomous vehicles are expected to revert to a safe state if their ODD is exceeded. People often make the choice to take a risk when they should not. Acceptance of autonomous vehicles will depend on their ability to react to dynamic situations. A vehicle that cannot respond to the vast majority of situations presented to it will not be accepted. People are unlikely to buy a vehicle that is not reliable. Geographic realities will limit the market willing to purchase such vehicles. The likelihood of certain situations that may be encountered may also limit such a market. Construction on roadways; unpredictable behaviour in other drivers, pedestrians, and bicyclists; and even a flat tire are all situations that are not "normal" but are certainly common enough to require consideration in design. The ability of autonomous vehicles to respond to a wide variety of situations will affect their marketability and the speed at which they are adopted.

At SAE Level 3, significant risks with issues surrounding attention span exist. Drivers are at their best when they are fully engaged in the

---

10 Charles J Kahane & Jennifer N Dang, "The Long-Term Effect of ABS in Passenger Cars and LTVs," DOT HS 811 182 (August 2009), online: *National Highway Traffic Safety Administration, Department of Transportation* https://crashstats.nhtsa.dot.gov/Api/Public/ViewPublication/811182.

task of driving. Distracted driving is a serious concern. With conditional automation allowed by SAE Level 3, there is a greater risk of distraction. Overreliance on autonomous technology to the detriment of the driving task has been seen in numerous collisions, some of which are reviewed in Appendix 1. Ensuring that adequate systems are in place to monitor and enforce driver attention is key to safe operation of vehicles at SAE Level 3. This begins with education on the limitations of technology and why this level is defined as conditional, not full, automation. Drivers at SAE Level 3 are still required to keep their attention on the driving task. Vehicle manuals devote a significant amount of text to reviewing the importance of this, but the message does not seem to reach some people. Just as a pilot is expected to maintain focus on the task of flying, even while autopilot is engaged, a driver at SAE Level 2 or 3 is required to stay vigilant. Drivers have died as a result of their lack of care, consideration, or knowledge relating to these systems. Recognizing that humans are not good at monitoring monotonous situations, which these levels of automation turn most of the driving experience into, is important to note in the design and limitations on the use of such systems. Although designers are expected to keep the human in the loop, making sure that this happens is not easy.

chapter 7

PHILOSOPHICAL CONSIDERATIONS: THE GHOST IN THE MACHINE

Autonomous vehicles will be driven largely by the algorithms programmed into them. This means that the vehicle can access its decision-making capabilities from the start. These capabilities may be upgraded or programmed to learn from experience, but the capability to learn allows for testing through simulation in a manner that has more variables than testing human experience on a person-by-person basis. Since not every conceivable situation can be programmed for, and because driving can involve inconceivable situations, programs must be developed to provide for a decision to be made even when it has not been specifically considered and a response predetermined by programmers.

A. WHAT IS AN ALGORITHM?

An algorithm is a set of rules to be followed in problem solving. The algorithm determines the method with which an action is to be considered. Algorithms can vary in complexity, from simple—"If an object is detected in the vehicle's path, then stop the vehicle"—to vastly complex, with numerous variables. Consider the number of steps and assessments a person must undertake to answer a question such as "How does the vehicle determine which item to strike if multiple objects enter the roadway and avoidance of all is impossible?" Both methods approach the issue of an object in the vehicle's path but engage different complexity. However, the difference between a situation where the vehicle can simply slow, stop, or steer around a single obstacle and one where it must decide between numerous obstacles is much more nuanced. The difference between hitting a plastic bag that has blown onto the road and hitting a pedestrian is vastly different. A fully autonomous vehicle must be able to (1) assess a dynamic situation; (2) weigh the possibilities and outcomes; and (3) come up with a "correct" decision, all within seconds. However, a "right" decision, in an ethical or moral sense, cannot be made in many situations. So how does the system deal with that dilemma?

The simplest algorithms are the easiest to understand but can only deal with the simplest situations. Cascading decision making, a process similar to that in which a human engages, must be programmed into the design to prevent simple tricks from compromising the designed function of the vehicle. Consider a vehicle that is programmed never to cross the solid dividing line on a highway. This makes sense; it follows the rules of the road. This algorithm is a simple and effective way of stopping the vehicle from driving into oncoming traffic. Left this simple, it achieves many aims, but it will struggle to deal with the complex issue of avoiding a pedestrian who wanders into traffic unless an overriding rule is also written in that it prioritizes avoiding the pedestrian over the strict adherence to the rule. Even strict rules are open to exploitation. Although only a prank, consider the situation in Figure 7.1, where the algorithm was exploited to incapacitate an autonomous vehicle in its testing phase through use of a trail of road salt to create what the vehicle sensed as a solid line it was not allowed to cross. The vehicle refused to move.

B. THE DIFFERENCES BETWEEN TRADITIONAL ALGORITHMS AND MACHINE LEARNING

Traditional algorithm design presumes that systems are programmed to react to certain parameters in a particular way; change the parameters and you may change the outcome. Easy to understand, these designs can be limited in their imagination and thus their ability to react to less

FIGURE 7.1. AUTONOMOUS VEHICLE TRAPPED BY ITS ALGORITHM. (AUTONOMOUS TRAP 001 (2017), JAMES BRIDLE, COURTESY OF THE ARTIST.)

predictable situations. As well, they are fixed, and modifications must be made if they are to react differently should a problem be identified.

Owing to these limitations, machine-learning designs are being preferred in many autonomous vehicles that allow the vehicles to learn from the situations they encounter. The designs are not so rigid in their structure that differing outcomes to the same parameters are possible, and the program may learn after they have left the factory. This learning can come from situations encountered, preferences or reactions preferred by a human driver/occupant, or updates from the manufacturer. How the vehicle learns may affect the assignment and apportionment of blame in a criminal or civil matter.

Machine learning can accrue from real-world occurrences, but it can also be enhanced through learning by example. In situations that an autonomous vehicle may not encounter regularly in the real world, the software can be given examples to learn from while it is still in a simulated environment. This allows the system to learn how to deal with complex scenarios and create solutions without endangering people in the real world. Situations such as encountering yellow left-turn arrows, turning left from a one-way street onto another one-way street at a red light, or entering non-traditional intersections may not be common, but autonomous vehicles must nonetheless have learned enough in order to respond.

An important legal issue with different types of design is to determine fault if an accident were to occur. Initial programming, system design failures, and user inputs may all affect blameworthiness. Proper maintenance, including ensuring that regular updates to software and hardware are made, will be the responsibility of the user or owner. Product updates and recalls will be ongoing concerns for manufacturers. Predicting dynamic situations and creating acceptable reactions, including designing for automatic reversion to a minimal-risk condition when the system is straining to deal with a situation, will be the responsibility of programmers. Programmers will undoubtedly be caught between the desire to minimize risk and the need to increase functionality. Since the safest way to avoid an accident is not to get in a car, some risk will always be inherent in driving. Assessing the blame for risks taken is the task of courts. Determining who is to blame and to what degree will be increasingly difficult and may necessitate reference to complex decision-making processes in software design rather than reference to the common human experience of driving. Assignment of blame in a legal context may be too complicated to ground a finding of criminal or civil liability without reference to significant expert testimony.

C. THE TROLLEY PROBLEM

This philosophical problem, introduced in 1967 by Philippa Foot, deals with a problem that has implications for autonomous vehicles. The situation to consider is that of a runaway trolley that is currently on track to run over five people. You are standing near the track and see this. You have the ability to do nothing and let events run their course or to intervene and shift the trolley to another track, where it will kill only one person. The decision between action and inaction is often important at law. A person is responsible for their actions but often not for their inaction. When considering this, the person who chooses to save the five at the expense of the one may be considered a murderer under the law subject to certain defences, such as self-defence or defence of another, although it is unclear if the currently worded section 34 of the *Criminal Code* would apply in this fact scenario. The person who remained inactive was not legally responsible for the events that occurred and so is not liable. How this sort of decision making may apply to an autonomous vehicle will need to be considered at some point. The utilitarian decision that may be programmed into the decision-making process may not be the most legally defensible decision. How to apportion blame in a legal system will thus be complicated by the competing moral and legal interests.

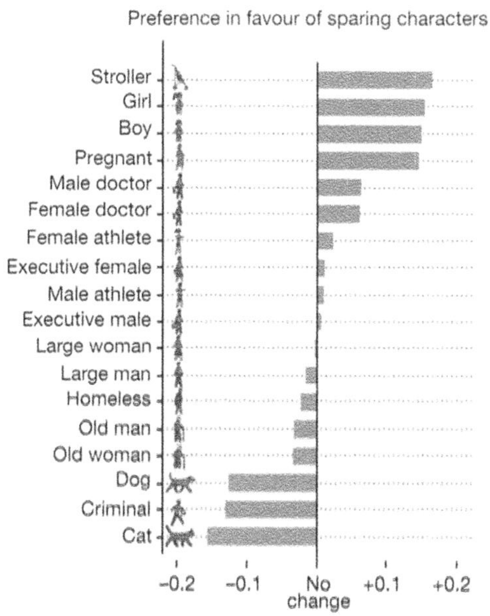

FIGURE 7.2.
THE MORAL MACHINE

Decision making in morally difficult circumstances is a very personal process. It varies from person to person and, very significantly, is based on cultural and societal norms in the place where the person lives.[1] The "Moral Machine" experiment assessed personal decisions in a number of scenarios providing various personal, societal, cultural, and moral priorities to choose from, including sparing humans versus pets, passengers

1 Edmond Awad et al, "The Moral Machine Experiment" (2018) 563 *Nature* 59–64, online: www.nature.com/articles/s41586-018-0637-6.

versus pedestrians, the elderly versus youth, legal versus illegal jaywalkers; higher versus lower social status; male versus female. Some scenarios provided additional characteristics, such as pregnancy, criminality, income status, or education of the possible victims (see Figure 7.2).[2]

Hundreds of thousands of decisions were surveyed from around the world. The variation in decisions is quite interesting. The results in sparing characters suggest a preference globally to preserve more youthful individuals, such as children; the educated; the affluent; and the athletic over the homeless, the overweight, and the elderly. In deciding who to prioritize, this means that avoiding running into criminals ranked higher than avoiding cats but lower than avoiding dogs. However, these global trends are not held universally across the world. The study found that

> participants from individualistic cultures, which emphasize the distinctive value of each individual, show a stronger preference for sparing the greater number of characters. Furthermore, participants from collectivistic cultures, which emphasize the respect that is due to older members of the community, show a weaker preference for sparing younger characters.[3]

This raises the issue of how systems should be designed. A programmer may have differing viewpoints based on the culture from which they come. As well, a company may have competing interests in such designs to follow either a morally or a financially relevant decision-making process. Companies in different parts of the world may need to program their decision-making systems to accommodate regional variances on both legal and ethical grounds. It is likely that the first time an autonomous vehicle is forced to make such a decision that leads to a death or significant injuries, the process will be scrutinized widely and at many levels. Instead, considerable pre-deployment simulation would allow for analysis and debate of reactions without the need to deal with an actual event. Adaptation of the program rules from there could be undertaken.

---

2 *Ibid* at 61.

3 *Ibid* at 62.

Implementation of autonomous vehicles will shift ethical and moralistic decision making away from the person occupying the vehicle at the moment of dilemma to the person involved at a design stage. This does not take the human element out of the equation but merely shifts it to another person. The issue of "who decides" is impactful at law in assessing blame. If such moral choices are made outside the control or input of the owner/occupant, then criminal punishment could shift to the designer/manufacturer. Corporate responsibility may necessitate a shift in insurance programming and civil responsibility when accidents take place. It will be in the best interest of designers/manufacturers to shift this responsibility to the consumer through comprehensive end-user licence agreements. How this will occur and to what degree remain to be seen.

Other issues will continue to arise in assessing decisions made. Although a vehicle may be programmed to react in a particular way, that process may change over time because of the machine-learning design of such functions. As well, if the user can have input, for example, by allowing a person to change the settings in their vehicle, the decision-making process may shift back to the end-user. Companies may require a person to undergo a decision-making process similar to that of the Moral Machine exercise to input their own preferences and thus insulate the manufacturer from direct involvement in such decisions. It may be uncomfortable to consider how a decision may change if the pedestrian's age can be determined or the survivability of each individual involved can be measured. However, such factors may need to be taken into account when programming. A hierarchy of interests will need to be established based on numerous facts. Consider that the best answer of who to prioritize and what damage to cause them, if striking a pedestrian is unavoidable, from a torts perspective, may be a death as the damages are often less than those of paralyzing a person. From a criminal law perspective, penalties for offences causing bodily harm are typically less than those where a death occurs. Along with the hierarchy of factors surrounding the event to be considered, a separate hierarchy of best results will need to be determined. Since such decisions are relative to the person involved, it may not be possible to come to a single conclusion for all users.

The decision-making process will be further affected by how someone values their own life. If the vehicle has no other choice but to hit a person who jumps out in front of it or drive itself into the ditch, then considering the survivability of each situation and the valuing of one person over another may be required. Does the choice change based on a purely utilitarian basis, based on the number of lives involved? If a vehicle could strike a person, killing them with 100 percent certainty versus a 50 percent fatality risk for the vehicle occupants, does the choice change based on the number of occupants? From a purely utilitarian point of view, it would change, with one outcome for a singular occupant, another for three occupants, and a split decision for two. A driver may decide to value their own life over the seemingly suicidal person jumping in front of the fast-moving vehicle, whereas a programmed system may assess things differently.

An assessment in programming may also need to be undertaken with regard to whose interests should rule. The decision-making process of an occupant will be different from that of the pedestrian they may hit. It is even more important to determine what should happen in situations where the owner is not the occupant (for example, corporate or shared ownership). What makes the most sense to an outside party may not be the decision that those involved in the particular situation may prefer. Programming decisions to avoid criminal and civil liability may be the functions preferred by the programmer/manufacturer over the ethical or moral decisions that the involved parties may prefer. This sort of tension will need to be resolved in order to allow consumer confidence to a degree that promotes adoption of autonomous vehicles. If people do not trust these vehicles, then they are unlikely to use them. If designs reflect interests that are not shared by the wider community, then adoption is unlikely. When dynamic scenarios occur, how they are handled will be considered in a wider forum than the courts, and public interest is likely to be high. The court of public opinion will have significant sway as it will likely affect the valuation of companies based on the decisions these autonomous vehicles make.

The standardization of decision making inherent in autonomous vehicles is presumed to lead to fewer risks and a safer driving environment for all. However, in the aggregation of knowledge comes an aggregation of risk as well. Autonomous vehicles will have similar logic built into them. This is beneficial because it allows all autonomous vehicles to learn from the mistakes of any single situation affecting any single autonomous vehicle. If a risky situation is identified, then the programming can be updated across a large number of vehicles. Companies can expose their program to an uncommon situation in a number of simulations to give their programs exposure to a particular situation and learn from it without exposing it to the risks inherent in a real-world scenario. This ability to effectively teach through experience without the risks in the real world is a great benefit of autonomous vehicles. However, as vehicles are taught how to handle certain situations, the machine must necessarily identify a hierarchy of priorities in its decision-making process. As a result, there is a risk that certain situations effectively become blind spots, or worse. The aggregation of knowledge means that similar situations should be dealt with in a similar and predictable fashion. That is at the heart of much of the reasoning behind adopting autonomous vehicles.

This standardization of risk assessment can lead to concerns of discrimination on a systematic scale. Another way of viewing crash optimization (determining what action to take if a crash is unavoidable) is by stating that avoiding certain obstacles means that other obstacles are essentially targeted. Crash optimization is a choice by exclusion of ranked worse options, but it is a choice nonetheless. Although human drivers are forced to make such choices in each crash, the decision is an individualized one. Theoretically, the human driver makes their own decision of prioritization, although, in reality, the decision may be made in such a short time frame that no real reasoning or logic enters into the decision-making process. With autonomous vehicles, the faster computer brain may be able to weigh factors to a finer degree. As a result, patterns in choices made during crashes will aggregate toward a particular type of solution. If autonomous vehicles share data as presumed, then the centralization of decision making makes patterns more likely. Even if each vehicle makes its own choice, similar algorithms are likely to lead to similar outcomes.[4]

4 Hin-Yan Liu, "Three Types of Structural Discrimination Introduced by Autonomous Vehicles" (2018) 51 *UC Davis Law Review Online* 149, online (pdf): https://lawreview.law.ucdavis.edu/online/vol51/51-online-Liu.pdf.

The inherent danger in justifying algorithmic preferences is that over time this can lead to a systemic discriminatory effect. For example, an algorithm which prioritizes the individuals on the basis of survivability may through its opaque learning function end up discriminating on the basis of age, sex, or race based on medical responses in the community in which it is operating. Failing to see the pattern that occurs can possibly lead to repeated but undesirable responses: "[A]lgorithmic preferences can be defended on the basis that each individual decision is justifiable so long as the overall policies are designed to minimize overall harm since any discriminatory effect is seemingly tangential due to a lack of intention."[5]

When considering crash optimization, the detail to which the autonomous vehicle can consider in order to make decisions will be key to understanding the decisions eventually made. Certainly, vehicle manufacturers have a vested interest in keeping the occupants of the vehicle safe. It would be difficult to sell consumers on the notion that their vehicle could prioritize another person to the detriment of the occupant. Human drivers have a similar vested self-interest in deciding between potentially dangerous situations and may choose an option that is less utilitarian but may increase their own survivability.

In a fully connected society, where an autonomous vehicle has access to data about everyone around it, the autonomous vehicle may be able to assess factors that a human driver could not. Consider the possibility of linking an autonomous vehicle with a large-scale data trawl that collects publicly available data about people it identifies. A programmer, or even an owner who provides input into the vehicle's settings, could prioritize people with certain characteristics over others, such as children. This would necessarily discriminate against the elderly. Consider another risk, however: the development of an "immunity device"[6] that allows the holder to be prioritized over others. Vehicle manufacturers could offer these programs to provide added protections to the wealthy, or society could offer them as rewards for socially laudable actions.[7] Certainly, if such devices

5 *Ibid* at 162.

6 *Ibid* at 164.

7 See, for example, Alexandra Ma & Katie Canales, "Chain's 'Social Credit' System Ranks Citizens and Punishes Them with Throttled Internet Speeds and Flight Bans if the

are created, a regulatory structure surrounding them will be required. Consideration of what factors should or should not be allowed to enter into such a decision-making process could form the basis of a significant philosophical text. An advantage of system design in the decision-making process is that the system can learn from the various experiences of all vehicles rather than just the experiences of a single driver.

Of course, the Trolley Problem has no single "right" answer. That is what makes it so interesting to study and why results can differ based on small changes to the circumstances. No program will ever be able to assess every possible permutation of events and come to the same answer every time, just as no human will either. Instead, consider that such events are highly contrived and that the best way to solve such situations is to avoid being put into them in the first place. Programming to make such complex decisions is best wholly avoided. By creating an autonomous car that can predict and avoid being out in such a situation, and by enhancing the sensing and reaction ability of such a vehicle, the need to choose can be avoided. A vehicle need not make a morally difficult decision if it can already sense the obstacle and avoid it. Although accidents may occur due to a number of factors, a lack of imagination is the real threat. By imagining, considering, and implementing safety planning into the design of vehicles, these situations can be eliminated. Proper planning prevents poor performance.

The use of vehicle-to-everything (V2X) technology will allow vehicles to comprehend information in a networked fashion, which will allow for even greater predictive behaviour. A system that can recognize and react to a dynamic situation by avoiding it in the first place will be best suited to safe decision making. Rather than deciding whether to strike a pedestrian, a connected vehicle will be able to sense the cellphone in the pedestrian's pocket and take evasive action before a dynamic situation can arise. Rather than considering the best outcome for a particular vehicle, a larger system

---

Communist Party Deems Them Untrustworthy" *Business Insider* (9 May 2021), online: www.businessinsider.com/china-social-credit-system-punishments-and-rewards-explained-2018-4.

can seek a more egalitarian solution[8] by knowing the decision-making process of all other vehicles. Not only will the vehicle be able to take steps to try to avoid an accident, but it can also communicate with other objects to let them understand the unfolding incident and react in a predictable way that maximizes outcomes. This would be like the driver steering to avoid the accident, but the object also being able to understand what the vehicle's next decisions will be and to instruct the pedestrian, the other vehicle, or any other object to take a parallel action to maximize outcomes. Through cooperation in the system, better outcomes are possible.

Further systematic discrimination can take place as a result of design and cost, especially in the early days of autonomous vehicles. As V2X technology presupposes installation of communication technology, its adoption will not be instant and universal. Poorer neighbourhoods will likely see the longest period until installation. This could lead to limitations in vehicles being able or willing to travel to certain areas, which would affect commerce, housing, and economic growth in those areas.

Although many situations are highly contrived and seem impossible, the law is often called upon to deal with seemingly implausible fact scenarios. The usual driving experience does not involve the dynamic situations that must be considered and designed for. Repairing harm done to an individual in the civil process, or society in the criminal process, is often relatively straightforward because the common law is pliable enough to apply to a wide variety of situations. The reason matters often go to court is because the situations are unique to a degree that they require the application of principles rendered with good judgment.

In dynamic situations, a decision must be made in fractions of a second. Which way to steer, how to react, and a course of action are all decided in a moment. Perception and reaction in humans take time. To assess a complex set of parameters in the way that is discussed in the Trolley Problem can form the basis of years of consideration without reaching a definitive conclusion. To expect a machine to make a morally correct decision is unfair. Expecting an autonomous vehicle to make a decision

---

8 Most drivers could be considered self-interested and would make a choice that saves themselves at the expense of others. Autonomous vehicles may weigh the competing interests of drivers with others outside the vehicle.

that is accepted by all is an impossibility. This standard is not expected of a human driver and should not be expected of an autonomous vehicle. Instead, like human drivers, autonomous vehicles need to be programmed in a way to avoid unethical decisions.[9]

If it is accepted that driving has social utility but also that risks exist, then the question shifts to what an acceptable level of risk is and how such risk should be apportioned when a risk is eventually realized. Criminal liability presupposes a degree of intention or at least significant negligence by failing to advert to a risk coupled with a risk to traditionally protected areas, "such as peace, order, security, health and morality, or to another similar interest."[10] It will be difficult to prove such intent to the criminal standard of beyond a reasonable doubt. The civil justice system, which seeks to redress wrongs in a way to put a person back in the position they were in before a harm was visited upon them, with its standard of a balance of probabilities, will still require significant consideration of who is to blame when an autonomous vehicle fails. If an autonomous vehicle with machine learning is involved in an accident, an analysis of the system programming may need to be undertaken. The consequences of a learned reaction rather than a preprogrammed one may further complicate the assessment of foreseeability of harm. Although difficult, courts will likely be called upon to answer such a question in both civil and criminal trials in the not-too-distant future. As with other technologies, the pervasiveness of their adoption and societal familiarity may change the assessment of their function over time.

Since a standard of perfection is unrealistic, the question of how good autonomous vehicles must be before they will be accepted is important. "Aviation automation, an area much in the news lately, is child's play compared to surface vehicles, and we're still debugging aircraft software, some 70 years later!"[11] Although aviation automation is decades old, it

---

9 See Alexander Hars, "Top Misconceptions of Autonomous Cars and Self-Driving Vehicles" (2016) 2016-09 *Thinking Outside the Box: Inventivio Innovation Briefs*, online (pdf): *Inventivio* www.inventivio.com/innovationbriefs/2016-09/Top-misconceptions-of-self-driving-cars.pdf.

10 *Reference re Genetic Non-Discrimination Act*, 2020 SCC 17 at para 68.

11 *Collision Between Vehicle Controlled by Developmental Automated Driving System and Pedestrian, Tempe, Arizona, March 18, 2018*, NTSB/HAR-19/03, PB2019-101402 (reissued

still fails. However, aviation is safer than surface transportation on a kilometre-over-kilometre basis. People know that automation is involved in flying. They understand that there are risks. Crashes happen, yet the risk is willingly taken daily. Clearly, adoption prior to perfection is possible. Human error in aviation incidents is widely recognized. As a result, automation has been accepted. Continual education of pilots has been key to understanding and implementing automation in a manner that promotes safety. There is no reason to believe that automation in surface transportation will be any different. Ongoing conversations about the benefits and limitations of automation are key. The National Highway Traffic Safety Administration crash reports reviewed in Appendix 1 speak to the problems that occur when there is an overreliance on automation, especially in vehicles at SAE Level 2. Companies such as Waymo (formerly Google Self-Driving Car Project) actively engage in discussions in an attempt to make automation better understood.[12] Although this benefits their self-interest in many ways, such informational steps will be key if autonomous vehicles are to achieve mainstream acceptance. There is a very strong belief, which is not statistically well founded, in your own driving ability. The example of the aviation industry continually improving by learning from incidents is another useful behaviour to model.

Ethical consideration must be given to situations where safety is involved. Lessons learned can be shared. When new safety enhancements to vehicles are created, such as seatbelts, airbags, and the like, they are typically pioneered by one or more vehicle manufacturers. This often happens in more expensive models, for individuals who are able and willing to pay more for such safety measures. Over time, as these enhancements become more widely accepted and their cost is reduced, they are adopted more widely or regulated as required equipment in all vehicles. This process can vary, but such adoption is usually measured in years if not decades. In situations where a company learns of a problem with the ability of a class of vehicle to deal with a particular situation, there may be moral culpability if this information is not shared. Companies may

26 June 2020), online (pdf): *National Transportation Safety Board* www.ntsb.gov/investigations/AccidentReports/Reports/HAR1903.pdf.

12 Waymo's online public education site can be found at: www.ltad.com.

have a financial interest in identifying such flaws with their programs, but sharing the solutions may not be financially incentivized in a similar way. Companies may seek protection under intellectual property law in the design of programs to deal with certain, less common scenarios. However, there may be a societal interest in the breaking down of such barriers. Consideration will need to be given to the open sharing of information in a way that protects companies' financial investments in the development of a patch but also a way to ensure that such information is shared to protect the driving public. New regulation of corporate information sharing will need to be considered to balance these competing interests, especially in fields of converging design, to allow continuous improvement in autonomous driving systems. Such convergent design may occur through different methods, but it will be important that companies freely acknowledge design failures so that the industry as a whole can better itself.

The competing societal, personal, and legal interests in determining worst-case scenario decision making will need to be assessed and accounted for. Far from being an esoteric philosophical question, these issues will have real-world implications for the designers and programmers who shape the decision-making processes in autonomous vehicles.

chapter 8

FUTURE HURDLES

The impact of autonomous vehicles will stretch beyond civil and criminal law, reaching into all aspects of society. In North America, where driving is a cornerstone activity, change to that activity changes society. It will take significant legislation to properly address the issues considered in earlier chapters.

Automated vehicles rely on predictable conditions. They struggle to appreciate poor decision making by human drivers and expect other vehicles to act and react predictably. With improvements over time, automated systems will be better able to appreciate the situations in which they may find themselves.

One issue that will affect autonomous vehicles will be their reliance on their sensors. Vehicles that rely on sensing technology may be thwarted by inclement weather. Snow in particular is an enemy to the automated vehicle. It can blind optical sensors, and it can confound radar, light detection and ranging (LiDAR), and sonar systems. Snow changes the vehicle's grip on the road and necessitates a change in the method of driving. It blocks the ability to see road markings and confuses distances between vehicles. This is a hurdle to be overcome through careful design—it is not an absolute bar. Human drivers already operate their vehicles in less than ideal situations. Adaptability to allow the system to rely on the data that is available to it, much in the same way that a human driver does, will help an automated vehicle continue to operate in situations such as those posed by inclement weather. Unlike the human driver, the automated vehicle can also rely on the more detailed Global Positioning System (GPS) and sensors that may reach into the non-visible spectrum of light to allow the system to observe, perceive, and react to things that a human could not. It will first be up to designers to implement multiple sensing systems that can deal with such interference and then programmers to implement a system that reacts to conditions in an appropriate way.

Another hurdle in the Canadian implementation of automated vehicles will be that, outside major population areas, roads are less likely to be mapped in the same detail and may lack the markings that current systems rely upon. This may mean that Level 5 automation may take longer to be adapted outside areas with greater population density. According to Statistics Canada, more than 80 percent of the Canadian population lives in an urban setting of some sort.[1] A quick perusal of Google Maps shows how encompassing Google's Street View has been in providing photographic mapping of roads (see Figure 8.1). A more industry-wide attempt or one that uses government imaging as well may fill in the gaps. Although not every road is programmed into a GPS device, most people would agree that GPS devices are useful aids in navigation.

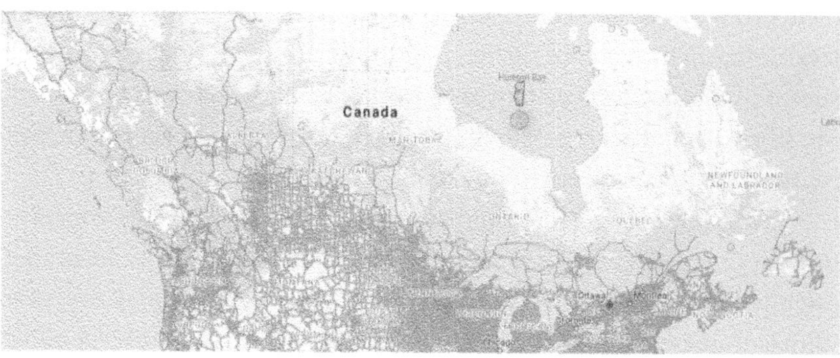

FIGURE 8.1. CURRENT GOOGLE MAPS' STREET VIEW COVERAGE

1 "Canada's Rural Population Since 1851" (23 July 2018), online: *Statistics Canada* www12.statcan.gc.ca/census-recensement/2011/as-sa/98-310-x/98-310-x2011003_2-eng.cfm.

The advent of automated vehicles may have unintended consequences, which will require further consideration and legislation. The efficacy and environmental impact of these vehicles may have the potential to be game changers, as previously discussed. Ideas of ownership of vehicles and city planning will need to change.

Changes in parking behaviours may have environmental impact. With the ability of a vehicle to loiter and wait for the driver, the concept of parking will change. There are two main ways this may happen, and legislative intervention may be required to decide which is appropriate in particular circumstances. Vehicles programmed to loiter and wait for the driver may clog streets by continuing to operate. However, with inventive programming, roadside parking may be a thing of the past. A vehicle that can rejoin traffic and leave curb lanes currently reserved for on-street parking vacant may increase the capacity of overtaxed streets. As well, vehicles could find themselves a parking spot while they wait rather than loiter by continuing to operate or circle the block. This will need to be realized in the design and programming of vehicles. Although a loitering vehicle may be most convenient for the owner, it would be worse for the environment and would add to congestion.

A different impact on parking is the potential for better use of parking garages, which may allow a vehicle to immediately travel to the nearest available garage and take itself out of use, becoming convenient for the owner to recall when needed and so help lessen congestion. This is high-level design, which is even further into the future and would require some sort of communication system to allow the vehicle to know where to park. But it is within design possibilities moving forward, especially in urbanized and well-mapped environments.

Another less considered impact of autonomous vehicles concerns how they may affect things that rely on motor vehicle accidents. Insurance premiums may be lowered as safety increases. Litigation may decrease. With a decrease in the number of accidents, there will be a corresponding decrease in the numbers of people injured or killed. As a result, there is expected to be some impact on the field of organ donation, which relies, in some measure (between 10 and 15 percent in the United States), on fatal collisions.[2] Although other developments, such as better technology in artificial organ design, may be able to fill this gap, a reduction in available organs will have an impact. Legislation to change from an opt-in system, as most jurisdictions currently have, to an opt-out system, like that of Nova Scotia, may be needed to ensure that such an important resource is not wasted. In the meantime, signing an organ donor card, or the provincial equivalent, will be that much more important.

The current state of technology in partial automation creates problems unique to this middle ground where neither driver nor system is usually controlling all aspects of driving at a particular time. Current levels of automation in commercially available vehicles do not exceed SAE Level 3, conditional automation. This level presupposes human intervention if the vehicle exceeds its operational design domain (ODD). Some manufacturers have changed tack in systems that assess driver engagement. Instead of the system merely relying on driver interaction with the steering wheel, cameras can assess the driver's eye focus on the roadway. Further work at keeping drivers engaged and focused will be important. Rather than maintaining current designs, where distractions such as cellphones and texting are separate from the driving system, full integration to set limits on their use while maintaining focus may be a better strategy. Programs such as Apple's CarPlay and Android Auto are allowing drivers to use functionality in limited ways to enhance their attention rather than compete for it. A number of manufacturers incorporate heads-up display (HUD), which allows drivers to display information on the windshield to maintain focus ahead rather than look down at a screen. This look-through ability maintains more focus on the road and allows the vehicle to shut down the HUD if a situation develops.

Licensing of drivers will need to take new technologies into account. Currently, some jurisdictions allow the use of parking assist (automatic parking) technologies during licensing examinations. Others do not. Whether a driver must prove an actual ability to perform a certain act,

---

2 "Organ Procurement and Transplantation Network: National Data," online: *Organ Procurement and Transplantation Network, Health Resources and Services Administration* https://optn.transplant.hrsa.gov/data/view-data-reports/national-data/#.

like parallel parking without the use of the technological aid, is going to change as the option becomes more common in vehicles.

In addition to determining which competencies must be shown to obtain a driver's licence, connected vehicles will allow for a greater ability to monitor driving. With the ability to contrast human driving against decisions that a system would have made, the assessment of competence to drive may change in both method and standards including on an ongoing basis. It may be that the learner's permit of the future allows for the monitoring of driving by licensing authorities so they can review driving decisions to ensure the competency of drivers by assessing their real-world driving behaviour. A constant and automated assessment of driving behaviours could lead to a new licensing regime that assesses drivers regularly, if not continuously, much like insurance companies currently do by recording speed and other driver behaviours, which, if deemed safe and legal, may lead to a premium discount.

Drivers generally become better as a result of experience. Shifting driving tasks completely away from the human may create a situation where future drivers are less capable of operation should it be required. Non-drivers and bad drivers will have to be considered in the design and development of Level 4 and 5 autonomous vehicles. Will knowledge of autonomous systems and how to operate them become part of the licensing test? If an automated system is not understood but the driver can recover and take a legitimate course of action to deal with a situation, this may be sufficient. It is for pilots using autopilot.[3]

Autonomous vehicles must also be contrasted with remote-controlled vehicles. Although some autonomous vehicles will have features that seem to be remote controlled, such as a summons feature, their function is better defined as remote ordered as the care and control of the vehicle rest with the onboard systems, not with the individual. The individual using the summons feature, for example, does not decide the route, speed, or decisions of the vehicle in any real way. Nonetheless, they may be responsible at law for the vehicle's actions.

3 See *Canada (Attorney General) v Annon*, 2013 FC 5 at paras 18–19.

The differing responsibilities in criminal and civil law may reflect differing responsibilities and consequences when dealing with remote-controlled functions. Many autonomous vehicles may eventually have remote-controlled functionality. Certainly, vehicles may have occupants who lack the ability to take control if the vehicle faces a situation that exceeds its ODD. One possibility of achieving a minimal-risk condition would be to have functionality where control is exercised by an off-site driver. The impact of allowing remote driving is significant, and given the difficulties of creating autonomous vehicles, some companies may seek to mimic autonomous function through the use of remote human operators.[4]

As with the adoption of most technology, disruption in the job market can be expected. The greatest disruption is likely to occur in the most directly impacted industries, such as freight transportation and taxi services. The elimination of the driver is hugely advantageous in these industries as labour costs account for a significant proportion of expenses. Although significant portions of these industries will be affected, the job losses may be offset by the development of different sorts of jobs, ranging from different forms of maintenance required on autonomous vehicles to increased demand in loading and unloading as trucking becomes more cost-effective. Labour savings based on elimination of certain jobs will not necessarily lead to a corresponding decrease in the labour market but may instead shift demand to other areas, such as fulfillment centres and warehouses. The labour required to design, build, and install the infrastructure to support autonomous and connected vehicles will be considerable.

How people drive is directly impacted by the human component in decisions made while driving. Many driving methods currently used are a result of the human driving experience. As human drivers are replaced, some of these methods will be reimagined. Traffic control, speed of travel, and roadway use all come to mind. The stoplight may become a thing of the past if vehicles are eventually able to communicate sufficiently with one another through vehicle-to-everything (V2X) technology. Traffic would flow in the most efficient pattern. This may eliminate the need for stopping

---

4 Conor Grant, "Human-Guided Burrito Bots Raise Questions About the Future of Robo-Delivery" *The Hustle* (3 June 2019), online: https://thehustle.co/kiwibots-autonomous-food-delivery.

as vehicles would be able to sense and avoid each other with enough time to ensure a smooth trip. Waiting for the light to turn when no traffic is coming could be eliminated. Speed on many roads is limited by the inability of a human driver to perceive, react, and respond in an appropriate way if a dynamic situation were to arise. By increasing perception and lowering reaction time, autonomous vehicles will be able to travel in safety at much higher speeds. Coupling this with a scenario in which autonomous vehicles can travel closer together due to ongoing communication between the vehicles and faster reaction times will reduce the amount of space required for a travelling vehicle. Such reductions will allow a greater number of vehicles to travel in the same space. Other reductions of physical space demands, such as a reimagining of parking space requirements, may allow current road spaces to accommodate greater traffic flow with the same infrastructure spaces currently being used.

Automated vehicles may continue to have an impact beyond transportation. With greater connection available through V2X technology, automated vehicles stand to become communication hubs. The remote-sensing opportunities to collect and aggregate data are huge. Detection of weather conditions, traffic conditions, pollution, noise levels, and other data points may allow for a more finely tuned assessment of our world. Increased data should lead to better predictive technologies, such as weather forecasting. Reaction to the detection of snow or ice on a roadway may allow a municipality to better respond to inclement weather. The possibilities are extensive.

Connected vehicles may also be able to be used as data relay points.[5] Just as cellular technology has expanded to include a greater set of relays throughout most of Canada, each vehicle could become a relay, greatly increasing access to broadband technology. Data muling, or the transportation of data, is also possible where direct links cannot be obtained, allowing a new connectiveness to previously unconnected areas. Linked computing has previously used home computers during their downtime for data analysis spread over a large number of systems, effectively achieving

5 Autonomous Vehicle Innovation Network, "Opportunities for Connected Vehicles Beyond Transportation" (2019) at 9, online (pdf): www.avinhub.ca/wp-content/uploads/2021/04/avin_quarterly-specialized-report_july-2019.pdf.

super-computing methods by harnessing thousands of smaller processors to achieve the same result as a much faster processor. Processing capacity not in use, such as parked vehicles, could be leveraged for cloud computing.[6]

Opportunities through data collection through the connectivity of autonomous vehicles to an increasing number of devices can create new modes of interacting with occupants, in both positive and negative ways. Cookies allow websites to track particular data and target advertising based on previous behaviour. Imagine the targeting that may occur where a vehicle has access to the occupant's location and travel habits and potentially conversations taking place in the vehicle. Interests in privacy and the limits on its invasion will be considerations for consumers and regulators moving forward.

Certain opportunities to engage vehicle occupants in non-driving actions arise from the use of autonomous vehicles. As vehicles disengage drivers from the task of driving, opportunities to advertise may be opened to users, especially in shared vehicles. Taxis already create further revenue streams through advertising, and targeted advertising for restaurants or other amenities in the area being travelled is possible in autonomous vehicles. The costs of ride sharing could be lowered through advertising.

Autonomous vehicles have the power to significantly impact many important areas of our society. Their expected impact should not be underestimated, but it need not be negative. By recognizing the opportunities offered, plans can be made to capitalize on the change they represent. New fields of research, new modes of business, and new areas of law will be created. Overcoming—and exceeding—the challenges presented by this technology will be a generational opportunity and those prepared to accept the challenges presented will reap the rewards.

6 *Ibid* at 12.

GLOSSARY

adaptive cruise control (ACC). *See* **traffic-aware cruise control (TACC).**

advanced driver assistance system (ADAS). A system of partial automation focused on a particular task. Examples include AEB or TACC.

Advanced Technologies Group (ATG). Formerly the self-driving division of the tech company Uber. Acquired by Aurora Innovation Inc in December 2020.

automated driving system (ADS). A term defined by SAE International to include any system that has a sustained action in the automation of driving tasks, including varying supports from Levels 1 to 5. Excludes Level 0, which has no ADS.

automated lane-keeping system (ALKS). An automated system that uses remote-sensing technology, typically image sensing, to detect lane lines and maintain a programmed distance between them or a set distance from one of them. Higher evolutions of this system are expected to use hyperprecise GPS to accommodate much the same function or to work with built-in image-sensing technology to enhance accuracy considerably.

automation. The shifting of a driving control burden from human-required interaction to a system or computer control that does not require direct human input.

autonomous emergency braking (AEB). Collision-avoidance technology that relies on a system of sensors to detect obstacles in the path of a motor vehicle and apply the brakes in a function designed to prevent collisions. This is usually performed by a distance-detecting sensor, such as radar, LiDAR, or a camera with image recognition. When a threat is detected, the system will automatically apply the brakes and slow the vehicle. Typically, this cannot be overridden by the driver. *See also* **forward collision warning (FCW).**

autonomous vehicle (AV). A conveyance with some level of automation, which can range from minimal aid, such as cruise control, to a fully driverless convenience that operates from start to finish with no human control input.

Autonomous Vehicle Innovation Network (AVIN). A Government of Ontario–sponsored collaboration initiative that seeks to bring AV talent together in the fields of research and development, training, and design of systems that can be adapted to winter environments. It seeks to put Ontario at the forefront of AV development.

Canadian Council of Motor Transportation Administrators (CCMTA). A committee of provincial and federal representatives who seek to coordinate motor vehicle and highway safety across Canada.

Canadian Motor Vehicle Safety Standards (CMVSS). The federal standards that all vehicles made for sale or import to Canada must meet. a. Made pursuant to the *Motor Vehicle Safety Act*, SC 1993, c 16.

connected automated vehicle (CAV). A vehicle that links its automated systems to other connected technologies through V2X technology to allow the AV to make decisions based not only on its own internal sensors but also data harvested from other sources.

dynamic driving task (DDT). One of the actual tasks of driving, including control over steering, speed, OEDR, planning, and proper communication through signalling.

Electronic Autonomous Shuttle project (ELA). A western Canada-based autonomous minibus pilot project operated by Pacific Western Transportation.

electronic data recorder (EDR). EDR is referred to colloquially as a "black box" in reference to the flight data recorders that aircraft carry. Sometimes referred to as an airbag control module or ACM, each manufacturer has its own name for such a unit.

- RCM: Restraint Control Module (Ford)
- PCM: Powertrain Control Module (Ford)
- SDM: Sensing and Diagnostic Module (GM)
- ORC: Occupant Restraint Controller (Chrysler)
- ACU: Airbag Control Unit (Nissan)
- ACSM: Advanced Crash Safety Module (BMW)
- CABS: Center Airbag Sensor (Toyota)

end-user licence agreement (EULA). The legal contract between the user of software and the developer or seller. It tends to set out in detail the rights and restrictions in the use of the software. This is often done through a simple click to accept. Such agreements often contain limitations on liability for the developer or seller, warnings about appropriate use, and choice of jurisdiction should an issue arise. Questions relating to informed consent in such agreements are significant. EULAs can be dozens of pages long and written in highly technical and legalistic wording.

fail-safe. A design state intended to deal with a failure or an inability of a system to deal with a problem—a safe state to which a system is to revert in the event of a failure of the system. For example, an AV may fail-safe by coming to a safe stop at the side of a road when it cannot determine another safe reaction to conditions on the roadway.

fallback. A design feature to provide an alternative function in the event of a particular event—a return to an earlier or simpler function. For example, an AV may have a fallback function calling for the occupant to take control if certain parameters are met.

Federal Motor Vehicle Safety Standards (FMVSS). American national requirements for safety compliance in vehicles.

forward collision warning (FCW). A system that relies on sensors to detect obstacles in a vehicle's path and provide a warning to the driver. Unlike AEB, which automatically reacts and applies brakes, FCW will alert the driver but not react of its own accord.

geofence. A defined boundary in which an AV can operate. Typically part of the ODD of an autonomous system design, a geofence is most commonly used to allow AVs to operate in a more controlled environment, where higher-resolution mapping is available or dynamic situations can be controlled.

global positioning system (GPS). A satellite-based location system that provides time and geolocation by providing a signal to a receiver. Based on the distance from multiple satellites (at least four), a location can be provided, typically within 30 centimetres with current technology. GPS is a purely receiver-based system, with no information being uploaded, but is often augmented with cellphone technology to provide even more accurate locations or locations where the line of sight to satellites is blocked by geographic features such as mountains or buildings. Although GPS operates globally, it is owned by the government of the United States. Similar systems have been deployed by Russia (GLONASS), the European Union (Galileo), and China (BeiDou), operating on similar principles.

highly automated vehicle. A vehicle that meets SAE International's Level 4 or 5 definition of AV.

human–machine interface (HMI). The manner in which a person interacts to control the machine or system. Traditionally, this would include the steering wheel, pedals, etc., but in the future this may change to resemble video game controls, touch screens, or other methods to lessen space requirements while enabling control when needed.

lane-keeping assist. A system that controls the lateral movement of the vehicle through the use of sensors to maintain travel by the vehicle in its current lane by staying inside the sensed lane lines.

light detection and ranging (LiDAR, also LIDAR). A system that sends out a light beam and, based on the time it takes for the beam to travel and be reflected or interfered with, calculates the distance or range to an object.

Data can be collected and used to create a map of the environment, as shown in Figure 1 (note that false colouring reflects distance or interference measurements).

FIGURE 1. WHAT LiDAR "SEES"

minimal-risk condition (MRC). The fail-safe condition that an automated system is expected to revert to should its ODD be exceeded. It may include transition to human control, either in person or remotely, or the vehicle pulling over and stopping until the ODD conditions can revert to a condition the system can handle.

Ministry of Transportation of Ontario (MTO). The provincial regulator of highway traffic matters in the province of Ontario, including matters related to driver licensing, motor vehicle safety, and rules of the road.

motor transport administrator (MTA). A member of the CCMTA, which includes provincial and federal government representatives and representatives of companies and organizations with an interest in transportation-related issues.

***Motor Vehicle Safety Act* (MVSA).** SC 1993, c 16. The federal Act that governs motor vehicle safety. *See also* **CMVSS.**

National Highway Traffic Safety Administration (NHTSA). The American organization that determines and enforces performance standards in motor vehicles. It is a federal agency that provides funds to state governments and can influence states by granting funding only if certain standards are met. The NHTSA establishes safety requirements for vehicles, examples of which include a national speed limit and a national per se alcohol limit of 80 mg of alcohol/100 mL of blood. These requirements are often adopted in law elsewhere, including in Canada. The NHTSA also performs investigations and research into vehicle safety and crashes and then issues recommendations or standards as a result.

National Transportation Safety Board (NTSB). The American investigative agency that deals with civil transportation accidents. Although well known for its investigations into aircraft crashes, the NTSB is responsible for all civilian accident investigations that warrant federal review. As a result, it also investigates train, shipping, and even motor vehicle accidents, where appropriate, and makes recommendations. Although the industry is not required to adopt such recommendations, the failure by manufacturers to adopt them may increase civil liability in the future.

object and event detection and response (OEDR). This is part of the DDT that includes the monitoring of and response to the driving environment. It is achieved by the human driver through observation and decision making and at a higher-level ADS through sensors and computer processing.

operational design domain (ODD). Any one of the parameters in which the AV is allowed to operate. These could include limits on location or geography such as a geofence, weather, speed, type of road, etc.

Radar (also RADAR)– radio detection and ranging. Radar sends out a radio beam and, based on the time it takes for the beam to travel and be reflected or interfered with, calculates the distance or range to an object.

side collision warning. A sensor-based warning system that provides an audio or visual warning should an object be in the predetermined range of the sensor. Sometimes called blind-spot warning.

Société de l'assurance automobile du Quebec (SAAQ). Also known as Société. The provincial regulator of highway traffic matters in the province of Quebec, including matters related to driver licensing, motor vehicle safety, and rules of the road.

Society of Automobile Engineers International (SAE). An American-based worldwide organization that works to develop standards for engineering, with an emphasis on transportation industries. Its classification of levels of autonomy in motor vehicles has become the standard relied upon by most governments in describing vehicles in legislation as it is developed.

traffic-aware cruise control (TACC). Sometimes termed ACC (adaptive cruise control), an automated system that uses remote-sensing technology, such as radar, LiDAR, or image sensing, to detect obstacles on the roadway and adjust speed accordingly. Like conventional cruise control, the goal is to maintain a set speed. But unlike conventional cruise control, TACC will sense an object, such as a slower-moving car in front of the vehicle, and adjust speed accordingly to avoid a collision.

vehicle-to-everything (V2X). Integrated technology that allows communication between a vehicle and other objects around it. Most commonly discussed with V2V or V2I, the term encompasses interaction with any other object. It can allow communication of information, which can then be interpreted by either automated or human-controlled systems. Examples include GPS location or other distance-measuring communication to warn of obstacles, such as a vehicle stopped on the roadway; communication with infrastructure, such as traffic lights, to allow responses by the vehicle; or communication with a parking facility, to determine the most efficient solution to finding a parking spot.

vehicle-to-infrastructure (V2I). See **vehicle-to-everything.**

vehicle-to-vehicle (V2V). See **vehicle-to-everything.**

appendix 1

ANNOTATED BIBLIOGRAPHY

A. GOVERNMENT POSITION PAPERS

US, National Science & Technology Council and Department of Transportation, "Ensuring American Leadership in Automated Vehicle Technologies: Automated Vehicles 4.0" (January 2020), online (pdf): *Department of Transportation* www.transportation.gov/sites/dot.gov/files/2020-02/EnsuringAmericanLeadershipAVTech4.pdf

This report builds on and evolves upon the principles stated in the three earlier automated vehicle reports the US Department of Transportation was involved in drafting. The initial paper provided a guidance framework, the second added technical assistance and best practices to states for testing and integration, and the third provided principles for innovation of all surface transportation modes. The newest report is structured around three areas: (1) principles of autonomous vehicles, (2) administration efforts to support growth, and (3) opportunities for collaboration.

The report highlights a number of opportunities for near-future adoption of automated technologies, including in farming, mining, and transit. It reviews opportunities with expanding connectivity through 5G networks and the importance of standardized infrastructure, including signs and signals that can be connected to vehicles.

"Preparing for the Future of Transportation: Automated Vehicles 3.0" (October 2018), online (pdf): *Department of Transportation* www.transportation.gov/sites/dot.gov/files/docs/policy-initiatives/automated-vehicles/320711/preparing-future-transportation-automated-vehicle-30.pdf

This document recognizes the fast pace at which automated vehicles are learning and being developed. It identifies the US government's role in establishing voluntary standards and targeting research to promote safe integration. It notes that federal regulations may be waived during certain testing of autonomous vehicles, such as those surrounding human safety for occupants if no occupant will be present during testing (for example, removing seatbelts to allow greater room when no person will be in the vehicle).

An interesting point raised is that with the rise of autonomous vehicles, the way in which people interact with vehicles will change in both driving and non-driving scenarios. Vehicles operating autonomously could begin moving at any time that they are called. Emergency workers will need to be trained to deal with these vehicles and may require an override of some sort to ensure that the vehicle is shut down if damaged to prevent unpredictable behaviour on the part of the vehicle.

Expanded road testing is recognized as significant in determining actual safety statistics relating to autonomous vehicles. Only in a real-world situation can their strengths and weaknesses be assessed. This is not to say that testing should not begin in closed courses and systems but instead recognizes that the eventual goal must be on-road testing.

This report also reviews the history of automation in the aviation workforce. As automation technology has advanced, pilots have not been made moot. Manual control is still required in certain situations. However, safety has been greatly enhanced through the use of automation. Lessons can be learned, including the importance of interface design to ensure that important information is communicated effectively to the driver. Fully autonomous vehicles strive to take this process further and eliminate the need for a driver, but a mixed human–machine interface such as that in aviation may be the next step.

US, Department of Transportation and National Highway Traffic Safety Administration, "Automated Driving Systems 2.0: A Vision for Safety" (September 2017), online (pdf): *National Highway Traffic Safety Administration* www.nhtsa.gov/sites/nhtsa.dot.gov/files/documents/13069a-ads2.0_090617_v9a_tag.pdf

This document was created in an attempt to provide strong guidance by prioritizing twelve safety design elements in autonomous vehicles. It reviews elements that provide goals and approaches to reach those goals.

1) *System Safety.* Robust design and validation of systems are needed. Risk assessment and remediation should be considered throughout the entire system. Designs should be related to these risks and address them. Testing, validation, and verification of subsystems and the system as a whole should be undertaken, along with documentation of such steps.
2) *Operational Design Domain (ODD).* Consideration needs to be given to when and where each automated function can and should be used. This information should be designed into the program and provided to operators/users. Minimum specifications suggested include the roadway type, geographic area, speed, and environmental conditions. The system must be able to operate safely in the defined ODD. Where a dynamic situation takes the vehicle outside the ODD, it should fail-safe. Such methods could include bringing the vehicle to a safe stop or transitioning control to the human driver.
3) *Object and Event Detection and Response (OEDR).* The system must be able to detect and react to circumstances around it that are relevant to the task of driving. Designing a system to perform a task in a singular way is very different from creating a system capable of reacting to the changing and sometimes dynamic situations that occur while driving. Again, assessment, testing, and validation are encouraged, along with documentation of the same. Normal driving may require reaction to things as varied as other vehicles, pedestrians, bicyclists, animals, and other objects on the road. As well, less common but still expected scenarios, such as construction, police directing traffic, or first-responder vehicles, must be programmed for. Crash-avoidance capabilities to predict and, where necessary, respond to situations such as loss of control, road departure, and low-speed situations have to be dealt with. Although these are the least common situations, they have the greatest risk of harm to the occupants.
4) *Fallback, or Fail-Safe, and Minimal-Risk Condition (MRC).* A documented process for transitioning to a safe state is needed. In lower forms of automation, this may take into account inattentive humans who are supposed to retake control in such situations. The ability to transition safely from system to human control in a safe manner is important.
5) *Validation Methods.* Validation of systems may take different forms, including deployment on public roads, test tracks, or simulation. Testing in the public sphere is encouraged only after safety has otherwise been shown.
6) *Human–Machine Interface.* In all situations, the vehicle should be able to provide information to the occupant about the system's intentions and the vehicle's performance. This is especially important in automation, where human input or control may be needed in dynamic situations, such as in a Level 3 vehicle.
7) *Vehicle Cybersecurity.* Continued work to minimize cybersecurity threats is necessary. Security designs will need to take this into account. Reporting of

any discovered incidents, exploits, or threats is encouraged. The importance of industry sharing of such information is noted.

8) *Crashworthiness.* Occupant safety in a crash is still an important safety design feature, and designers must not lose sight of this even as internal vehicle spaces may be redesigned in response to the fact that a person may not need to be looking ahead if they are no longer driving. Compatibility with conventional vehicles and use of data that sensors in the vehicle have access to in order to minimize harm to occupants will be useful.
9) *Post-Crash Automated Driving System (ADS) Behaviour.* Design consideration for how a vehicle will respond if it is involved in a crash is reviewed. Depending on the severity of the crash, the vehicle may need to take safety steps, from shutting off the fuel pump to moving the vehicle from the roadway. Data sharing is encouraged to help improve industry-wide design.
10) *Data Recording.* A documented process for testing, validating, and collecting data is encouraged. The only way to learn from a crash, or any event, is to be able to review the data and determine how and why things unfolded as they did. Promotion of continual learning is encouraged. The ability to recover data and to share it is identified. This will require both technical and legal considerations.
11) *Consumer Education and Training.* Documented training programs for numerous groups, including employees, dealers, and consumers, are identified. Topics such as the functional intent of ADS, its operational parameters, and its capabilities and limitations will be important. Thought should be given to on-road or on-track training. These programs should be evaluated regularly.
12) *Federal, State, and Local Laws.* How designers plan on dealing with each level of regulation should be documented. In situations where a vehicle may have to temporarily violate a law (such as crossing a double line on a roadway to give room to a pulled-over vehicle if safe to do so), then the validation and testing of such plausible scenarios should be recorded. The ability to adapt to changes in law and update vehicles to change with the law is needed.

This document does not mandate anything but merely provides best-practice guidance to industries looking to work in this area. It may nonetheless be relevant in assessing civil responsibility and establishing the standard of care expected in relation to autonomous vehicles. It goes on to review the division of powers in the United States between federal and state authorities in law making and suggests best practices for legislatures. These include promoting a "technology-neutral" environment where non-motor vehicle manufacturers could develop ADSs, providing licensing and registration procedures and reporting and communication methods, and reviewing traffic laws and regulations that may serve as barriers to autonomous vehicles.

US, Department of Transportation and National Highway Traffic Safety Administration, "Federal Automated Vehicles Policy: Accelerating the Next Revolution in Roadway Safety" (September 2016), online: *Homeland Security Digital Library* www.hsdl.org/?view&did=795644

This is the 1.0 document upon which the above documents were built. It states from the outset that it is meant to be a living policy that evolves over time. It reviews design suggestions with specific review of privacy and security of information. Suggestions are made to provide transparency, choice, respect for context, de-identification, limited retention, data security, defined access, and accountability as principles to be upheld when considering privacy.

Crashworthiness, security from takeover, and post-crash behaviour are all reviewed as important considerations. The review of post-crash behaviour indicates that there will be times when sensing equipment may become damaged, and reversion to an MRC should be the default. This highlights the concern that a damaged sensor may eliminate a vehicle's ability to operate. Redundancy must therefore be built into sensing, or a human interface must continue to exist to allow the vehicle to be taken for servicing. Otherwise, mechanics may have to perform more fixes at the roadside or at an owner's home if the vehicle will not operate with the damaged sensing equipment.

The dichotomy of legal versus ethical decision making is briefly touched upon. This report recognized that the most strictly legal decision may not be the most ethical decision in certain circumstances. Maintaining a lane versus hitting a pedestrian who jumps in front of the vehicle would be decided one way legally and another ethically. Autonomous vehicles will need to be able to prioritize things in similar ways to a human to allow the right decision to be made.

A list of "normal" driving conditions is provided. It includes detecting and responding to speed limit changes and advisories; merging; parking; detecting and responding to oncoming vehicles; passing other vehicles in safe and legal ways; detecting and responding to other vehicles, both moving and stopped; navigating intersections, traffic signals, roundabouts, work zones, parking, and detours; following right-of-way decisions; pulling over (police or first-responder overrides); dealing with construction hazards; responding to police or others directing traffic after a third-party accident; and dealing with pedestrians and bicyclists, including in all of the above situations. These conditions were taken from research performed in California.[1]

---

1 Christopher Nowakowski et al, "Development of California Regulations to Govern the Testing and Operation of Automated Driving Systems" (14 November 2014), online: *American Association of Motor Vehicle Administrators* www.aamva.org/WorkArea/DownloadAsset.aspx?id=6296.

Fallback or MRC is discussed. This is a fail-safe protocol in which the vehicle takes itself out of service if an issue is identified that the vehicle cannot safely handle. Recognition that the human driver may be available is important but not sufficient on its own. Concerns that "human drivers may be inattentive, under the influence of alcohol or other substances, drowsy, or physically impaired in some other manner" (at 30) mandates that the vehicles cannot merely rely on transitioning to human control but that other fail-safe modes must also be built in.

A model state policy is included. As the authors are both federally mandated organizations and control over regulating drivers is a state function, the authors recognize the conflict but hope that standardized rules can apply. This is a similar issue that will occur in Canada, where most safety compliance is required at a national level, but driver regulation and traffic control are accomplished at a provincial level. Will the autonomous systems be considered more akin to equipment installed in a vehicle, such as airbags, seatbelts, and other safety items that are approved through national safety organizations? Alternatively, will regulation of the autonomous functions be more akin to regulating a driver who requires licensing and testing at a provincial level? This constitutional question will need to be considered, and power may be shared as development continues and as both levels of government may be involved to differing degrees. Incidental overlap will inevitably occur.

The report concludes with a review of existing legislative tools. Of specific interest is Appendix II, which reviews regulatory tools used by the Federal Aviation Administration. It again brings home the fact that autonomous systems are largely in use in air travel, and interpretation and guidance can be obtained by reviewing those tools and procedures.

Myra Blanco et al, "FMVSS Considerations for Vehicles with Automated Driving Systems: Volume 1," Report No DOT HS 812 796 (April 2020), online (pdf): *National Highway Traffic Safety Administration* www.nhtsa.gov/sites/nhtsa.dot.gov/files/documents/ads-dv_fmvss_vol1-042320-v8-tag.pdf

This report reviews twelve Federal Motor Vehicle Safety Standards (FMVSS) that have been identified as needing consideration in the field of autonomous vehicles. It recognizes that certain standards may be unnecessary or may lead to unintended consequences when applied to autonomous vehicles, especially during testing phases where there may be no human occupants. These are also important if vehicles such as freight transport are developed with the specific intention of eliminating any human occupant. The report notes that something as simple as "front" and "rear" may be tripping points in definitions as future vehicles may be bidirectional or multidirectional in the same way that a train might. This can affect design, including crashworthiness.

Terminology will need to be adapted as autonomous vehicles enter the marketplace. As well, the authors offer a number of different opportunities, such as redesigning the interior space of the vehicle cabin. Instead of all seats pointing forward, because there is no need for a driver to look out the front window, a layout more akin to that of passengers on a train may be adopted. This will have a knock-on effect to safety design. Another possibility is that in post-accident or post-sensor failure, a manual control may be required to allow for the use of the vehicle to seek maintenance. Designing for this and the ability to turn off parts of the autonomous systems while maintaining others may be needed. Interfaces in manual control may change from what is standard now, and space-dependent controls such as a steering wheel may be replaced by smaller controls, such as a joystick or smaller deployable steering wheel. All of this affects safety and the FMVSS. A remote-controlled system from an external source to take over should a sensor issue arise is considered as well.

Although many people consider an automated vehicle as being very similar to conventional vehicles in the way we will interact within them, they may eventually reach a point where they see riding in an autonomous vehicle as more like riding in a private subway or train. Things such as windshield wipers or window defrosters may become less relevant in fully autonomous vehicles. If the driver is never intended to take control, say in a Level 6 automated vehicle without an adult occupant, then the layout of the interior can be reimagined. In uses such as trucking, where elimination of the human occupant is intended to save labour costs, the elimination of the space may allow for redesigning of the distribution of the engine and other equipment. Much the way a "cab over" (flat-faced transport truck) design allowed for longer trailers by moving the traditional locations of the driver and the engine in a freight vehicle, eliminating the cabin may allow for larger spaces for freight. The utility of such a design can increase the volumes carried and the efficiency of trucking while maintaining similar vehicle sizes.

B. CRASH ANALYSES

"Collision Between a Car Operating with Automated Vehicle Control Systems and a Tractor-Semitrailer Truck Near Williston, Florida, May 7, 2016," NTSB/HAR-17/02, PB2017-102600 (reissued 12 October 2017), online (pdf): *National Transportation Safety Board* www.ntsb.gov/investigations/AccidentReports/Reports/HAR1702.pdf

On 7 May 2016, a Tesla Model S car operating in semi-autonomous mode collided with a tractor-semitrailer truck near Williston, Florida. The National Transportation Safety Board (NTSB) released its report, which made a number of observations and recommendations as a result of the accident. The facts surrounding the accident are that the Tesla was operating with its traffic-aware cruise control (automated braking) and lane-keeping systems both engaged. This equates to a Level 2 automation based on SAE terminology as the automated systems exercised both lateral and longitudinal control.

The report provides a comprehensive review of how such systems operate (at 8–16). A series of sensors in the vehicle detects objects in front of the vehicle and automatically applies the brakes if an object is detected. The lane-keeping system operates by detecting lane markings, such as the lines on the road, to ensure that the vehicle does not sway across them. Both automations are designed to enhance safety. The driver is expected to remain attentive, but this did not occur in the particular case. The vehicle attempts to ensure vigilance by requiring the driver to keep their hands on the wheel, as detected through a torque system. If the driver does not keep their hands on the wheel, then a warning is issued, first visually by the instrument panel indicating "Hold Steering Wheel," then audibly with progressively louder chimes. If the driver does not interact with the steering wheel, then the automated systems will slow down and stop the vehicle.

The manuals for the Tesla vehicle warn not to use these systems where traffic conditions may change, such as on city streets, where bicycles or pedestrians may be present, or anywhere else where traffic conditions are unpredictable (at 13). As was noted, however, most people do not read their vehicle manual. The report notes that automatic braking systems, through model year 2016 specifically, do not perform reliably in all crash modes, including crossing-path collisions, which accords with the warning in the manual.

In this situation, the tractor-trailer turned across the road in front of the Tesla vehicle. Unfortunately, the automated braking system did not have sufficient time to detect and react to the threat of a vehicle turning across the roadway. The tractor-trailer posed an observable issue for approximately seven seconds, but the driver failed to react. Seven seconds is a significant amount of time to observe and react to an issue, and the failure of the driver to do so confirms a lack of attention.

Regarding driver attentiveness, the NTSB found that "[s]imply checking whether the driver has placed a hand on the steering wheel gives little indication of where the driver is focusing his or her attention" (at 34). The report indicates that this is largely because people fail to realize the limitations of automation and do not pay attention to tasks requiring passive vigilance. People stop paying attention with automation. Rather than use the freed-up attention span to focus on safer driving, they devote attention to non-driving tasks and actually become worse drivers. Companies are now developing new means of determining if a driver is still paying attention. Toyota and Volvo are two companies that are pursuing technology that tracks the driver's head and eye positions to make sure that a driver is looking where they are driving if the automation systems are to be engaged. The NTSB determined that the probable cause of the accident was the "prolonged disengagement from the driving task and [the driver's] use of the automation in ways inconsistent with guidance and warnings from the manufacturer" (at vi). The report recommends that manufacturers develop more effective ways of monitoring driver engagement.

The report asserts: "Although system designers understand the limits of partial automation, the driving public may not" (at 27). The impact of this in law and the assessment of negligence are important. The standard of care of a person being weighed against an objective standard will consider the expectations of an average person to some degree. When entering an unfamiliar vehicle, a driver would be expected to familiarize themselves with the fittings of the vehicle. In most cars, this may only require adjusting the mirrors and determining where some of the controls are. In an automated vehicle, especially when only partially automated, the learning curve for the driver will be steeper than usual. A driver might never review the owner's manual for a new vehicle, yet that may be the manner in which the manufacturer intends to communicate the limits of an automated system. Where designers know that their intent is not being communicated effectively to the end-user, there may be liability for both the designer who fails to effectively communicate and the user who fails to take steps to inform themselves of the risk they are posing. Tesla has specifically stated that Autopilot use should be restricted to preferred road environments. However, the design did not restrict it to these. As a result, the system could be used on roads for which it was not intended. This sort of a design flaw may give rise to liability to the manufacturer that provides a system that it knows will be used outside the design specifications. Even the name of the system, "Autopilot," connotes a level of automation not intended in the design. The NTSB recommends the implementation of methods to verify use of automation systems that are limited to parameters for which they are designed (at 34).

The NTSB report provides some other interesting information. In 2010, 92 percent of light vehicles had an electronic data recorder (EDR) (at 36). However, that number has been falling. There is no requirement for EDRs to be in a vehicle, and many companies are foregoing them in favour of their own proprietary data technology. Owing to the requirements that EDRs collect certain information and that the software to download it must be commercially available, companies are opting to collect different data and not provide the ability for others to download it.

Of interest with the Tesla is that it did not contain an EDR but did collect significant data, including images at different times, although none at the crash. This means that the car was taking and recording photographs without the driver necessarily knowing. Performance data in the Tesla Model S included steering angle, accelerator pedal position, driver-applied brake pedal application, vehicle speed, automated system states, and lead vehicle distance, among others. All parameter data is given a time-stamp using a Global Positioning System (GPS)-derived clock time. The data is stored in the vehicle on an SD card and is also intermittently uploaded to Tesla. The NTSB was able to download system performance data, including data surrounding the Traffic-Aware Cruise Control and Autosteer lane-keeping systems. The forward collision warning and automatic emergency braking (AEB) systems were of particular note in this case because the vehicle collided with an object directly in front of it, which is exactly the situation that AEB is designed to prevent.

The NTSB has made a number of recommendations. One of the most impactful is the suggestion that the development of vehicle-to-vehicle (V2V) technology be emphasized. V2V technology allows vehicles to communicate with each other to recognize the locations of other vehicles to avoid crashes. Crashes at intersections are the most frequent and fatal, and this sort of technology could go a long way to avoiding them. Although this technology may seem far-fetched, other innovations, such as airbags, backup cameras, and even seatbelts, seemed unlikely to gain wide adoption at different points in history. Certainly, security issues inherent in vehicles communicating with each other and the ability to hack such a system will be key in ensuring the safe development and adoption of this technology. The NTSB specifically recommends that the National Highway Traffic Safety Administration "[d]evelop minimum performance standards for connected vehicle technology . . . require this technology to be installed on all newly manufactured highway vehicles" (at 44).

The NTSB report also recommends the implementation of "enhanced EDRs" that would collect a greater amount of data, which could be used for accident reconstruction and analysis. The further data in enhanced EDRs would continue to expand the privacy interest of owners and operators by going further toward a person's core biographical data.

"Rear-End Collision Between a Car Operating with Advanced Driver Assistance Systems and a Stationary Fire Truck, Culver City, California, January 22, 2018," NTSB/HAB-19/07 (22 August 2019), online (pdf): *National Transportation Safety Board* www.ntsb.gov/investigations/AccidentReports/Reports/HAB1907.pdf

An individual operating a Tesla Model S vehicle was travelling in the high-occupancy vehicle lane. The Tesla Autopilot system was engaged. The vehicle in front of him, which the system was pacing, changed lanes to go around a parked fire truck. The Autopilot system sensed more space in front of it and began to accelerate. It rear-ended the fire truck at a speed of 31 miles per hour (50km/h).

The driver in this case acknowledged that although he had received an owner's manual upon purchasing the car, he had never read it. The manual specifically warned that the driver must "stay alert, drive safely, and be in control of the vehicle at all times" (at 7). What occurred in this case is called a "cut-out scenario" (at 10). The adaptive cruise control (ACC) system accelerated when it could no longer detect a lead vehicle. When the system detected the stationary fire truck as an obstruction (approximately 2.5 to 3.5 seconds after the lead vehicle cut out), it displayed visual and auditory warnings to the driver, but it was too late. The report indicates that "the limited time a stationary vehicle is in the car's field of view challenges the system's ability to assess a threat and apply AEB" (at 11). The report notes that the driver was not attending to the driving task. This is similar to the driver in the Williston crash. The recommendation from that report—that manufacturers develop more effective methods to sense driver engagement—had received acceptable responses from VW, BMW, Nissan, Mercedes-Benz, and Volvo, but no response had yet come forward from Tesla. This could have a significant impact on the apportionment of civil liability.

"Collision Between Car Operating with Partial Driving Automation and Truck-Tractor Semitrailer, Delray Beach, Florida, March 1, 2019," NTSB/HAB-20/01 (22 January 2020), online (pdf): *National Transportation Safety Board* www.ntsb.gov/investigations/AccidentReports/Reports/HAB2001.pdf

Similar to the Willison crash above, the facts in this case involve a tractor-trailer across the roadway. The Tesla Model 3 did not detect this and drove under the trailer while its Autopilot was engaged. Tesla's Autopilot was not designed for such roadways, but the company has not implemented or noted a limitation on such use. Tesla was quoted in the report as saying that ODD "limits are not applicable . . . because the driver determines the acceptable operating environment" (at 13).

The tractor-trailer should not have been across the road, the driver of the Tesla was not paying the required level of attention, and Tesla's refusal to limit ODD were all found to have contributed to the collision.

"Collision Between Vehicle Controlled by Developmental Automated Driving System and Pedestrian, Tempe, Arizona, March 18, 2018," NTSB/HAR-19/03, PB2019-101402 (reissued 26 June 2020), online (pdf): *National Transportation Safety Board* www.ntsb.gov/investigations/AccidentReports/Reports/HAR1903.pdf

This crash involved an Advanced Technologies Group (ATG, Uber) automated vehicle striking and killing a pedestrian. After taking methamphetamines, the pedestrian crossed at night at a location without a crosswalk. However, the autonomous vehicle did not manage the risk appropriately. The pedestrian was walking beside his bicycle. The system struggled to identify the pedestrian and at different times classified him as a bicyclist or an unknown object, each of which is dealt with differently. Another factor was ATG's failure to retroactively monitor its operators. A human operator was in the vehicle in order to take control if an issue arose, but the person was watching a movie on her cellphone. ATG had monitoring in the vehicle but rarely used it.

The vehicle's ADS was fully in control of all driving tasks. It used a light detection and ranging (LiDAR) system as well as a radar system; a camera system; and telemetry, positioning, monitoring, and telecommunication systems. This included GPS, twelve ultrasonic sensors, and an inertial measurement system.

The system operates by identifying, then predicting, the expected behaviour of an object. Objects classified as "other" were deemed static. Pedestrians were not assigned a behaviour unless they were identified as a pedestrian and had a trajectory that might indicate a midblock crossing. The system classified the pedestrian as a vehicle, other, and a bicyclist at different times. This failure to classify led to a failure to predict the behaviour.

Volvo had built-in sensors and automation (that was disabled) in favour of the ATG system. Testing showed that the Volvo system would have avoided the crash seventeen out of twenty times. In the remaining three times, the collision would have been at a speed of less than 10 miles per hour and less serious. Further modifications to the ATG system now allow it to work in conjunction with Volvo's built-in system.

This report also reviews the automated vehicle regulatory systems in California and Pennsylvania, finding that their safety requirements to be more comprehensive than those in Arizona. It encourages Arizona and other jurisdictions to look to these states as examples.

"Collision Between a Sport Utility Vehicle Operating with Partial Driving Automation and a Crash Attenuator, Mountain View, California, March 23, 2018," NTSB/HAR-20/01, PB2020-100112 (reissued 20 March 2020), online (pdf): *National Transportation Safety Board* www.ntsb.gov/investigations/AccidentReports/Reports/HAR2001.pdf

The crash in this case involved a Tesla SUV driving into the crash attenuator (sometimes called a bull nose) at the end of the guardrails that separated the highway and the exit ramp. The vehicle was operating with its Autopilot function engaged. The driver was not paying due attention. The traffic markings were in the shape of a V, but the right side of the V was faded. The Autopilot followed the left side of the V directly into the crash attenuator, which it did not detect. The driver allowed himself to become distracted due to overreliance on the automation.

Tesla Autopilot limits the maximum speed at which the ACC can be set to 5 miles per hour above the speed limit to a maximum of 90 miles per hour. If no speed limit is detected, then a maximum speed of 45 miles per hour is imposed.

This report briefly touches on the importance of software updates. The vehicle in the crash had not updated its software due to connectivity issues. Although this was not a factor in this crash, it nonetheless demonstrates that the only way the vehicle can benefit from experiences and fixes is by ensuring that software upgrades take place.

Brandon Schoettle & Michael Sivak, "A Preliminary Analysis of Real-World Crashes Involving Self-Driving Vehicles," UMTRI-2015-34 (October 2015), online (pdf): *University of Michigan Transportation Research Institute* www.umich.edu/~umtriswt/PDF/UMTRI-2015-34.pdf

Comparing the abilities of autonomous vehicles to those of conventional vehicles is an important step in determining how far the technology has progressed. It helps identify the strengths and weaknesses of automation and will likely impact adoption of the technology more broadly. This study conducted this comparison. The authors note that "self-driving vehicles have a higher crash rate per million miles traveled than conventional vehicles" (at i) but that "self-driving vehicles were not at fault in any crashes they were involved in [and that] the overall severity of crash-related injuries involving self-driving vehicles has been lower than for conventional vehicles" (at i).

By analyzing the data provided by Audi, Delphi, and Google relating to their self-driving cars, the authors conducted a comparison with conventional vehicles. There are a number of interesting points to take from this comparison. One is the identification of the situation where an autonomous vehicle identifies an event it cannot handle. At that point, the vehicle transitions to conventional mode, and the driver is expected to take over. Two crashes were identified where the incident was reported as occurring during conventional driving, but the critical event that the system could not handle occurred during autonomous driving mode. The crash occurred after the system decided it could not handle the event and was transitioning control to the user. This sort of situation will tax both criminal and civil lawyers in the future. How a driver is trained to perceive and react to these situations will be integral to determining liability. The design of each vehicle and the instructions provided to the user will be key.

Autonomous vehicles were determined to have a crash rate of 9.1 crashes per million miles in comparison with conventional vehicles at 1.9 per million miles. Although the difference is significant, the autonomous vehicles were not at fault in any of the accidents. This is attributed to autonomous vehicles not responding in the manner that other drivers may expect.[2] Human drivers engage in non-logical

---

2 See, for example, "Low-Speed Collision Between Truck-Tractor and Autonomous Shuttle, Las Vegas, Nevada, November 8, 2017," NTSB/HAB-19/06 (2017), online (pdf): *National Transportation Safety Board* www.ntsb.gov/investigations/AccidentReports/Reports/

driving at times, such as in attempts to merge. An aggressive lane merge by a human driver may lead to another human swerving into another lane, and the autonomous vehicle may not expect the human to illegally merge.

The study acknowledges that the relatively small number of miles driven by autonomous vehicles at the time of the study may lessen the conclusions that can be drawn. As well, autonomous vehicles are required to report every accident, whereas human drivers may not report a minor accident involving only property damage. The authors note that "60% of property-damage-only crashes and 24% of injury crashes go unreported each year" (at 14). Adjusted rates as a result of this estimate overlap, leaving uncertainty as to whether autonomous vehicles are involved in more accidents. At the time of the study, autonomous vehicles did not operate in adverse conditions such as snow or ice, so the accident rate may change as autonomous vehicles venture further afield to places where these inclement conditions are more common. Accident and injury rates are expected to rise as autonomous vehicles begin to undertake more demanding driving tasks.

The vast majority (73 percent) of accidents involving autonomous vehicles occurred while the vehicle was stopped or proceeding at 5 miles per hour or less. Most involved the autonomous vehicle being rear-ended, whereas the remaining involved the autonomous vehicle being sideswiped or hit at an angle. Head-on collisions did not occur. These types of collisions are often the deadliest. As well, no autonomous vehicles collided with any non-vehicular objects, such as pedestrians or buildings. They all involved another vehicle hitting it. The severity of injuries occasioned by accidents involving autonomous vehicles was lower than for those involving conventional vehicles, and no fatalities occurred.

C. IDENTIFIED RISKS

Stephen Checkoway et al, "Comprehensive Experimental Analyses of Automotive Attack Surfaces" in *SEC '11: Proceedings of the 20th USENIX Conference on Security* (2011), online (pdf): *Center for Automotive Embedded Systems Security* www.autosec.org/pubs/cars-usenixsec2011.pdf

This study reviews the different ways in which a motor vehicle may be attacked via electronic intervention. It highlights a number of ways in which current motor vehicles are already vulnerable to attack. It begins by acknowledging that "while previous research has shown that the *internal* networks within some modern cars are insecure, the associated threat model—requiring *prior physical access*—has

HAB1906.pdf, where a tractor-trailer driver backed into an autonomous shuttle because he thought a human driver would have stopped earlier or backed up to allow him to reverse into an alley.

justifiably been viewed as unrealistic" (at 1; emphasis in original). This highlights the fact that if a person already had physical access to the vehicle, there are a number of ways in which the vehicle could be tampered with, and an electronic vulnerability was no more a concern than a physical vulnerability: "[A]ttackers with physical access can easily mount non-computerized attacks as well (e.g., cutting the brake lines)" (at 1). However, the study goes on to analyze external attack vulnerabilities. Exploitation was found to be feasible through a number of different methods, including via mechanics' tools, CD players, Bluetooth, and cellular radio.

Many of the vulnerabilities noted have similarities. This, the authors feel, is due to "systemic structural issues in the automotive ecosystem" (at 2). To put it another way, since external threats have not been fully understood, the same sorts of vulnerabilities exist across a number of different systems. Although this is concerning due to the different methods over which intrusion could take place, it means that similar fixes may be applicable across multiple systems. The authors noted that "very few operations are not mediated by computer control in a modern vehicle (with the parking brake and steering being the last holdouts, though semi-automatic parallel parking capabilities are available in some vehicles and full steer-by-wire has been demonstrated in several concept cars)" (at 2). Physical vulnerabilities that could be exploited include disc, USB, and iPod ports and the OBD-II, the scanning port that mechanics plug into to "read" the error message related to a "check engine" light. These all require physical access to the vehicle but could be corrupted at one point but not exploited until a later time.

Short-range wireless data entry points include Bluetooth, remote key fobs, Wi-Fi, and even tire pressure monitoring systems. Long-range data entry points can include things such as onboard telematics systems (think GM's OnStar, BMW Assist, or Toyota's Safety Connect), GPS, or satellite radio.

The authors were able to "obtain complete control over the vehicle's systems" (at 6) via a number of these pathways, including cell calls to the car, Bluetooth, and using audio media, such as a CD inserted into the stereo. Using Bluetooth, for example, the authors were able to quickly take control via a paired device. But although they were still able to conduct a takeover without such access, it proved much more time-consuming. This highlights the importance of the user recognizing possible exploits and avoiding them. By not pairing an unknown Bluetooth accessory to a car, the user can create a situation where the sheer amount of work to allow a takeover may deter a potential hack.

Although the authors admit that there have been no known electronic attacks "in the wild" using such exploits, they realize that the potential for harm exists and is significant. Theft of vehicles would be simplified through the disabling of security in the vehicle. Surveillance via the vehicle's onboard systems allows for recording via the in-cabin microphone as well as GPS and other data. Attacks ranging from targeted takeover of single vehicles to harm a particular individual to widespread takeover in a terrorist act are possible. The authors note the danger of a simple program to disable the braking systems in a car as an example.

The report likens current automobile technology to the status of personal computers in the 1990s. Although vulnerabilities existed, it was not until widespread networking via the internet occurred that computer vulnerabilities were exploited. Motor vehicles are now approaching that level of networking, and the risk of vulnerabilities being exploited is growing.

The authors assert that vulnerabilities may be addressed through a number of methods. Hiving off certain functions into stand-alone computing modules that are not connected to vulnerable input vectors, such as cellular services and Bluetooth, would provide a physical barrier to a takeover. As well, software developments to close vulnerabilities would be another possibility.

What this study raises more than anything is the fact that current automobiles are already vulnerable to attack. Further automation may increase networking capabilities and give greater visibility to such weaknesses that already exist and are not currently being exploited. This does not mean that it should not be of concern, but it does recognize that automation may not signal as significant an increase in the threat of hacking that some believe.

Bryan Reimer et al, "Behavioral Impact of Drivers' Roles in Automated Driving" in *AutomotiveUI '16: Proceedings of the 8th International Conference on Automotive User Interfaces and Interactive Vehicular Applications* (New York: Association for Computing Machinery) at 217, online: *ACM Digital Library* https://dl.acm.org/doi/pdf/10.1145/3003715.3005411

This study reviews the effects of minor changes in automation on drivers' attention to the driving task. It compares conventional, semi-automated, and fully autonomous driving modes. It found that the greater the level of automation, the less attention was paid to the task of driving. At even greater levels of automation, drivers were more likely to take their hands off the wheel and engage in another activity. As well, the amount of time that a driver's gaze was not on the road increased with automation. The more automation, the shorter time passed until a person picked up a "distractor"—or the greater the belief in the automation, the more likely and more quickly a person will stop paying attention to driving.

Dorothy J Glancy, "Privacy in Autonomous Vehicles" (2012) 52:4 *Santa Clara Law Review* 1171, online: https://digitalcommons.law.scu.edu/lawreview/vol52/iss4/3

This article considers the difference between self-contained and networked autonomous vehicles. The privacy perspective shifts where a person believes their information is only being gathered and interpreted by their own vehicle compared to a situation where vehicle-to-everything (V2X) technology is being used. In what manner V2X technology may allow data to be shared, to what degree, and for what retention period all have an impact on a person's privacy interest. Anonymizing such data, along with strict use and retention periods, will be key considerations for designers. These options may not be considered in a significant way by end-users. Consider the number of people who already consent to data being collected in mapping apps on phones. The author refers to "surveillance by design" and mentions that the Ontario Privacy Commissioner's Office broadened its focus to include this in 2012.[3] Understanding how data is collected and disseminated will be a new area of consumer education in the future. A review of the end-user licensing agreement (EULA) and the uses to which data can be put may need to be highlighted to consumers in order to make such contracts valid.

When considering networked transportation grids, freedom of travel may be affected in different ways for the elderly, children, or disabled persons. Although these groups may enjoy greater mobility as a result of autonomous vehicles, the author questions whether they may be impacted by an interconnected network that optimizes travel based on time. Such a network may prioritize certain travel related to peak business or work hours and in doing so require travel by other individuals at off-peak times. This can be dealt with through different methods of prioritization of travel but must be considered. A higher cost to travel at certain times could be imposed to encourage travel in off-peak periods, although this would affect individuals of different socio-economic backgrounds differently. Roads are generally available equally for all people, although tolls do have a similar effect currently.

The author discusses how, in the United States, "third-party doctrine" can allow the state to easily access an individual's personal information that is in the hands of another without the need for a warrant or other judicial authorization. Although this issue is dealt with very differently in Canada, for data that may be stored outside Canada, this issue becomes more significant. Consider a motor vehicle that communicates with or stores data with the US-based headquarters of the vehicle's manufacturer. A person may lose their privacy without even knowing.

The article reviews the use of data by non-state actors. It is in the best interest of many companies seeking to market products to have access to personal data. Targeted advertisements already exist in many places, including social media. Consider the degree of targeting that may arise when an even greater amount of data

3 Referring to Ann Cavoukian, Information and Privacy Commissioner of Ontario, Introductory Address at Symposium: "Beware of 'Surveillance by Design': Standing Up for Freedom and Privacy" (27 January 2012) [unpublished].

may be harvested and the value this offers to companies that can market products based on direct behavioural observation. There is also a corresponding risk to the holder of such private information.[4]

D. IMPACTS OF AUTONOMOUS VEHICLES

Alexandra Cutean, "Autonomous Vehicles and the Future of Work in Canada" (2017), online (pdf): *Information and Communications Technology Council* www.ictc-ctic.ca/wp-content/uploads/2018/01/ICTC_-Autonomous-Vehicles-and-The-Future-of-Work-in-Canada-1-1.pdf

This study reviews a number of important considerations, including a history of automation and the identification of specific opportunities and hurdles in Canada. One of the greatest hurdles is that many designs for fully autonomous vehicles rely on the most modern cellular functions, specifically 5G technology. Another limitation is the expectation of highly detailed maps. Both issues are specifically difficult in rural Canada. A lack of large-scale 5G availability is noted as a possible limiter for autonomous vehicles. The sheer geography of Canada limits the availability of such technology and makes mapping more difficult and resource intensive as well. The impact on the job market, specifically trucking, taxi, and chauffeur jobs, is noted. This includes a high level of impact for individuals with less education. The article reviews other jobs that would see a rise in demand, along with the educational requirements.

Brandon Schoettle & Michael Sivak, "Potential Impact of Self-Driving Vehicles on Household Vehicle Demand and Usage," UMTRI-2015-3 (February 2015), online (pdf): *University of Michigan Transportation Research Institute* https://deepblue.lib.umich.edu/bitstream/handle/2027.42/110789/103157.pdf

This report addresses the impact that autonomous vehicles may have on automobile ownership and use in the United States. It suggests that the technology, "in the most extreme hypothetical scenario, could reduce average ownership rates by 43% [and] would result in a 75% increase in individual vehicle usage" (at 12). This demonstrates that although fewer vehicles would be required to meet demand, each vehicle would be used to a greater degree as a result.

It is anticipated that autonomous vehicles will shift driving patterns along with behaviours. Many households have multiple drivers who require a vehicle but whose demands for the vehicle do not necessarily overlap. Consider the parent going to work at one time, the child who needs to be picked up at another time, and another

---

4 Consider the tort of breach of privacy as in *Hopkins v Kay*, 2015 ONCA 112, where the tort was open for consideration in a case where hospital employees having improper access to health records was being considered.

parent running errands during the day. This could all be achieved by one vehicle that self-piloted to the next user in the household who needed the vehicle. Although this does not help where there are overlapping demands, it may reduce a significant number of vehicles required to meet a household's demands. With the changing landscape presented by the COVID-19 pandemic and the shift to greater telecommuting and work from home, this sort of demand shift may increase.

As well, autonomous vehicles may give rise to a greater number of current "non-drivers" becoming users. A vehicle that does not require a driver enables children to get to activities or elderly drivers to access transportation where health considerations might otherwise prevent such independence.

The use of fewer autonomous vehicles to replace a greater number of non-automated vehicles would also lead to an increase in the number of kilometres a particular vehicle has to drive. Currently, vehicles sit parked, awaiting their driver. However, in the hypothetical scenario advanced by the authors, the automated vehicle would have to drive empty after dropping one person off in order to pick up the next person from the household for their trip. The increased wear and tear on the vehicle and the environmental impact of unoccupied vehicles travelling the roadways are identified as important but unaddressed issues in the report. The authors do note that this would likely lead to a shorter lifespan for vehicles but posit that "[o]ne possible silver lining to decreased vehicle lifespan (in years) involves the more rapid introduction of new technology into the on-road fleet" (at 11). This could lead to the adoption rate of autonomous vehicles growing exponentially rather than sequentially.

The authors recognize weaknesses in their calculations, including unknowns such as what users will accept as delays between trips by different members of the household, the degree of acceptance of automated vehicles more broadly, and changing vehicle-sharing strategies within households.

Daniel J Fagnant & Kara Kockelman, "Preparing a Nation for Autonomous Vehicles: Opportunities, Barriers and Policy Recommendations" (2015) 77 *Transportation Research Part A: Policy and Practice* 167, online: *ScienceDirect* www.sciencedirect.com/science/article/abs/pii/S0965856415000804

This article highlights a number of potential benefits to autonomous vehicles while also identifying hurdles to their eventual adoption. It discusses concerns with liability law, security concerns, and privacy implications. Benefits around safety, crash reduction, faster travel times, environmental impacts, and parking benefits are quantified through dollar estimates to be contrasted with the concerns. The initial costs for early adopters are noted as one of the biggest barriers to widespread use. The article concludes by suggesting a federal framework that could provide consistency across states. More so than in Canada, the division of powers between state and federal governments in the United States, along with the sheer number of states, creates an amplified version of the problems Canada may see if provinces do not cooperate among themselves and with the federal government in legislating in the area of autonomous vehicles. The paper's main goals are identified as recognizing the potential benefits, acknowledging barriers to implementation, and then concluding with policy recommendations.

Mobility options that autonomous vehicles can provide to the elderly or disabled may lead to a greater number of people using private transport options. However, the increased fuel efficiency through optimized speeds, drafting ("slipstream sharing"), and less idle time for a vehicle can offset this increased use of private vehicles from an environmental standpoint. A move from personal ownership to on-demand service is considered. The change that this may have on travel choices and use patterns and the impact on necessary infrastructure developments are briefly addressed at the outset. Although a joint ownership or subscription service for vehicle use may seem bizarre, consider a service such as Netflix, which has moved many from ownership of physical media such as DVDs to a subscription service. The key will be service and the ability to meet demand in seamless ways that satisfy the consumer.

High costs currently "hamper large-scale production and mass consumer availability" (at 168). This is common to virtually every technology as it develops. The differences are those of scale and safety. Safety measures in vehicles are often implemented through early adopters. Airbags, backup cameras, and blind-spot detectors, for example, were once expensive add-on features. The first two are now mandated as required equipment. Their development was funded by early adopters, and, as costs lowered, they became standard equipment.

Another issue reviewed is how the lack of consistency and predictability across states has hampered the development of some autonomous vehicles, preventing them from moving beyond the testing phase. As larger and more populous states such as California begin to adopt requirements, there could be a de facto federal or international standard, in much the way that California emissions standards became the norm for vehicles in many states. Most states are currently focused on standards for the testing of autonomous vehicles, but, as technology moves forward, the first states with sufficient markets for sales will have a significant impact on regulation.

The annual economic cost of vehicle crashes in the United States is USD$277 billion. Safety is a driver of costs from a quantitative standpoint, along with such qualitative measurements as the value of human life. Although autonomous vehicles are not perfect, it is important to remember that the human driver is not either; driver error is the critical error in more than 90 percent of all crashes. The leading cause of death of fifteen- to twenty-four-year-olds is traffic accidents, and more than 40 percent of "fatal crashes involve some combination of alcohol, distraction, drug involvement, or fatigue. Self-driven vehicles would not fall prey to human failings, suggesting the potential for at least a 40% fatal crash-rate reduction" (at 169). The value of automation is not in achieving the perfect but in achieving the better. Although change will not occur if autonomous vehicles are merely as good as or slightly better than human drivers, the safety they provide may be significantly better well before these vehicles achieve perfection. Perfect is the enemy of good. Given the complexities of driving, some human interaction will be required in the foreseeable future. The authors identify another impediment: the rate at which human control is needed will be a substantial factor in the safety of these vehicles.

Reduction of traffic issues is a key benefit of automation. Vehicles that allow for smoother braking and speed adjustments, drafting to reduce wind resistance, and the ability to know what is coming up and adapting accordingly will lead to fuel savings, shorter commute times, and less time on the road. Technologies that allow greater communications will be key to this. Most phones already have apps that can show upcoming traffic issues and rely on data shared between phones being analyzed. In short, the technology exists and is in use already, and the ability to use this data in a finer way will allow automated vehicles to work better. We all can see the traffic jam approaching, but we fail to use this knowledge in the best way. As well, non-automated vehicle use prevents the best use of this data as human reaction times prevent the degree of control that automated systems can provide. Technologies that already exist in cellphones can be added to vehicles and other items to create V2V, vehicle-to-infrastructure (V2I), or V2X communication routes. Combine this with systems such as automated braking and many traffic accidents can be eliminated. Waiting at a stoplight could become a thing of the past as the vehicle automatically knows when the light is turning green and accelerates immediately. The second vehicle in line may also accelerate simultaneously as the vehicles can predict each other's movements rather than wait for vehicles to begin moving one by one. The knock-on or "shock-wave propagation" effect is significant.

Who can drive will be affected. Autonomous vehicles can offer transportation for individuals who otherwise would be unable to drive, such as those too young, the elderly, or the disabled. As well, cost sharing may make such transportation more available than current modes, such as taxis. Parking patterns will be disrupted as vehicles may eventually be programmed to return home or detect the nearest parking spot without needing to search for it.

As with many technological innovations, the earliest adopters may be industry. Freight transportation can be hugely affected by the elimination of the cost of drivers, enhanced fuel efficiency through drafting, optimized traffic avoidance, and integration into on-time delivery plans.

Although the high current cost of technology is considered, the estimated cost is expected to drop significantly as adoption increases. Potential impacts for safety are significant. The availability of such technologies for modes of transport such as motorcycles is lagging, and the impact in that sector is predicted to be slower in developing.

Infrastructure development will have to take automation into account. As more vehicles are automated, a significant reduction in highway congestion is expected. At a level where 90 percent of vehicles are autonomous, congestion is predicted to fall by 60 percent, almost doubling highway capacity. The impact of unoccupied vehicles travelling to their next pickup is not included in this estimate. An impact on real estate (such as changing land use, fewer roads, and greater options for commuting) and the freeing of space currently dedicated to parking are possible.

Increased safety should translate into lower insurance rates for users. As well, civil litigation surrounding motor vehicle accidents may become increasingly rare. Questions of liability may shift to manufacturers or programmers who have programmed the decision-making mind of the car. Whether the car decides to hit an obstacle or run itself off a road to avoid it may no longer be in the control of the occupant. Owners may be able to program their settings in a way that affects this kind of decision making, which may create liability at that level. If manufacturers or programmers are liable, then they may wish to have an ownership or access right in data collected by the vehicle to defend themselves. The article briefly touches upon the issues of security and privacy of information.

The article concludes by calling for expansion of funding for research; the development of a set of federal guidelines for certification of autonomous vehicles; and the setting of standards for liability, security, and data privacy. Although autonomous vehicles are in their infancy, the authors note how quickly such technology can develop and the slow pace with which the law often moves.

Michele Bertoncello & Dominik Wee, "Ten Ways Autonomous Driving Could Redefine the Automotive World" (1 June 2015), online: *McKinsey & Company* www.mckinsey.com/industries/automotive-and-assembly/our-insights/ten-ways-autonomous-driving-could-redefine-the-automotive-world#

This article reviews the possible effects of the introduction of autonomous vehicles in the short, mid-, and long term. The authors posit that early adoption will be in controlled environments, such as mining and farming. The savings realized due to decreased labour costs and reduction in CO_2 emissions through optimized driving will be significant financial drivers to encourage adoption. The authors believe that initial use for highway purposes will most likely be in trucking and shipping as commercial fleets can be in controlled environments at their start and end points while travelling well-defined and mapped routes otherwise. Early company structures involving automated vehicle hailing and peer-to-peer car rentals are a natural evolution from existing structures such as Uber or Lyft.

In the mid-term era, the authors believe that vehicle ownership and insurance business models are likely to be affected. As the cost and risk of vehicle ownership may be shared over a larger group, with higher levels of vehicle use, independent ownership may be less and less attractive. If autonomous vehicles can be made as safe as expected, insurance models will need to adapt. Risks will shift from collision and driver liability to the coverage of jointly owned or temporarily licensed vehicles. The authors relate this shift to being somewhat similar to cruise lines or shipping companies in the expected model. Instead of insuring the driver, the vehicle and its occupant will be insured as the risks associated with a particular driver will have been eliminated. Optimized supply chain logistics are expected "to increase efficiency and flexibility" as labour costs are reduced, along with boosting utilization rates for equipment. Consider the value to a shipping company of having a truck that does not sit idle while a driver requires food or rest.

In the third era, as automated vehicles become fully mainstream, the authors consider impacts in other areas. If passengers exit at a location and the vehicle leaves to park itself, the parking space need not accommodate room for a door to open. This alone can reduce the physical footprint of a vehicle by 15 percent, allowing for greater use of parking space. Accident rates will be reduced, leading to savings in health care and impacting the economy as workers would no longer lose time due to traffic injuries. It is expected that as automation becomes more advanced, advances in other areas, such as artificial intelligence, robotics, and remote sensing, will occur as a side effect. The impact of autonomous vehicles will stretch beyond driving and into many different areas of life.

Alexander Hars, "Top Misconceptions of Autonomous Cars and Self-Driving Vehicles" (2016) 2016-09 *Thinking Outside the Box: Inventivio Innovation Briefs* at 9, online (pdf): *Inventivio* www.inventivio.com/innovationbriefs/2016-09/Top-misconceptions-of-self-driving-cars.pdf

This article considers eight misconceptions surrounding autonomous vehicles.

1) *Speed of Evolution of Autonomous Vehicles*. The article asserts that the difference between temporally short automation, such as self-parking, is significant. Gradual evolution will not be possible with fully autonomous vehicles because there will be little to no room for error. Once human attention is removed from the tasks of driving, the automated systems must be able to deal with almost any eventuality. A person cannot remain vigilant for long periods of time while the system drives. It is unrealistic to expect this. Thus, once vehicles become autonomous, they must have a very high ability to deal with a wide range of scenarios.

2) *Likely First Consumers.* According to the author, fleet operators will be the likely first consumers. This recognizes that certain parameters that make autonomous vehicles easier to design and control relate to controlled geography. A "network effect" allows greater use of a function. By reducing downtime, a fleet operator can reduce their capital expenditure on vehicles. The author considers a taxi company in a fair-weather location. Detailed mapping and location services in a limited geographic area will be cheaper and thus more cost-effective than an undefined or "unfenced" area. Long-haul operators can similarly benefit by limiting use to defined routes that can be mapped with hyperaccuracy while again limiting labour and capital costs. Further benefit identified in this model is the fact that long-haul vehicles often operate less in urban settings, where dynamic situations are more common.
3) *Expected Time Frames for Adoption.* The authors believed that adoption will be quick once it starts. Although initial costs are likely to be expensive, the earliest adopters of safety technology are often the most well off. This is because they have both the ability to pay and a higher self-valuation of their time and safety. By releasing a person from the constraint of driving, they are freed to conduct other, more highly remunerated tasks. As greater adoption drives costs down, an exponential adoption rate is expected.
4) *Expected Algorithm Designs.* In many situations, algorithm design is programmed as a series of "if-then" rules. If a certain set of parameters is presented, then the following actions are taken by the program. Driving decisions cannot be reduced to a few simple rules given the complexity of the tasks. As a result, the author believes that probabilistic reasoning is more likely to be adapted in the programming. As a result, autonomous vehicles may react differently even when presented with the same situation, which is no different than human drivers. Programs will be designed to learn from a set of situations that have been faced, and best outcomes will be judged as a result of previous experience rather than be controlled by a fixed set of instructions.
5) *Utility of Public Demonstration.* The utility of public demonstration is not to provide an indication of the capabilities of autonomous vehicles. At this time, public demonstrations tend to be in highly controlled situations and environments. The current "maturity" of autonomous vehicles "is impossible to judge" (at 5). Instead, reviewing the experiences the systems have faced and how well they were able to react provides a better assessment.
6) *Ethical Judgment Expectations.* In a dynamic situation, a driver is required to make snap ethical decisions. For example, if an accident in unavoidable but a decision as to whether to hit another vehicle or a pedestrian occurs, a decision may need to be made instantly. However, taking such situations into account when designing a program can be artificial. Human decision making in the

moment is far from perfect. There may be no "right" choice, and what is "right" may be subjective. These dilemmas connote certain knowledge and facts that cannot be known in a particular circumstance. Certainly, exact knowledge of a person's age, health, and survivability is not known to a human driver, so expecting an automated system to take such factors into account would be an unfairly high burden. The probability of such a dilemma is incredibly rare, and the examples tend to be contrived. With proper design, their likelihood decreases further. Making a singularly "right" decision is impossible, as being "right" is a fluid concept. Instead, the vehicle must avoid ethically wrong decisions and, by doing so, avoid being in such situations in the first place.

7) *Requirements of Proof Surrounding Safety.* Assessing safety and the requirements of proof of safety does not require as many miles of safe driving as one might think, according to the author. The failure rate is a statistical analysis. Significant confidence levels can be reached in relatively low distances driven by autonomous vehicles. Complications surrounding non-independent variables need to be analyzed, but the driving examples can be shortened by correlating data properly. The failure rate of autonomous vehicles need not be zero to nonetheless provide great confidence in such a system. Human drivers are the default and currently have a significant failure rate. In fact, most people overestimate their own driving ability. A spotless record is often as much out of luck as skill. Although the adoption of autonomous systems will require a prime mover, such as a significant safety difference, once adoption begins it is likely to accelerate quickly. As well, learning by autonomous vehicles is a system-wide exercise. What one accident teaches can be applied throughout all vehicles through a software update, whereas human experience is slower and individual. If a failure is noted and cannot be fixed, then the whole fleet can be shut down or instructed to avoid such an eventuality by avoiding certain preconditions. This could affect saleability as no one will want to purchase an unreliable vehicle, but it will also put more pressure on manufacturers and programmers to continually upgrade their systems. It may evidence itself in future civil judgments. An assessment of not just accidents but also their severity and impact will be necessary to properly measure the best ethical decision-making capabilities of an automated vehicle.

8) *Impact on Traffic Congestion.* Traffic congestion relating to autonomous vehicles will have an effect in both directions. On the one hand, a greater number of people may access transportation as a result of autonomous vehicles and unoccupied vehicles may return home or park without anyone being in them, adding to congestion. On the other hand, greater use of road space and parking space and convoy driving may lessen congestion. The eventual impact may shift either way depending on design.

Bryan Reimer, "Driver Assistance Systems and the Transition to Automated Vehicles: A Path to Increase Older Adult Safety and Mobility?" (2014) 24:1 *Public Policy & Aging Report* 27, online: https://academic.oup.com/ppar/article/24/1/27/1566999

This article reviews the implementation of autonomous vehicles, especially with regard to the elderly. It reviews "human-centered considerations" and the issues that arise with trust and interaction with an autonomous system. It demonstrates that "[t]he fact that we cannot create a perfect automated driving system is a major barrier to trust." Since people overestimate their own abilities, they have difficulty accepting the change that technology represents, even in cases where it is safer. This distrust is likely to be reinforced as autonomous vehicles become more prevalent. The first time an autonomous vehicle makes a decision that leads to a serious accident will likely add to this distrust, even if a human driver would have made the same or a worse decision and even if the incidence of such accidents is much lower than that of accidents caused by human drivers.

The author discusses how automation of at least some tasks will be required if driving is to progress to greater speeds and greater numbers. Recognizing that the interface between driver and vehicle will likely change, the author states: "[T]he basic human–machine interface has changed very little in the history of the car but it is about to transform significantly." Optimizing these interfaces "to support driver attention, not fight for it" is key. Education surrounding autonomous vehicles is identified as required both to build trust, which will lead to adoption, and to enhance understanding, which will create technologically literate drivers as modes of transportation change.

appendix 2

ONTARIO REGULATION 306/15

ONTARIO REGULATION 306/15
made under the
HIGHWAY TRAFFIC ACT
Made: September 16, 2015
Filed: October 13, 2015
Published on e-Laws: October 13, 2015
Printed in *The Ontario Gazette*: October 31, 2015

PILOT PROJECT—AUTOMATED VEHICLES

INTERPRETATION AND APPLICATION

Interpretation

1.(1) In this Regulation,

"approval" means approval to test automated vehicles issued under section 9;

"automated driving system" means a system that performs dynamic driving tasks to operate a vehicle with limited or no need for any dynamic driving task to be performed by a human driver;

"automated vehicle" means a motor vehicle or a street car, excluding a motorcycle or motor-assisted bicycle, with an automated driving system that operates at driving automation Level 3, 4 or 5;

"drive", in relation to an automated vehicle, includes driving or causing the operation of the automated vehicle, with or without the automated driving system being engaged;

"dynamic driving task" includes a task required for the operational aspect of driving, such as steering, braking, accelerating and monitoring the vehicle and roadway, and a task required for the tactical aspect of driving, such as responding to events and determining when to change lanes, turn or use signals, but does not include a task required for the strategic aspect of driving, such as determining destinations;

"Level" means an automated driving system's level of driving automation for on-road vehicles, as defined in SAE Standard J3016;

"owner", in the case of a commercial motor vehicle, includes the operator, within the meaning of subsection 16 (1) of the Act;

"Registrar" means the Registrar of Motor Vehicles;

"SAE Standard J3016" means SAE International Standard J3016: Taxonomy and Definitions for Terms Related to On-Road Motor Vehicle Automated Driving Systems, issued on January 16, 2014 and available on SAE International's website.

(2) The Levels of driving automation are the following:

1. Level 0—no automation.
2. Level 1—driver assistance.
3. Level 2—partial automation.
4. Level 3—conditional automation.
5. Level 4—high automation.
6. Level 5—full automation.

(3) A person seated in the driver's seat of an automated vehicle is considered to be driving the automated vehicle, and to be the driver of the vehicle, with or without the automated driving system being engaged.

Application

2.(1) This Regulation applies to an automated vehicle, with or without the automated driving system being engaged.

(2) This Regulation does not apply to a motor vehicle with an automated driving system that operates at driving automation Level 0, 1 or 2.

PILOT PROJECT

Pilot project established

3.(1) A pilot project to evaluate the use of automated vehicles on highways is established.

(2) The Minister shall conduct and complete an evaluation of the use of automated vehicles on highways under the pilot project before the tenth anniversary of the day this Regulation comes into force.

(3) The Minister may from time to time during the course of the pilot project conduct interim evaluations of the use of automated vehicles with an automated driving system that operates at driving automation Level 3 or 4 to determine if there is a need to continue to evaluate such vehicles under the pilot project.

PROHIBITION AND PERMITTED USE

Prohibition

4. No person shall drive or permit the operation of an automated vehicle on a highway, except as permitted by this Regulation.

Permitted use of automated vehicles

5. A person may drive or permit the operation of an automated vehicle on a highway if,

(a) the owner of the vehicle has been approved under section 9 to test automated vehicles;
(b) the vehicle meets the requirements of sections 11 and 12;
(c) the vehicle is in good working order;
(d) the driver holds any of the following that authorizes him or her to drive the vehicle:
 (i) A valid Class A, B, C, D, E, F or G driver's licence.
 (ii) A valid driver's licence issued by another jurisdiction.
 (iii) A valid International Driver's Permit;
(e) the driver complies with section 13; and
(f) the vehicle is being driven only for testing purposes under the pilot project established by this Regulation.

Application of Act

6. The Act applies to the operation of an automated vehicle, to a person who drives an automated vehicle and to the owner of an automated vehicle.

APPROVAL TO TEST AUTOMATED VEHICLES

Who may apply for approval

7.(1) The owner of one or more automated vehicles, if the requirements of subsection (2) or (3) are satisfied, may apply to the Registrar for approval to test the vehicles under the pilot project.

(2) For vehicles that were originally manufactured as automated vehicles,

(a) the owner must also be the original manufacturer of the vehicles; and
(b) the owner must be a company, within the meaning of the *Motor Vehicle Safety Act* (Canada), that,
 (i) is authorized under that Act to apply a national safety mark to the vehicles, or
 (ii) is a foreign manufacturer registered under that Act.

(3) For vehicles that were not originally manufactured as automated vehicles but were converted into automated vehicles,

(a) the owner must also be the person that converted the vehicles into automated vehicles;
(b) the owner must be an original manufacturer of automated vehicles or a technology company, an academic or research institution or a manufacturer of parts, systems, equipment or components for automated driving systems; and
(c) the Registrar must be satisfied that the owner has the expertise to properly convert vehicles into automated vehicles.

Required information and documents

8.(1) An application for approval must include the following information and documents:

1. The name and business address of the applicant.
2. The name, business address, business telephone number, business fax number and business e-mail address of the applicant's contact person for the purposes of this Regulation.
3. Proof satisfactory to the Registrar of the applicant's ownership of the vehicles.
4. The total number of vehicles of any make, model and class to be tested.
5. Declaration by the applicant that the vehicles are covered by automobile insurance, as defined in subsection 1 (1) of the *Compulsory Automobile Insurance Act*, in respect of any one accident, to the limit of at least $5,000,000, exclusive of interest and costs, against liability resulting from bodily injury to or the death of one or more persons and loss of or damage to property.
6. Declaration by the applicant that the vehicles,
   i. comply with the requirements of sections 11 and 12,
   ii. are in good working order,
   iii. meet the statutory and regulatory requirements applicable to motor vehicles or street cars, as the case may be, and
   iv. are capable of being driven safely in Ontario.
7. Declaration that the applicant will conduct the testing of the vehicles safely and in accordance with the law.
8. Any other information relevant to the applicant, the vehicles, the testing or the drivers that the Registrar may request.

(2) If requested to do so by the Registrar, an applicant shall demonstrate that an automated vehicle complies with subparagraph 6 iii or iv of subsection (1).

Approval of application

9. (1) The Registrar may approve an application that meets the requirements of section 11 subject to any conditions that the Registrar may impose, including any condition that the Registrar considers necessary to ensure that the testing will be conducted safely and in accordance with the law.

(2) The Registrar may refuse to approve an application if he or she is not satisfied that the testing will be conducted safely and in accordance with the law.

(3) If the Registrar imposes conditions in an approval, the owner shall comply with the conditions and shall ensure that the testing is conducted in compliance with the conditions.

Revocation of approval

10. (1) The Registrar may revoke an approval if, in his or her opinion,

(a) false or inaccurate information, or information that was incomplete in a material respect, was provided in the application;
(b) the person to whom the approval was issued,
    (i) does not comply with a condition of the approval, or
    (ii) ceases to meet the requirements set out in section 7;
(c) the testing of the vehicles has not been conducted,
    (i) in compliance with this Regulation, or
    (ii) in compliance with any conditions of the approval; or
(d) the testing of the vehicles has not been or will not be conducted safely and in accordance with the law.

(2) Notice of the revocation of an approval is sufficiently given if it is given to the owner's contact person referred to in paragraph 2 of subsection 8 (1) by any of the following methods:

1. Personal delivery to the contact person at the latest address for that person provided by the owner.
2. Regular mail addressed to the contact person at the latest address for that person provided by the owner.
3. Fax to the contact person at the latest fax number for that person provided by the owner.
4. E-mail to the contact person at the latest e-mail address for that person provided by the owner.

(3) Unless the contact person establishes that he or she did not, acting in good faith, through absence, accident, illness or other cause beyond the person's control, receive the notice,

(a) notice given by regular mail is deemed to have been received on the fifth day after it was mailed; and
(b) notice given by fax or by e-mail is deemed to have been received on the first business day after it was sent.

(4) The approval is revoked on the day the notice of the revocation is received or deemed to have been received.

AUTOMATED DRIVING SYSTEM

Automated driving system requirements

11.(1) For a vehicle that was originally manufactured as an automated vehicle, its automated driving system,

(a) must comply with any applicable requirements of the Act and the regulations;

(b) must comply with any requirements of the *Motor Vehicle Safety Act* (Canada) that apply to automated driving systems for the vehicle's year of manufacture; and

(c) must comply with SAE Standard J3016.

(2) For a vehicle that was not originally manufactured as an automated vehicle but was converted into an automated vehicle, its automated driving system,

(a) must comply with any applicable requirements of the Act and the regulations;

(b) must not render the vehicle non-compliant in any respect with the *Motor Vehicle Safety Act* (Canada) or the *Motor Vehicle Safety Regulations* made under that Act; and

(c) must comply with SAE Standard J3016.

Mechanisms and systems included in automated driving system

12. For every automated vehicle, its automated driving system must be equipped with the following mechanisms and system:

1. A mechanism, easily accessible to the driver, that engages and disengages the automated driving system.
2. A system that,
   i. safely alerts the driver if a failure of the automated driving system is detected while it is engaged, and
   ii. does either of the following when an alert is given:
      A. requires the driver to take over all the dynamic driving tasks required to operate the vehicle, or
      B. if the driver does not or is unable to take over all the dynamic driving tasks required to operate the vehicle, causes the vehicle to safely move out of traffic and come to a complete stop.
3. A mechanism that allows the driver to take over all the dynamic driving tasks required to operate the vehicle if the automated driving system fails or if the driver disengages the automated driving system.

DRIVER'S DUTIES

Driver's duties

13.(1) The driver of an automated vehicle shall remain at all times in the driver's seat of the vehicle and shall monitor the vehicle's operation.

(2) The driver of an automated vehicle shall carry a copy of the approval in the vehicle.

(3) The driver of an automated vehicle shall present a copy of the approval upon the demand of any police officer or officer appointed for enforcing or carrying out the provisions of the Act.

(4) In the event of a collision or traffic stop, the driver of an automated vehicle shall advise the attending police officer or officer appointed for enforcing or carrying out the provisions of the Act that the vehicle is an automated vehicle and is being tested under the pilot project established by this Regulation.

REPORTS AND RECORDS

Changes in information

14.(1) An owner to whom an approval has been issued shall notify the Registrar of any change in the information provided to the Registrar in the application for approval no later than 10 days after the day the change occurs.

(2) Without limiting the generality of subsection (1), an owner to whom an approval has been issued shall notify the Registrar,

(a) if a vehicle listed in the original application for approval, identified by its make, model and class, is no longer being tested;

(b) if a vehicle not listed in the original application for approval, identified by its make, model and class, is being tested; and

(c) if a vehicle described in clause (b), identified by its make, model and class, is no longer being tested.

Collision reports

15. An owner to whom an approval has been issued shall notify the Registrar of any collision involving an automated vehicle no later than 10 days after the day the collision occurs and shall include the following information respecting the particulars of the collision:

1. The vehicles involved, identified by their vehicle identification numbers.
2. The persons involved.
3. The location of the collision.
4. The apparent cause of the collision.
5. The details and extent of any personal injury or damage to property caused by the collision.
6. Any other relevant information that the Registrar may request.

Records retention

16.(1) An owner to whom an approval has been issued shall retain any record that relates to its use of automated vehicles, including information requested under section 15, until the third anniversary of the day this Regulation is revoked.

(2) The owner shall retain the records at its principal place of business in Ontario, if any, or, if the owner has notified the Registrar that it keeps records at other specified premises in Ontario, at those other premises.

(3) Despite subsection (2), records in electronic form need not be retained at the premises described in that subsection if those records can be retrieved in a usable electronic or paper form promptly upon request.

(4) The owner shall ensure that it maintains the capacity to retrieve its electronic records throughout the retention period described in subsection (1).

Reports to Minister

17.(1) If requested to do so by the Minister, an owner to whom an approval has been issued shall report in writing to the Minister on its use of automated vehicles under the pilot project, or on any aspect of that use that may be specified by the Minister.

(2) If requested to do so by the Minister, the owner shall give the Minister any record referred to in subsection 16 (1) that the Minister may require to evaluate the pilot project.

REVOCATION AND COMMENCEMENT

Revocation

18. This Regulation is revoked on the tenth anniversary of the day it comes into force.

Commencement

19. This Regulation comes into force on the later of January 1, 2016 and the day this Regulation is filed.

appendix 3

SAFETY ASSESSMENT FOR AUTOMATED DRIVING SYSTEMS IN CANADA

ANNEX A: SAFETY ASSESSMENT WRITER'S GUIDE

Questions identified in the Safety Assessment Writer's Guide are meant to provide further clarity and direction to ADS developers as they review the safety of their ADS equipped vehicles. The questions provide a non-exhaustive list of considerations that ADS developers are encouraged to reflect upon as they produce their Safety Assessment reports. Specific questions have been developed for each of the 13 expected outcomes identified in the Safety Assessment tool.

Transport Canada recognizes that not all questions may be relevant or applicable to all ADS technologies, and it is incumbent upon ADS developers to produce reports that reflect their unique products. Some ADS developers may choose to focus their Safety Assessment reports on the safety elements they deem most critical. However, entities are encouraged to provide some minimal explanation as to how they have achieved each of the 13 expected outcomes.

ADS CAPABILITIES, DESIGN, AND VALIDATION

1. **ADS Level of Automation and Intended Use**

a. What ADS features is the vehicle equipped with? What is their level of automation?

b. How is the ADS identified (e.g., does it have a specified hardware version, software version, etc.)?

c. Is the driver/user responsible for any portion of the DDT including fallback? Under what conditions?

d. What is the intended use of the vehicle (transportation of goods vs. people; highway vs. low-speed; urban vs. rural; etc.)? Is the vehicle intended for private ownership or will it be managed by a ride-share program? Will you, the ADS developer, be operating the ride-share program, or will the vehicles be marketed to a third-party for this purpose?

2. Operational Design Domain

a. How is ODD of each ADS feature defined? Please include any domain constraints (weather, road type, speed restrictions, traffic conditions, etc.).
b. How does the vehicle respond when the limits of the ODD are exceeded?
c. Is it possible to activate or engage the ADS outside of the ODD?

3. Object Event Detection and Response

a. What systems are used for OEDR? How does the vehicle perceive its surroundings to determine if there is an object or event (computer vision, sensor fusion, sensor suite and integration, localization/recognition and decision software/route planning)?
b. What is the range of view of the sensors? What is the range of object detection?
c. How does the system treat unknown objects or objects it cannot classify?
d. What are the known sources of interference with the operation of your system?
e. Can the vehicle identify and react safely to:
   i. Pedestrians (adults, children, individuals with mobility devices)
   ii. Other vulnerable road users (cyclists, motorcycles)
   iii. Law enforcement or emergency services vehicles and officers
   iv. Canadian signs and road infrastructure
   v. Vehicle types that are commonly found on Canadian roadways (logging trucks, snow plows, etc.)
   vi. Other service providers (e.g., construction workers, crossing guards, utility service providers, waste collection, snow plows, public transit vehicles, school buses, etc.) with occasional responsibilities to direct traffic, or that require specific behaviours (e.g., stopping, yielding right-of-way)
   vii. Other vehicles or road users that do not respect traffic laws (e.g., vehicles that are speeding, do not stop, do not signal, etc.)
   viii. Animals/wildlife

4. International Standards and Best Practices

a. What safety risks were considered in the design of the vehicle? Which industry standards, voluntary guidance, best practices, design principles and original approaches were employed to mitigate safety risks (e.g., ISO 26262 functional safety process standard for road vehicles, etc.)? If applicable, please describe the subsystems to which the standards were applied.

b. Have you deviated from international standards in the design of the ADS-equipped vehicle? If so, why?

5. Testing and Validation

a. What design and validation processes have been used to manage safety risks (e.g., critical systems test scenarios, on-road testing, lab testing, model in the loop, software in the loop, hardware in the loop, driver in the loop, etc.)?

b. Snow, ice, freezing rain, low temperatures, snow/ice accumulation on sensors/vehicles, gravel and dirt roads, among others, are all common conditions in Canada that could pose additional risks to the safe operation of the vehicle and the ADS features. What measures have been taken to mitigate these risks?

c. How have factors related to extreme seasonal variability (changing topography due to snow accumulation, variable light conditions due to changes in foliage, road markings hidden by snow and ice, etc.) been factored into the testing and validation of the vehicle?

d. How did you arrive at the determination that testing was sufficient and safety risks were appropriately mitigated?

USER-CENTERED SAFETY

6. Safety Systems

a. What safety-critical systems are provided with redundancies and why? How are the redundant systems designed (sensor level, hardware level, software level), and how do they interact? Do they continually contribute to decision-making, or are they only activated in the event of a malfunction?

b. How do the ADS features perform fault detection? What will happen in the event of a fault detection, sub-system malfunction or failure (e.g., limp mode, restricted ODD, ADS becomes unavailable)? Will the driver/user be able to take over at any point? Is there an emergency override built into the system?

c. What does the vehicle consider to be a minimal risk condition? Recognizing the choices will be situation dependent, what options will the vehicle consider for its minimal risk condition (e.g., stop in-lane; stop on shoulder; stop at next available rest-stop)?

d. How will the vehicle determine that a minimal risk condition is achieved? What actions will the vehicle take after a minimal risk condition is achieved? If this is an ADS-dedicated vehicle, how will the vehicle be put back into service? Does it need a signal from an occupant to resume or will it do so when the conditions place it back within its ODD?

7. **Human-Machine Interface and Accessibility of Controls**

a. What processes and best practices were used to ensure vehicle controls are intuitive and easy for drivers/users to understand? What measures are in place to prevent the unsafe misuse of the vehicle's features?

b. How does the vehicle communicate critical messages to users/drivers and other passengers? How will indicators show:
   i. When the ADS is functioning as intended?
   ii. When the system is malfunctioning, or sensors need to be recalibrated?
   iii. When the ADS is on?
   iv. When ADS functions are available/unavailable for use (if applicable)?
   v. A request for the operator to resume/assume the dynamic driving task (if applicable)?

c. Is the vehicle equipped with systems that allow occupants to seek assistance in the event of an emergency or when more information is needed?

d. Is the vehicle accessible to passengers with special needs (e.g., with mobility impairments, hearing/vision impairments, service animals, children, mobility devices)? What design features have been developed to meet the needs of these users?

e. What measures have been taken to ensure vehicle actions are intuitive to other road users?

Additional questions for vehicles equipped with SAE level 3 ADS features:

e. [*sic*] If the ODD boundaries are exceeded or if the driver must take over dynamic driving task, how much time is given for a take-over request?

f. Is the system equipped with risk mitigation features that will bring the vehicle to a minimal risk condition if the driver does not take over the dynamic driving task?

g. How will the vehicle react in the event of a critical situation involving an imminent hazard when there is not enough time to facilitate a safe transition of the dynamic driving task?

h. Is the vehicle equipped with systems to monitor the availability of a take-over-ready driver (e.g., weight in the driver seat, fastened seat belt, eye-movement monitoring, etc.)?

8. **Public Education and Awareness**

a. What measures have been/will be taken to ensure drivers/users are aware of the capabilities and limitations of the vehicle's ADS, including any domain constraints?

b. How will drivers/users and owner/operators be informed of critical tasks related to safe operation and maintenance of the vehicle (e.g., in-car tutorials, training or education programs for sales representatives)?
c. How will drivers/users be informed of critical system updates, and particularly how system updates may change or affect the way they are expected to operate the vehicle?
d. Have measures been taken to ensure other road users (drivers, pedestrians, cyclists, etc.) know:
   i. That the vehicle is equipped with ADS(s)?
   ii. How to interact with the vehicle?
   iii. How the vehicle will react to them?

9. User Protections during Collisions or System Failures

a. What are the vehicle's crash avoidance design features and capabilities? What pre-crash scenarios can the vehicle detect?
b. What active and passive safety measures are in place to protect occupants and other road users?
c. What design considerations have been used to ensure crash compatibility with existing vehicles on roadways?
d. What actions/system responses will occur immediately before, during, and after a crash to protect occupants? Will the actions/system responses vary depending on the severity of the crash?
e. How will the vehicle systems be brought to a safe state following a crash?
f. Does the ADS seek to minimize external damages and impacts on pedestrians or vulnerable road users during a crash?
g. How will first responders and emergency service providers be protected and informed about the hazards and procedures associated with the vehicle? Consideration should be given to how safety messages will be transmitted to emergency responders and first on scene (members of the public).

CYBER SECURITY AND DATA MANAGEMENT

10. Cyber Security

a. What methods are available to interface external systems or software with the vehicle through wired (ODB, USB, memory card, etc.) or wireless (V2X, Wifi, 4G/LTE, etc.) means?
b. What testing has been done to ensure system intrusion safety? How segregated are the various systems?
c. In addition to any international standards adhered to (see Expected Outcome 4), are additional measures in place to address cyber security threats

(e.g., self-audits, regular software updates, forensic support, aftermarket risk mitigation, etc.)?

d. How will the vehicle systems detect a potentially malicious cyber event?
e. What action will the vehicle take in the event of a cyber incident? Does the vehicle have means of executing safe behaviours when encountering unsafe or compromised sensor information (i.e., GPS spoofing, sensor modification etc.)? How will vulnerabilities and/or safety risks be communicated to occupants?
f. Will government agencies (Transport Canada, Canadian Centre for Cyber Security) be informed of cyber incidents, including those occurring outside of Canada?
g. Is there a vehicle cyber security program and/or plan in place to support the response to a cyber event affecting the vehicle and ADS (e.g., a designated team, governance structure, protocols, testing, training, etc.)?
h. How will vulnerabilities (software and/or hardware) that are observed as vehicles are deployed be addressed?

11. System Updates and After-Market Repairs/Modifications

a. Is the vehicle equipped with an auditable version control system that shows the system version in operation, past and/or pending updates? How is the information presented or accessed?
b. In the event of a system update, after-market repair or modification to the software or hardware of the vehicle, what tests will be performed to ensure other systems are not compromised and continue to function as intended (i.e., that subsystems still interact correctly and existing functions are not affected)?
c. In the event of an update conducted by the ADS developer, what regression testing will be conducted to ensure system performance is not degraded by the update prior to its implementation (e.g., simulation, track test, real-world)?
d. What measures are in place/will be taken to ensure OTA updates are completed securely, safely and in full (e.g., the integrity of the communication link to the vehicle is safeguarded and maintained throughout the update; the vehicle is not in operation while the update is being performed, etc.)? How will the ADS developer ensure the update is legitimate and/or that no code has been modified, added or removed from the update?
e. Does the vehicle need to be off for a certain period of time during or after the update is installed? If the vehicle is electric, does it need to have a certain level of power remaining? How will this information be conveyed to drivers/users?

12. User Privacy

a. Is personal information of occupants or other road users transmitted to the ADS developer during normal operation, or only during servicing? What kind of personal information is being transmitted (video, sound, GPS, other sensor data)?

b. How will drivers/users consent to the collection and use of their personal information? What processes are in place to ensure drivers/users are aware of what personal information is being collected and how it is being used?
c. What measures are in place to safeguard occupants' and road users' personal information and prevent its loss, theft, or unauthorised access, use or disclosure?
d. How will occupants and other road users be made aware of any loss, theft, or unauthorised access, use, or disclosure of their personal information?

13. Collaboration with Government Agencies and Law Enforcement

a. What systems within the vehicle collect and store data on the vehicle's operation? Where are these systems located? What tools are required to retrieve this data?
b. Is data collection constant, or it is triggered by a set of events (rapid lateral or longitudinal change, ADS disengagement, etc.)? If the latter, what is the amount of time pre and post event that is captured? How long is this information stored?
c. What assistance will be provided to law enforcement or collision investigators to retrieve data needed to support investigations?
d. Are there processes in place to enable data sharing with vehicle owner/operators when requested, for example, to facilitate insurance claims? How will vehicle owners be made aware of these processes?

INDEX

Numbers in italics refer to images and/or their captions.

ABOUT THE AUTHOR & CONTRIBUTOR

Nathan Baker is a criminal law practitioner who focuses on impaired-driving matters. He also holds the role of standing agent for the Public Prosecution Service of Canada in Peterborough, prosecuting matters under the *Controlled Drugs and Substances Act*, in addition to his private practice. Since 2012, he has produced the Drug Recognition Exercise/Standardized Field Sobriety Testing Netletter for practitioners to keep them abreast of developments related to drug-impaired driving. He has developed and presents a CPD course in consultation with DRE officers. In 2015, he was a panel member on the Law Society of Upper Canada's annual Drinking and Driving CPD and authored the paper provided to participants. Nathan received training to conduct SFST and DRE training at seminars in Atlanta and New Orleans in 2014 and 2016, and has also completed the NCDD Mastering Scientific Evidence Course. He believes that the law is often slower to evolve than technology, but hopes to lead the way in adapting law to autonomous vehicles.

Jaye Hooper has been a litigation lawyer specializing in personal injury, professional liability, and insurance litigation for over twenty years. She has appeared before all levels of court, including the Court of Appeal and the Supreme Court of Canada. A past president of the County of Carleton Law Association and the Federation of Ontario Law Associations, Jaye is a leader at the Ontario bar. She has been a presenter at various continuing professional development panels, including matters focusing on civil litigation as well as professionalism. Jaye works to be accessible to those in need of legal services and strives to provide individualized care to those she serves.

Printed and bound by CPI Group (UK) Ltd, Croydon, CR0 4YY

15/09/2026

14962402-0002